T0192254

Lecture Notes in Computer Science 12245

More information about this series at http://www.springer.com/series/7409

Jérôme Darmont · Boris Novikov ·
Robert Wrembel (Eds.)

Advances in Databases and Information Systems

24th European Conference, ADBIS 2020
Lyon, France, August 25–27, 2020
Proceedings

 Springer

Editors
Jérôme Darmont (iD)
ERIC (Research Unit 3083)
Université Lumière Lyon 2
Lyon, France

Boris Novikov (iD)
National Research University, Higher
School of Economics
St. Petersburg, Russia

Robert Wrembel (iD)
Poznan University of Technology
Poznań, Poland

ISSN 0302-9743   ISSN 1611-3349   (electronic)
Lecture Notes in Computer Science
ISBN 978-3-030-54831-5   ISBN 978-3-030-54832-2   (eBook)
https://doi.org/10.1007/978-3-030-54832-2

LNCS Sublibrary: SL3 – Information Systems and Applications, incl. Internet/Web, and HCI

Obituary

In Memoriam: Sherif Sakr

Sherif Sakr was a rising star in the constellation of database researchers. After obtaining a BSc and MSc degrees in Computer Science from the Faculty of Computers and Information at Cairo University in 2001 and 2003, respectively, he joined the ranks of the Computer and Information Science of Konstanz University, where he obtained a doctorate in 2007 for his research on XQuery Processing on top of relational databases. He then joined NICTA Research Centre (now CSIRO Data61 Lab) and University of New South Wales, where he developed a research agenda in the field of graph indexing and querying.

Following these appointments, he joined the ranks of the Department of Health Informatics at King Saud bin Abdulaziz University for Health Sciences (KSAU-HS), Saudi Arabia, where he pursued various applications of graph processing and big data technologies in the medical field. Along the way, he held visiting researcher and scholar appointments at Microsoft Research, Redmond, USA (2011), Nokia Bell Labs, Ireland – Formerly Alcatel-Lucent Bell Labs (2012), Humboldt-Universität zu Berlin, Germany (2015), University of Zurich, Switzerland (2016), and Technical University of Dresden, Germany (2016). This infatigable research journey led him to write the *Handbook of Big Data Technologies* (2017) and later the *Encyclopedia of Big Data Technologies* (2019), which will remain as one of his most notable legacies to the field of database research.

In 2018, Sherif joined University of Tartu's Institute of Computer Science in 2018 funded by a Top Researcher grant from the Estonian Research Council. During his two-years tenure, he created and led a Data Systems Research Group, which he grew from 1 to 16 researchers and research students in less than 24 months. During this time, he developed and spread his vision. He imagined a highly scalable engine for distributed event processing. His efforts immediately produced notable results: at CAiSE 2019 his work on stream analytics earned a Best Paper Award. Sherif was a tireless researcher. In fact, he started in parallel a research stream on explainable machine learning. At ADBIS 2019, he presented a hybrid local-global approach for generating explanations from black-box machine learning models.

Sherif Sakr will be remembered for generously giving his time to his community. During his career, Prof. Sakr was associate editor of the *Cluster Computing* journal and *Transactions on Large-Scale Data and Knowledge-Centered Systems* (TLDKS). He served as an editorial board member and guest editor for several reputable top-ranked scientific journals. He toured the world as a distinguished speaker of both the ACM and the IEEE Computer Society. Prof. Sakr published more than 150 refereed research publications in international journals and conferences. He was also author of six books, including *Big Data 2.0 Processing Systems* (2016). His research received more than 4,000 citations[1]. In 2019, he received the Best Arab Scholar Award from the Abdul Hammed Shoman Foundation.

Above and beyond all of the above, Sherif Sakr was a good person. The kind of person one would like to meet both personally and professionally. He cared that everyone felt comfortable and approached life with enthusiasm. He forged a group upon his values: hard work, intellectual honesty, and mutual support. His colleagues will remember Sherif as a passionate and visionary scientist, and someone who had time for everyone, devoting much time to ensuring that his students were aiming high and pushing them to maximize their potential.

Sherif Sakr was due to organize the ADBIS conference in Tartu in 2021. Unfortunately, he passed away during the night on March 24, 2020. His team will take over his mission to host ADBIS 2021.

June 2020

Marlon Dumas
Riccardo Tommasini

---

[1] cf. Google Scholar 2020.

Preface

The 24th European Conference on Advances in Databases and Information Systems (ADBIS 2020) was set to be held in Lyon, France, during August 25–28, 2020, in conjunction with the 24th International Conference on Theory and Practice of Digital Libraries (TPDL 2020) and the 16th EDA days on Business Intelligence & Big Data (EDA 2020). However, because of the worldwide COVID-19 crisis, ADBIS, TPDL, and EDA had to take place online during August 25–27, 2020. Yet, the three conferences joined their forces to propose common keynotes, workshops, and a Doctoral Consortium.

ADBIS established itself as a highly recognized conference in Europe. It aims at providing an international forum for exchanging research achievements on databases and data engineering, both from practical and theoretical perspectives. ADBIS also aims at promoting the interaction and collaboration of the database and data engineering as well as information systems research communities worldwide.

Previous ADBIS conferences were held in Saint Petersburg (1997), Poznan (1998), Maribor (1999), Prague (2000), Vilnius (2001), Bratislava (2002), Dresden (2003), Budapest (2004), Tallinn (2005), Thessaloniki (2006), Varna (2007), Pori (2008), Riga (2009), Novi Sad (2010), Vienna (2011), Poznan (2012), Genoa (2013), Ohrid (2014), Poitiers (2015), Prague (2016), Nicosia (2017), Budapest (2018), and Bled (2019).

ADBIS 2020 attracted 82 paper submissions, which were reviewed by an International Program Committee constituted of members from 28 countries. The Program Committee selected 13 long research papers for inclusion in this volume (acceptance rate: 16%). The selected papers span a wide spectrum of topics related to the ADBIS conference from different areas of research in database and information systems, including big data and social media analysis, business intelligence, and machine learning.

This volume also includes extended abstracts of the three keynotes that related most to ADBIS' topics, which were given by Amr El Abbadi, from the University of California (USA), Johann Gamper, from the Free University of Bozen-Bolzano (Italy), and Ioana Manolescu from Inria Saclay–Île-de-France and École Polytechnique (France).

Finally, we would like to express our sincere gratitude to everyone who contributed to make ADBIS 2020 a successful event:

- authors, for submitting their research papers to the conference;
- keynote speakers who honored us with their talks at ADBIS 2020;
- members of the Program Committee and external reviewers, for dedicating their time and expertise to build a high-quality program;
- members of the ADBIS Steering Committee for their trust and support, and especially its chair Yannis Manolopoulos;
- our academic and private sponsors and partners: the Universities of Lyon 2 and Lyon 3, IDEXLYON, the ERIC laboratory, OnlyLyon, Springer for publishing

these proceedings, the Coalition for Networked Information, as well as our PCO Insight Outside;
- last but not least, all members of the Organizing Committee, who had to switch from a physical organization to an online organization in troubled times.

June 2020   Jérôme Darmont
                                                                     Boris Novikov
                                                                     Robert Wrembel

Organization

General Chair

Jérôme Darmont   Université Lyon 2, France

Steering Committee Chair

Yannis Manolopoulos   Open University of Cyprus, Cyprus

Steering Committee

Ladjel Bellatreche	ENSMA Poitiers, France
Andras Benczur	Eötvös Loránd University, Hungary
Maria Bielikova	Slovak University of Technology in Bratislava, Slovakia
Barbara Catania	University of Genoa, Italy
Jérôme Darmont	Université Lyon 2, France
Johann Eder	Alpen Adria Universität Klagenfurt, Austria
Theo Haerder	Technical University Kaiserslautern, Germany
Mirjana Ivanović	University of Novi Sad, Serbia
Hannu Jaakkola	Tampere University of Technology, Finland
Marite Kirikova	Riga Technical University, Latvia
Rainer Manthey	University of Bonn, Germany
Manuk Manukyan	Yerevan State University, Armenia
Tadeusz Morzy	Poznan University of Technology, Poland
Boris Novikov	National Research University, Higher School of Economics in Saint Petersburg, Russia
George Papadopoulos	University of Cyprus, Cyprus
Jaroslav Pokorný	Charles University in Prague, Czech Republic
Boris Rachev	Technical University of Varna, Bulgaria
Sherif Sakr	University of Tartu, Estonia
Bernhard Thalheim	Christian Albrechts University, Germany
Goce Trajcevski	Iowa State University, USA
Valentino Vranić	Slovak University of Technology in Bratislava, Slovakia
Tatjana Welzer	University of Maribor, Slovenia
Robert Wrembel	Poznan University of Technology, Poland
Ester Zumpano	University of Calabria, Italy

Program Committee Chairs

Boris Novikov   National Research University, Higher School
                                  of Economics in Saint Petersburg, Russia
Robert Wrembel   Poznan University of Technology, Poland

Program Committee

Alberto Abelló   Universitat Politècnica de Catalunya, Spain
Bernd Amann   Sorbonne Université, France
Andreas Behrend   University of Bonn, Germany
Ladjel Bellatreche   ENSMA Poitiers, France
András Benczúr   Eötvös Loránd University, Hungary
Fadila Bentayeb   Université Lyon 2, France
Maria Bielikova   Slovak University of Technology in Bratislava,
                                  Slovakia
Sandro Bimonte   IRSTEA Clermont-Ferrand, France
Miklos Biro   Software Competence Center Hagenberg, Austria
Pawel Boiński   Poznan University of Technology, Poland
Omar Boussaid   Université Lyon 2, France
Drazen Brdjanin   University of Banja Luka, Serbia
Albertas Caplinskas   Vilnius University, Lithuania
Barbara Catania   University of Genoa, Italy
Tania Cerquitelli   Politecnico di Torino, Italy
Ajantha Dahanayake   Lappeenranta University of Technology, Finland
Jérôme Darmont   Université Lyon 2, France
Christos Doulkeridis   University of Piraeus, Greece
Johann Eder   Alpen Adria Universität Klagenfurt, Austria
Markus Endres   University of Passau, Germany
Werner Esswein   Technische Universität Dresden, Germany
Georgios Evangelidis   University of Macedonia, Greece
Flavio Ferrarotti   Software Competence Centre Hagenberg, Austria
Flavius Frasincar   Erasmus University Rotterdam, The Netherlands
Johann Gamper   Free University of Bozen-Bolzano, Italy
Matteo Golfarelli   University of Bologna, Italy
Marcin Gorawski   Silesian University of Technology, Poland
Jānis Grabis   Riga Technical University, Latvia
Le Gruenwald   The University of Oklahoma, USA
Francesco Guerra   Università di Modena e Reggio Emilia, Italy
Giancarlo Guizzardi   Federal University of Espirito Santo, Brazil
Hele-Mai Haav   Tallinn University of Technology, Estonia
Tomas Horvath   Eötvös Loránd University, Hungary
Theo Härder   Technical University Kaiserslautern, Germany
Marko Hölbl   University of Maribor, Slovenia
Mirjana Ivanović   University of Novi Sad, Serbia
Hannu Jaakkola   University of Tampere, Finland

Stefan Jablonski	University of Bayreuth, Germany
Aida Kamišalić Latifić	Universtiy of Maribor, Slovenia
Dimitris Karagiannis	University of Vienna, Austria
Zoubida Kedad	University of Versailles, France
Attila Kiss	Eötvös Loránd University, Hungary
Michal Krátký	Technical University of Ostrava, Czech Republic
Julius Köpke	Alpen Adria Universität Klagenfurt, Austria
Dejan Lavbič	University of Ljubljana, Slovenia
Wolfgang Lehner	Technical University Dresden, Germany
Daniel Lemire	Université du Québec à Montréal, Canada
Sebastian Link	The University of Auckland, New Zealand
Yurii Litvinov	Saint Petersburg State University, Russia
Federica Mandreoli	University of Modena, Italy
Yannis Manolopoulos	Open University of Cyprus, Cyprus
Manuk Manukyan	Yerevan State University, Armenia
Patrick Marcel	Université de Tours, France
Bálint Molnár	Eötvös University of Budapest, Hungary
Angelo Montanari	University of Udine, Italy
Tadeusz Morzy	Poznan University of Technology, Poland
Martin Nečaský	Charles University, Czech Republic
Boris Novikov	National Research University, Higher School of Economics in Saint Petersburg, Russia
Kjetil Nørvåg	Norwegian University of Science and Technology, Norway
Andreas Oberweis	Karlsruhe Institute of Technology, Germany
Carlos Ordonez	University of Houston, USA
George Papadopoulos	University of Cyprus, Cyprus
András Pataricza	Budapest University of Technology and Economics, Hungary
Jaroslav Pokorný	Charles University in Prague, Czech Republic
Giuseppe Polese	University of Salerno, Italy
Alvaro E. Prieto	University of Extremadura, Spain
Miloš Radovanović	University of Novi Sad, Serbia
Heri Ramampiaro	Norwegian University of Science and Technology, Norway
Franck Ravat	Université de Toulouse, France
Stefano Rizzi	University of Bologna, Italy
Oscar Romero	Universitat Politècnica de Catalunya, Spain
Gunter Saake	University of Magdeburg, Germany
Kai-Uwe Sattler	Technical University Ilmenau, Germany
Milos Savic	University of Novi Sad, Serbia
Patrick Schäfer	Humboldt Universität zu Berlin, Germany
Timos Sellis	Swinburne University of Technology, Australia
Bela Stantic	Griffith University, Australia
Kostas Stefanidis	University of Tampere, Finland
Sergey Stupnikov	Russian Academy of Sciences, Russia

Olivier Teste	Université de Toulouse, France
Bernhard Thalheim	Christian Albrechts University Kiel, Germany
Goce Trajcevski	Iowa State University, USA
Raquel Trillo-Lado	Universidad de Zaragoza, Spain
Olegas Vasilecas	Vilnius Gediminas Technical University, Lithuania
Goran Velinov	UKIM, North Macedonia
Isabelle Wattiau	ESSEC, CNAM, France
Tatjana Welzer	University of Maribor, Slovenia
Marek Wojciechowski	Poznan University of Technology, Poland
Robert Wrembel	Poznan University of Technology, Poland
Anna Yarygina	Saint Petersburg State University, Russia
Vladimir Zadorozhny	University of Pittsburgh, USA
Jaroslav Zendulka	Brno University of Technology, Czech Republic

Additional Reviewers

Andrea Brunello	Nicolas Labroche
Alexandre Chanson	Christos Mettouris
Stefano Cirillo	Sergi Nadal
Vincenzo Deufemia	Demetris Paschalides
Senén González	Oszkár Semeráth
Anna Gorawska	Jakub Ševcech
Sergio Ilarri	Artem Trofimov
Igor Kuralenok	Willeme Verdeaux
Petar Jovanovic	Alexandros Yeratziotis

Proceeding Chairs

Fadila Bentayeb	Université Lyon 2, France
Elöd Egyed-Zsigmond	INSA Lyon, France
Nadia Kabachi	Université Lyon 1, France

Workshop Chairs

Ladjel Bellatreche	ENSMA Poitiers, France
Mária Bieliková	Slovak University of Technology, Slovakia
Christos Papatheodorou	Ionian University, Greece
Guilaine Talens	Université Lyon 3, France

Doctoral Consortium Chairs

Barbara Catania	University of Genoa, Italy
Elena Demidova	L3S Research Center, Germany
Oscar Romero	Universitat Politècnica de Catalunya, Spain
Maja Zumer	University of Ljubljana, Slovenia

Journal Special Issue Chair

Ladjel Bellatreche   ENSMA Poitiers, France

Publicity Chair

Selma Khouri   ESI Alger, Algeria

Organizing Committee

Fadila Bentayeb	Université Lyon 2, France
Omar Boussaïd	Université Lyon 2, France
Jérôme Darmont	Université Lyon 2, France
Fabien Duchateau	Université Lyon 1, France
Elöd Egyed-Zsigmond	INSA Lyon, France
Mihaela Juganaru-Mathieu	École des Mines de Saint-Étienne, France
Nadia Kabachi	Université Lyon 1, France
Omar Larouk	ENSSIB Lyon, France
Fabrice Muhlenbach	Université de Saint-Étienne, France
Habiba Osman	Université Lyon 2, France
Muriel Perez	Université de Saint-Étienne, France
Pegdwendé Sawadogo	Université Lyon 2, France
Guilaine Talens	Université Lyon 3, France
Caroline Wintergerst	Université Lyon 3, France

Keynote Speakers' Bios

The 24th European Conference on Advances in Databases and Information Systems (ADBIS 2020), the 24th International Conference on Theory and Practice of Digital Libraries (TPDL 2020), and the 16th EDA days on Business Intelligence & Big Data (EDA 2020) were "colocated" online during August 25–27, 2020, because of the COVID-19 crisis. This joint event was set to be held originally in Lyon, France.

Keynotes were common to all three conferences. This chapter introduces the five keynote speakers of high scientific profile who honored us with an invited speech. We thank them very much. Extended abstracts of keynotes by: Amr El Abbadi, Johann Gamper, and Ioana Manolescu are included in this LNCS volume. Extended abstracts of keynotes by Verónika Peralta and Elaine Toms are included in the EDA and TPDL proceedings, respectively.

Amr El Abbadi (University of California, USA)

Amr El Abbadi is a Professor of Computer Science at the University of California, Santa Barbara. He received his Bachelor in Engineering from Alexandria University, Egypt, and his PhD from Cornell University. His research interests are in the fields of fault-tolerant distributed systems and databases, focusing recently on Cloud data management and blockchain-based systems.

Prof. El Abbadi is an ACM Fellow, AAAS Fellow, and IEEE Fellow. He was Chair of the Computer Science Department at UCSB from 2007 to 2011. He has served as a journal editor for several database journals, including *The VLDB Journal* and *IEEE Transactions on Computers and The Computer Journal.* He has been Program Chair for multiple database and distributed systems conferences. He currently serves on the Executive Committee of the IEEE Technical Committee on Data Engineering (TCDE) and was a board member of the VLDB Endowment from 2002 to 2008.

In 2007, Prof. El Abbadi received the UCSB Senate Outstanding Mentorship Award for his excellence in mentoring graduate students. In 2013, his student, Sudipto Das received the SIGMOD Jim Gray Doctoral Dissertation Award. Prof. El Abbadi is also a co-recipient of the Test of Time Award at EDBT/ICDT 2015. He has published over 300 articles in databases and distributed systems and has supervised over 35 PhD students.

Johann Gamper (Free University of Bozen-Bolzano, Italy)

Professor Johann Gamper's main research areas are temporal databases, time series data, data warehousing and data analytics, approximate query answering, data summarization, and graph matching. His research concentrates on database technologies with a focus on processing and querying temporal data.

Johann Gamper is author of 120+ publications in international journals and conference proceedings, many of which are in the most prestigious outlets of database systems (TODS, VLDBJ, TKDE, SIGMOD, VLDB, ICDE). He regularly serves as reviewer for technical journals, PC member, and organizer of conferences.

Ioana Manolescu (Inria Saclay–Île-de-France et École Polytechnique, France)

Doctor Ioana Manolescu is a Senior Researcher who leads of the INRIA/LIX CEDAR project-team, focused on Rich Data Exploration at Cloud Scale. She is also part-time professor at École Polytechnique, Paris.

Her research interests include models, tools, and algorithms for data journalism and journalistic fact-checking; efficient ontology-mediated query answering; and cloud-based management of web data.

Ioana Manolescu is also member of the PVLDB Endowment Board of Trustees.

Verónika Peralta (University of Tours, France)

Verónika Peralta is Associate Professor at the University of Tours, France, and a member of the Fundamental and Applied Computer Science Laboratory (LIFAT), since 2008. She received her PhD in Computer Science from the University of Versailles and the University of the Republic of Uruguay in 2006. Her research interests include data quality, data warehousing, exploratory analysis, OLAP, query recommendation, and query personalization.

Her teaching mainly concerns databases, data warehousing, and information systems. She has taught multiple courses since 1996, in several universities of France, Uruguay, and Argentina. She has also several years of professional experience as a data warehouse developer and consultant.

Elaine Toms (University of Sheffield, UK)

Elaine Toms is currently Professor of Information Innovation Management, Management School, University of Sheffield, UK. She previously held posts at the iSchool, University of Sheffield; the Faculty of Management and School of Information Studies, Dalhousie University, Canada; and the Faculty of Information, University of Toronto, Canada. She was the first information scientist to be appointed to a Canada Research Chair.

Over the course of her career, she has held multiple administration roles (e.g., Director of Teaching Quality Enhancement and of Research); been actively engaged in professional associations including ASIST (serving on the Board of Directors); has served as program chair for multiple conferences (e.g., ASIST, Hypertext, and JCDL); and currently serves on the editorial board of IPM and is an associate editor of JASIST.

She completed her PhD at Western University, Canada, from which she went on to examine multiple facets of the information interaction problem from interface issues to interruptions and task, with a particular focus on evaluation. Her work has been funded by multiple groups on both sides of the pond (e.g., both the science and social science research councils in Canada, OCLC, Heritage Canada, Canada Foundation for Innovation, Horizon 2020).

She has been an investigator with multiple research networks (e.g., NECTAR, Network for Effective Collaboration Through Advanced Research; PROMISE, Participative Research labOratory for Multimedia and Multilingual Information Systems Evaluation).

Contents

Keynote Extended Abstracts

Blockchains and Databases: Opportunities and Challenges for the Permissioned and the Permissionless

Divyakant Agrawal, Amr El Abbadi$^{(\boxtimes)}$, Mohammad Javad Amiri, Sujaya Maiyya, and Victor Zakhary

Department of Computer Science, University of California, Santa Barbara, USA
{agrawal,amr,amiri,sujaya_maiyya,victorzakhary}@cs.ucsb.edu

1 Introduction

Bitcoin [12] is a successful and interesting example of a global scale peer-to-peer cryptocurrency that integrates many techniques and protocols from cryptography, distributed systems, and databases. The main underlying data structure is blockchain, a scalable fully replicated structure that is shared among all participants and guarantees a consistent view of all user transactions by all participants in the system. In a blockchain, nodes agree on their shared states across a large network of *untrusted* participants. Although originally devised for cryptocurrencies, recent systems exploit its many unique features such as transparency, provenance, fault tolerance, and authenticity to support a wide range of distributed applications. Bitcoin and other cryptocurrencies use *permissionless* blockchains. In a permissionless blockchain, the network is public, and anyone can participate without a specific identity. Many other distributed applications, such as supply chain management and healthcare, are deployed on *permissioned* blockchains consisting of a set of known, identified nodes that still might not fully trust each other. This paper illustrates some of the main challenges and opportunities from a database perspective in the many novel and interesting application domains of blockchains. These opportunities are illustrated using various examples from recent research in both permissionless and permissioned blockchains. Two main themes unite the various examples: (1) the important role of distribution and consensus in managing large scale systems and (2) the need to tolerate malicious failures. The advent of cloud computing and large data centers shifted large scale data management infrastructures from centralized databases to distributed systems. One of the main challenges in designing distributed systems is the need for fault-tolerance. Cloud-based systems typically assume trusted infrastructures, since data centers are owned by the enterprises managing the data, and hence the design typically only assumes and tolerates crash failures. The advent of blockchain and the underlying premise that copies of the blockchain are distributed among untrusted entities has shifted the focus of fault-tolerance from tolerating crash failures to tolerating malicious failures. These interesting and challenging settings pose great opportunities for database researchers.

© Springer Nature Switzerland AG 2020
J. Darmont et al. (Eds.): ADBIS 2020, LNCS 12245, pp. 3–7, 2020.
https://doi.org/10.1007/978-3-030-54832-2_1

2   Permissionless Blockchains

The recent adoption of blockchain technologies and open permissionless networks suggest the importance of peer-to-peer atomic cross-chain transaction protocols. Users typically own assets in different crypto-currencies and should be able to atomically exchange their assets across different blockchains without depending on centralized intermediaries such as exchanges. Recent peer-to-peer atomic cross-chain swap protocols use hashlocks and timelocks to ensure that participants comply with the protocol [1,10,13]. However, an expired timelock could lead to a violation of the all-or-nothing atomicity property. An honest participant who fails to execute a smart contract on time due to a crash failure or network delays might end up losing her assets. Although a crashed participant is the only participant who ends up worse off, current proposals are unsuitable for atomic cross-chain transactions in asynchronous environments where crash failures and network delays are the norm.

An **A**tomic **C**ross-**C**hain **T**ransaction, AC^2T, is a distributed transaction that spans multiple blockchains. This distributed transaction consists of sub-transactions and each sub-transaction is executed on a different blockchain. An **A**tomic **C**ross-**C**hain Commitment protocol is required to execute AC^2Ts. Such a protocol is a variation of traditional distributed atomic commitment protocols (e.g., 2PC [7,8]) and should guarantee both *atomicity* and *commitment* of AC^2Ts. **Atomicity** ensures the **all-or-nothing** property where either all sub-transactions take place or none of them are executed. **Commitment** guarantees that any changes caused by a cross-chain transaction are durable and once committed, these changes are permanent. Unlike in 2PC and other traditional distributed atomic commitment protocols, atomic cross-chain commitment protocols are also trust-free and therefore must **tolerate** maliciousness [10]. Existing solutions by Nolan [1,13] and generalized by Herlihy [10] do not guarantee the atomicity of AC^2Ts in asynchronous environments where crash failures, network partitioning, denial of service attacks and message delays are possible. In [14], we present an **A**tomic **C**ross-**C**hain **C**ommitment protocol that uses an open **W**itness **N**etwork. Events for redeeming and refunding transactions that exchange assets across permissionless blockchains are modeled as conflicting events. An open permissionless network of witnesses is used to guarantee that conflicting events could never simultaneously occur and either all smart contracts in an atomic cross-chain transaction are redeemed or all of them are refunded.

3   Permissioned Blockchains

Permissioned blockchains consist of a set of known, identified nodes that still might not fully trust each other. To be practical in real-life settings permissioned blockchains face multiple challenges regarding the *confidentiality, verifiability, performance,* and *scalability* requirements of distributed applications.

Confidentiality of data is required in many collaborative distributed applications, e.g., supply chain management, where multiple enterprises collaborate with each other following Service Level Agreements (SLAs) to provide different services. To deploy distributed applications across different collaborating enterprises, a blockchain system needs to support the internal transactions of each enterprise as well as cross-enterprise transactions that represent the collaboration between enterprises. While the data accessed by cross-enterprise transactions should be *visible* to all enterprises, the internal data of each enterprise, which are accessed by internal transactions, might be *confidential*. In Caper [2], each enterprise orders and executes its internal transactions locally while cross-enterprise transactions are public and visible to every node. In addition, the blockchain ledger of Caper is a directed acyclic graph that includes the internal transactions of every enterprise and all cross-enterprise transactions. Nonetheless, for the sake of confidentiality, the blockchain ledger is not maintained by any node. In fact, each enterprise maintains its own *local view* of the ledger including its internal and all cross-enterprise transactions. Since ordering cross-enterprise transactions requires global agreement among all enterprises, Caper introduces different consensus protocols to globally order cross-enterprise transactions.

Besides confidentiality, in many cross-enterprise systems, e.g., crowdsourcing applications, participants need to verify transactions that are initiated by other enterprises to ensure the satisfaction of some predefined global constraints on the entire system. Thus, the system needs to support *verifiability* while preserving the confidentiality of transactions. To address this problem, we have introduced Separ [6], a multi-platform blockchain-based crowdsourcing system that uses a token-based technique to ensure verifiability. A token can be seen as an entity that represents some property based on a global constraint, which need to be verified. For example, if a global constraint declares that a particular participant cannot initiate more than 20 transactions in a week, the system will assign 20 tokens to that participant and the participant consumes a token whenever it initiates a transaction. Depending on the requested global constraints, the tokens might need to satisfy different properties. First, tokens need to be non-exchangeable, i.e., different participants cannot exchange their tokens. Second, a token should expire after some predetermined amount of time, and third, a token cannot be consume more than once.

In addition to confidentiality and verifiability, distributed applications, e.g., financial applications, require high performance in terms of throughput and latency, e.g., while the Visa payment service is able to handle more than 10000 transactions per second, Multichain [9] can handle at most 200 transactions per second. SharPer [3,5] supports the concurrent processing of transactions by clustering nodes into clusters and sharding the data and the blockchain ledger. SharPer supports both intra-shard and cross-shard transactions and introduces flattened consensus protocols for ordering cross-shard transactions among the involved clusters.

Finally, scalability is one of the main obstacles to business adoption of blockchain systems. To support a distributed application, e.g., large-scale database, a blockchain system should be able to scale efficiently by adding more nodes to the system. While database systems use the sharding technique to improve the scalability of databases in a network of crash-only nodes, the technique cannot easily be utilized by blockchain systems due to the existence of malicious nodes in the network. ParBlockchain [4] introduces a new paradigm to support distributed applications that execute concurrently for workloads with some degree of contention. In ParBlockchain a disjoint set of nodes (orderers) establishes agreement on the order among transactions of different enterprises, constructs blocks of transactions, and generates a *dependency graph* for the transactions within a block. A dependency graph gives a partial order based on the conflicts between transactions and enables the parallel execution of non-conflicting transactions. Transactions are then executed following the generated dependency graph. While ParBlockchain supports contentious workloads, any non-deterministic execution of transactions will decrease its performance.

4   Back to Databases

As increasing amounts of data are currently being stored and managed on third-party servers. It is impractical for small scale enterprises to own their private datacenters, hence renting third-party servers is a viable solution. But the increasing number of malicious attacks, both internal and external, as well as buggy software on third-party servers may cause clients to lose their trust in these external infrastructures. While small enterprises cannot avoid using external infrastructures, they need the right set of protocols to manage their data on untrusted infrastructures. Fides [11], introduces a novel atomic commitment protocol, TFCommit, that executes transactions on data stored across multiple untrusted servers. This novel atomic commitment protocol executes transactions in an untrusted environment without using expensive Byzantine replication. Using TFCommit, we propose an *auditable* data management system, Fides, residing completely on untrustworthy infrastructure. As an auditable system, Fides guarantees the detection of potentially malicious failures occurring on untrusted servers using blockchain inspired tamper-resistant logs with the support of cryptographic techniques. Fides is scalable and incurs relatively low overhead that allows executing transactions on untrusted infrastructure.

Acknowledgement. This work is partially funded by NSF grants CNS-1703560 and CNS-1815733.

References

1. Atomic cross-chain trading (2018). https://en.bitcoin.it/wiki/Atomic_cross-chain_trading
2. Amiri, M.J., Agrawal, D., El Abbadi, A.: Caper: a cross-application permissioned blockchain. Proc. VLDB Endow. **12**(11), 1385–1398 (2019)
3. Amiri, M.J., Agrawal, D., El Abbadi, A.: On sharding permissioned blockchains. In: Second International Conference on Blockchain. IEEE (2019)

4. Amiri, M.J., Agrawal, D., El Abbadi, A.: Parblockchain: leveraging transaction parallelism in permissioned blockchain systems. In: 39th International Conference on Distributed Computing Systems (ICDCS), pp. 1337–1347. IEEE (2019)

5. Amiri, M.J., Agrawal, D., El Abbadi, A.: Sharper: sharding permissioned blockchains over network clusters. arXiv preprint arXiv:1910.00765 (2019)

6. Amiri, M.J., Duguépéroux, J., Allard, T., Agrawal, D., El Abbadi, A.: Separ: a privacy-preserving blockchain-based system for regulating multi-platform crowd-working environments. arXiv preprint arXiv:2005.07850 (2020)

7. Bernstein, P.A., Hadzilacos, V., Goodman, N.: Concurrency control and recovery in database systems (1987)

8. Gray, J.N.: Notes on data base operating systems. In: Bayer, R., Graham, R.M., Seegmüller, G. (eds.) Operating Systems. LNCS, vol. 60, pp. 393–481. Springer, Heidelberg (1978). https://doi.org/10.1007/3-540-08755-9_9

9. Greenspan, G.: Multichain private blockchain-white paper. http://www.multichain.com/download/MultiChain-White-Paper.pdf (2015)

10. Herlihy, M.: Atomic cross-chain swaps. In: ACM Symposium on Principles of Distributed Computing (PODC), pp. 245–254. ACM (2018)

11. Maiyya, S., Cho, D.H.B., Agrawal, D., Abbadi, A.E.: Fides: managing data on untrusted infrastructure. In: 40th International Conference on Distributed Computing Systems (ICDCS). IEEE (2020)

12. Nakamoto, S.: Bitcoin: a peer-to-peer electronic cash system (2008)

13. Nolan, T.: Alt chains and atomic transfers (2013). https://bitcointalk.org/index.php?topic=193281.msg2224949#msg2224949

14. Zakhary, V., Agrawal, D., El Abbadi, A.: Atomic commitment across blockchains. Proc. VLDB Endow. **13**, 1 (2020)

Processing Temporal and Time Series Data: Present State and Future Challenges

Johann Gamper$^{(\boxtimes)}$ ⓘ and Anton Dignös ⓘ

Free University of Bozen-Bolzano, Bolzano, Italy
{johann.gamper,anton.dignoes}@unibz.it

Abstract. Temporal data is ubiquitous, and its importance has been witnessed by the research efforts for several decades as well as by the increased interest in the last years from both academia and industry. Two prominent research directions in this context are the field of temporal databases and the field of time series data. This extended abstract aims at providing a concise overview about the state of the art in processing temporal and time series data as well as to discuss open research problems and challenges.

Keywords: Temporal databases · Time series

1 Introduction and Background

Research efforts on temporal information have been conducted for several decades, evolving the field and covering multiple aspects of time referenced data, e.g., in AI, Logic, and Databases. In the last decade, we have seen a renewed interest in temporal data from both academia and industry. This has several reasons: abundant storage has made long term archival of historical data feasible, and it has been recognized that temporal data holds the potential to reveal valuable insights that cannot be found by analyzing only a snapshot of the data.

The field of temporal databases focused on data with associated time periods, representing valid or transaction time. Research covered many aspect of data management: the design of SQL-based query languages, the development of efficient storage/index structures and algorithms, as well as standardization efforts. Data is processed by the classical database operators of the relational algebra. Conceptually, a temporal database is seen as sequence of snapshot databases, and operations are performed on each snapshot. The main intuition behind this scheme is that data is processed together only if it is valid at the same time.

A different variant of temporal data are time series (or more generally data series), representing a core abstraction to capture the dynamics of the world.

This work has partially been done in the context of the TASMA project, which is funded by the CRC research fund of unibz.

J. Darmont et al. (Eds.): ADBIS 2020, LNCS 12245, pp. 8–14, 2020.
https://doi.org/10.1007/978-3-030-54832-2_2

A key difference to temporal databases is that data is recorded at time points and the analysis operations have to consider time series as a whole (or subsequences thereof), rather than values at individual time points. As a consequence, most operations are based on similarity measures between sequences. Most of past research on time series in the database and data mining communities concentrated on similarity measures, indexing structures and individual operations, delivering highly efficient and specialized solutions.

In this extended abstract, we provide a concise overview about the state-of-the-art on classical temporal database research and on time series as a specific form of temporal data. We will then focus on current and future research challenges and relationships between the two fields.

2   Database Technologies for Temporal Data

State of the Art. The management and processing of temporal data in database management systems (DBMS) has been an active research area since databases were invented [5]. After studying basic concepts for modeling time in the early days of temporal database research, in the 1980s various query languages have been proposed to facilitate the formulation of temporal queries [7]. Different strategies have been adopted, such as extending SQL with new data types and associated predicates (e.g., TSQL2 [38]), point-based approaches in combination with timestamp normalization to transform between an interval-based representation and a point-based conceptual model (e.g., IXSQL [32], SQL/TP [39]), and the systematic construction of temporal SQL queries from nontemporal SQL queries (e.g., ATSQL [8]). In a subsequent phase, the focus shifted towards efficient algorithms and index structures for individual operators, such as aggregation and joins. Temporal aggregation has been studied in various flavors (instant, moving-window, and span temporal aggregation [6,31]) with dedicated algorithmic solutions, e.g., aggregation tree [26], balanced tree [34], SB-tree [42], and *MVSB-tree* [43]. Temporal joins [17] gained increased attention in recent years with a number of efficient solutions, e.g., lazy endpoint-based interval join [36], overlap interval partition join [13], disjoint interval partitioning join [10], and a forward-scan based plane sweep algorithm [9]. The timeline index is a general main memory index for temporal data and supports different operations [19].

The first approach to achieve systematic and comprehensive support for sequenced temporal queries in RDBMSs is the temporal alignment framework [14], which reduces temporal queries to the corresponding nontemporal queries. The approach allows a tight integration into the database kernel, leveraging existing query optimization and evaluation strategies for temporal queries.[1]

Temporal Support in SQL:2011 and DBMSs. The most important novelty in the SQL:2011 standard is the explicit support for the storage and manipulation of temporal data [27]. Tables can be associated with one or two time periods, representing application time and system time, commonly known as valid and

---

[1] An implementation in the kernel of PostgreSQL is here: tpg.inf.unibz.it.

transaction time, respectively. The standard also specifies the update behavior of temporal tables as well as primary and foreign keys. The support for querying temporal relations is essentially limited to simple range queries; more advanced operators are not supported. Following the SQL:2011 standard, major database vendors have started to offer temporal support in their database management systems, such as IBM DB2, Oracle DBMS, or PostgreSQL. Teradata DBMS [2] provides the best query support based on the concept of statement modifiers [8].

Future Challenges. Despite recent advancements in processing temporal data, there are a number of open challenges that call for further research. While temporal alignment [14] provides the first solid and sound framework for a tight integration of temporal query support in existing relational database systems, a number of improvements are required to achieve scalability for very large data. This includes, for instance, more targeted temporal alignment primitives that produce smaller intermediate relations, more accurate and optimistic cost estimates for the query optimizer based on statistics about the temporal distribution of data, as well as specialized query algorithms and equivalence rules.

Another important aspects concerns the support for two or more time dimensions, such as valid time and transaction time as specified in the SQL standard; currently, temporal alignment supports only valid time. While the key idea of temporal alignment an be generalized and extended to multiple time dimensions, the adjustment of timestamps becomes much more complex and demanding.

From the user perspective, more research in SQL-based temporal query languages is needed to facilitate the formulation of complex temporal queries; this aspect is not covered in the SQL:2011 standard.

3   Time Series Management and Analysis

State of the Art. Time series have been the subject of extensive studies for many years now and in several research communities. In the database community, we can observe an increased activity during the past decade due to the fast diffusion of sensors and the unprecedented speed at which such data is generated in different application domains, e.g., Industry 4.0, IoT, finance, medicine, etc. The study of time series has concentrated on different aspects, including similarity measures, preprocessing, indexing, and advanced query processing.

Most of the queries are based on similarity between time series or subsequences rather than on exact matches. Prominent distance measures are the Euclidean distance, Dynamic Time Warping distance [4], and the Fréchet distance [3]. To enable accurate and reliable time series analytics, a preprocessing phase is indispensable for at least two reasons: most of the methods require complete and clean input data, which is rarely the case in real-world applications, and data is often very huge and need to be compressed for an efficient analysis. Important preprocessing tasks are the imputation of missing values [25,41] and data summarization/representation. Representative examples of data summarization include piecewise aggregate approximation (PAA) [22], piecewise linear approximation (PLA) [24], symbolic aggregate approximation (SAX) [29], adaptive piecewise constant approximation (APCA) [21], discrete Fourier transform (DFT) [1], and discrete wavelet transform (DWT) [12]. To offer efficient access to time series, a variety of different indexing techniques have been proposed, most notably an entire family of indices based on the SAX representation of time series, e.g. iSAX [11], ADS [44], and ULISSE [30]. There has been a large body of research work on various advanced data analysis and mining tasks (cf. [15] for a survey), such as query by content [16], anomaly detection [40], motif discovery [28], finding discords [20], clustering [23], and prediction [33].

Time Series Management Systems. While relational DBMSs have been successfully deployed in many situations, they are not designed for time series data and hence are unsuitable to handle the huge amount of data and to offer appropriate query facilities. Hence, more recently various time series management systems (TSMSs) have been proposed, which are either implemented from scratch or extensions of existing DBMSs [18]. There have also been some works on extending SQL towards the support for time series, e.g., proposed SQL-TS for querying patterns in sequences of data stored in RDBMSs [37]. Finally, there exist several open-source TSMSs, such as OpenTSDB, InfluxDB, and TimescaleDB.

Future Challenges. Past research on time series has focused on specific analysis and mining operations in isolation, producing highly specialized solutions that make assumptions about the data that are rarely met in real-world applications. Practical case studies show that the preprocessing of data is of utmost importance for accurate downstream analyses. This is mainly an explorative task and is frequently done in a rather ad hoc manner. What would be needed by data analysts is a toolbox of preprocessing methods to support, for example, choosing the appropriate representation/summarization method and/or window size together with the required parameters for specific analytical tasks. A systematic study of the impact of preprocessing methods (such as time series representation/summarization and choosing the right window size) for follow-up analysis is therefore crucial.

Modern relational DBMSs are extremely powerful analytics engines. It would be interesting to investigate how existing technologies from (temporal) databases can be adopted for the processing of time series and to deeply integrate time series and database technologies. This will leverage existing technologies from both fields and advance SQL and relational database systems towards a powerful high-level shell for processing time series data in a declarative way. The need for a general-purpose TSMS has also been expressed in [35].

4   Conclusion

The processing of temporal data including time series is receiving renewed attention in the database community. In this work, we provide a concise overview of current results, and we identify new challenges to advance the state-of-the-art towards more comprehensive support for querying and analyzing such data.

While many works exist on individual aspects of temporal and time series data, the main challenge is to integrate these results into scalable, general purpose data management systems with comprehensive support for such data.

References

1. Agrawal, R., Faloutsos, C., Swami, A.N.: Efficient similarity search in sequence databases. In: FODO, pp. 69–84 (1993)
2. Al-Kateb, M., Ghazal, A., Crolotte, A., Bhashyam, R., Chimanchode, J., Pakala, S.P.: Temporal query processing in teradata. In: EDBT, pp. 573–578 (2013)
3. Alt, H., Godau, M.: Computing the fréchet distance between two polygonal curves. Int. J. Comput. Geom. Appl. **5**(01n02), 75–91 (1995)
4. Berndt, D.J., Clifford, J.: Using dynamic time warping to find patterns in time series. In: KDD Workshop, pp. 359–370. AAAI Press (1994)
5. Böhlen, M.H., Dignös, A., Gamper, J., Jensen, C.S.: Temporal data management – an overview. In: Zimányi, E. (ed.) eBISS 2017. LNBIP, vol. 324, pp. 51–83. Springer, Cham (2018). https://doi.org/10.1007/978-3-319-96655-7_3
6. Böhlen, M., Gamper, J., Jensen, C.S.: Multi-dimensional aggregation for temporal data. In: Loannidis, Y., et al. (eds.) EDBT 2006. LNCS, vol. 3896, pp. 257–275. Springer, Heidelberg (2006). https://doi.org/10.1007/11687238_18
7. Böhlen, M.H., Jensen, C.S.: Temporal data model and query language concepts. In: Encyclopedia of Information Systems, pp. 437–453. Elsevier (2003)
8. Böhlen, M.H., Jensen, C.S., Snodgrass, R.T.: Temporal statement modifiers. ACM Trans. Database Syst. **25**(4), 407–456 (2000)
9. Bouros, P., Mamoulis, N.: A forward scan based plane sweep algorithm for parallel interval joins. PVLDB **10**(11), 1346–1357 (2017)
10. Cafagna, F., Böhlen, M.H.: Disjoint interval partitioning. VLDB J. **26**(3), 447–466 (2017)
11. Camerra, A., Palpanas, T., Shieh, J., Keogh, E.J.: iSAX 2.0: indexing and mining one billion time series. In: ICDM, pp. 58–67. IEEE (2010)
12. Chan, K., Fu, A.W.: Efficient time series matching by wavelets. In: ICDE, pp. 126–133 (1999)
13. Dignös, A., Böhlen, M.H., Gamper, J.: Overlap interval partition join. In: SIGMOD, pp. 1459–1470 (2014)
14. Dignös, A., Böhlen, M.H., Gamper, J., Jensen, C.S.: Extending the kernel of a relational DBMS with comprehensive support for sequenced temporal queries. ACM Trans. Database Syst. **41**(4), 26:1–26:46 (2016)
15. Esling, P., Agon, C.: Time-series data mining. ACM Comput. Surv. **45**(1), 12:1–12:34 (2012)
16. Faloutsos, C., Ranganathan, M., Manolopoulos, Y.: Fast subsequence matching in time-series databases. In: SIGMOD, pp. 419–429. ACM (1994)
17. Gao, D., Jensen, C.S., Snodgrass, R.T., Soo, M.D.: Join operations in temporal databases. VLDB J. **14**(1), 2–29 (2005)
18. Jensen, S.K., Pedersen, T.B., Thomsen, C.: Time series management systems: a survey. IEEE Trans. Knowl. Data Eng. **29**(11), 2581–2600 (2017)
19. Kaufmann, M., et al.: Timeline index: a unified data structure for processing queries on temporal data in SAP HANA. In: SIGMOD, pp. 1173–1184 (2013)
20. Keogh, E., Lin, J., Fu, A.: HOT SAX: efficiently finding the most unusual time series subsequence. In: ICDM (2005)

21. Keogh, E.J., Chakrabarti, K., Mehrotra, S., Pazzani, M.J.: Locally adaptive dimensionality reduction for indexing large time series databases. In: SIGMOD, pp. 151–162 (2001)
22. Keogh, E.J., Chakrabarti, K., Pazzani, M.J., Mehrotra, S.: Dimensionality reduction for fast similarity search in large time series databases. Knowl. Inf. Syst. **3**(3), 263–286 (2001)
23. Keogh, E., Lin, J.: Clustering of time-series subsequences is meaningless: implications for previous and future research. Knowl. Inf. Syst. **8**(2), 154–177 (2004). https://doi.org/10.1007/s10115-004-0172-7
24. Keogh, E.J., Pazzani, M.J.: An enhanced representation of time series which allows fast and accurate classification, clustering and relevance feedback. In: KDD, pp. 239–243 (1998)
25. Khayati, M., Lerner, A., Tymchenko, Z., Cudré-Mauroux, P.: Mind the gap: an experimental evaluation of imputation of missing values techniques in time series. Proc. VLDB Endow. **13**(5), 768–782 (2020)
26. Kline, N., Snodgrass, R.T.: Computing temporal aggregates. ICDE **1995**, 222–231 (1995)
27. Kulkarni, K.G., Michels, J.: Temporal features in SQL: 2011. SIGMOD Rec. **41**(3), 34–43 (2012)
28. Lin, J., Keogh, E.J., Lonardi, S., Lankford, J.P., Nystrom, D.M.: Visually mining and monitoring massive time series. In: SIGKDD, pp. 460–469 (2004)
29. Lin, J., Keogh, E.J., Wei, L., Lonardi, S.: Experiencing SAX: a novel symbolic representation of time series. Data Min. Knowl. Discov. **15**(2), 107–144 (2007)
30. Linardi, M., Palpanas, T.: Scalable, variable-length similarity search in data series: the ULISSE approach. PVLDB **11**(13), 2236–2248 (2018)
31. López, I.F.V., Snodgrass, R.T., Moon, B.: Spatiotemporal aggregate computation: a survey. IEEE Trans. Knowl. Data Eng. **17**(2), 271–286 (2005)
32. Lorentzos, N.A., Mitsopoulos, Y.G.: SQL extension for interval data. IEEE Trans. Knowl. Data Eng. **9**(3), 480–499 (1997)
33. Matsubara, Y., Sakurai, Y.: Regime shifts in streams: real-time forecasting of co-evolving time sequences. In: SIGKDD, pp. 1045–1054 (2016)
34. Moon, B., López, I.F.V., Immanuel, V.: Efficient algorithms for large-scale temporal aggregation. IEEE Trans. Knowl. Data Eng. **15**(3), 744–759 (2003)
35. Palpanas, T.: Data series management: the road to big sequence analytics. SIGMOD Rec. **44**(2), 47–52 (2015)
36. Piatov, D., Helmer, S., Dignös, A.: An interval join optimized for modern hardware. In: ICDE, pp. 1098–1109 (2016)
37. Sadri, R., Zaniolo, C., Zarkesh, A.M., Adibi, J.: A sequential pattern query language for supporting instant data mining for e-services. In: VLDB, pp. 653–656 (2001)
38. Snodgrass, R.T. (ed.): The TSQL2 Temporal Query Language. Kluwer, Norwell (1995)
39. Toman, D.: Point vs. interval-based query languages for temporal databases. In: PODS, pp. 58–67 (1996)
40. Wei, L., Kumar, N., Lolla, V.N., Keogh, E.J., Lonardi, S., Ratanamahatana, C.A.: Assumption-free anomaly detection in time series. In: SSDBM, pp. 237–240 (2005)
41. Wellenzohn, K., Böhlen, M.H., Dignös, A., Gamper, J., Mitterer, H.: Continuous imputation of missing values in streams of pattern-determining time series. In: EDBT, pp. 330–341 (2017)
42. Yang, J., Widom, J.: Incremental computation and maintenance of temporal aggregates. VLDB J. **12**(3), 262–283 (2003)

43. Zhang, D., Markowetz, A., Tsotras, V.J., Gunopulos, D., Seeger, B.: Efficient computation of temporal aggregates with range predicates. In: PODS (2001)
44. Zoumpatianos, K., Idreos, S., Palpanas, T.: RINSE: interactive data series exploration with ADS+. PVLDB 8(12), 1912–1915 (2015)

Integrating (Very) Heterogeneous Data Sources: A Structured and an Unstructured Perspective

Ioana Manolescu[✉]

Inria and Institut Polytechnique de Paris, Palaiseau, France
ioana.manolescu@inria.fr
https://pages.saclay.inria.fr/ioana.manolescu/

Abstract. Data integration is a broad area of data management research. It has lead to the development of many useful tools and concepts, each appropriate in a certain class of applicative settings.

We consider the setting in which data sources have heterogeneous data models. This setting is of increasing relevance, as the (once predominant) relational databases are supplemented by data exchanged in formats such as JSON or XML, graphs such as Linked Open (RDF) data, or matrix (numerical) etc. We describe two lines of work in this setting. The first aims on improving performance in a *polystore* setting, where data sources are queried through a *structure, composite* query language; the focus here is on dramatically improving performance through the use of *view-based rewriting* techniques. The second data integration setting assumes that sources are much too heterogeneous for structured querying and thus, explore *keyword-based search* in an integrated graph built from all the available data.

Designing and setting up data integration architectures remains a rather complex task; data heterogeneity makes it all the more challenging. We believe much remains to be done to consolidate and advance in this area in the future.

1 Outline

The goal of data integration is to enable users and applications to make use of a set of data sources through a single point of access to the data. Among its earliest incarnations is the wrapper-mediator architecture [12]; subsequently, the area developed considerably, fueled also by the explosion of data (and of data exchange opportunities) on the Web [7]. A first classification of data integration platform separates *warehouse-style* integration, where all data sources are loaded into a single consolidated one, from *mediator-style*, where each source holds its data and the integration layer is developed on top. A second important dimension of classification concerns the *heterogeneity* of the sources. There may exist differences in the structure of the sources, in their semantics, and/or in their data model; along this last axis, structured (typically relational) data models

© Springer Nature Switzerland AG 2020
J. Darmont et al. (Eds.): ADBIS 2020, LNCS 12245, pp. 15–20, 2020.
https://doi.org/10.1007/978-3-030-54832-2_3

contrast with semistructured (JSON, XML, RDF) ones and, at the other end of the spectrum, with unstructured (text) data.

Data integration needs are made all the more pressing, first, because *data volumes keep increasing.* Digitization, an increasing trend which never seems to stop, drives the production of more and more data, by more and more actors. Further, there is a well-noted tendency to accumulate, but not delete, data: no organization readily departs with data sources it has invested energy and effort in building.

The second big driver for data integration is that *data heterogeneity keeps increasing.* An important reason for this is the accumulation of tools and platforms tailored to different data models; the NoSQL movement was a big contributor here. A second reason is the democratization of data production. As more and more tools which produce and manipulate electronic data are used in all lines of trade and for one's private life, each organization or individual gets to make a decision on what data to store, how to model it, and how to describe it.

Below, we outline the main motivations, results and perspectives in two lines of work in this area. The first, in the ESTOCADA project [1–3] considers a polystore setting; polystores can be seen as modern incarnations of mediator systems, with less focus on the design of a common schema and more on effectively integrating data from heterogeneous sources. The second line of work is a more recent, ongoing effort to support integration of data sources of any (semi)structured or unstructured format, into a form of *journalistic dataspaces* [6,11], following the DataSpace vision introduced in [8]. Here, the focus is on building an integrated graph and querying it with for connections among a set of given keywords.

2   The ESTOCADA Project: Materialized View-Based Query Rewriting in Polystores

Modern polystore architectures suffer from two performance limitations. First, they do not exploit possible data redundancy: the same data could be stored in several stores, some of which may support a query operation much more efficiently than others. Second, they are unable to take advantage of the presence of partially computed query results, which may be available in one or several stores (in the style of materialized views), when the data model of the queried dataset differs from the data model of the store hosting the view.

To overcome these limitations, we proposed [1,3] a novel approach for allowing an application to transparently exploit data stored in a set of heterogeneous stores, as a set of *(potentially overlapping) data fragments.* Further, if fragments store results of partial computations applied on the data, we show *how to speed up queries by using these fragments as materialized views.* This reduces query processing effort and seeks to take maximum advantage of the efficient query processing features of each store. Importantly, our approach does not require any change to the application code, which remains oblivious of the way in which the data is actually stored across the distributed store.

Integration Language and Views. We rely on a concrete integration language, called QBT^{XM}, which supports queries over several data stores, each with its own data model and query language. QBT^{XM} follows a *block*-based design, with blocks organized into a tree in the spirit of the classical Query Block Trees (QBT) introduced in System R. The main difference in our setting is that each block may be expressed in a different query language and carry over data of a different data model (e.g., SQL for relational data, key-based search API for key-value data, different JSON query languages etc.). We call the resulting language QBT^{XM}, for *cross-model QBT*.

Each materialized view V is defined by an QBT^{XM} query; it may draw data from one or several data sources, of the same or different data models. Each view returns (holds) data following <u>one</u> data model, and is stored in a data store supporting that model.

View-Based Query Rewriting. We reduce the cross-model rewriting problem to a single-model setting, namely *relational constraint-based query reformulation*, First, we *encode relationally* the structure of original data sets, the view specifications and the application query. Note that the relations used for the encoding are *virtual*, i.e., no data is migrated into them; they are also *hidden*, i.e., invisible to both the application designers and to users. They only serve to support query rewriting using relational techniques. The virtual relations are accompanied by *integrity constraints* that reflect the features of the underlying data models (for each model M, a set $enc(M)$ of constraints).

An incoming query Q over the original datasets $DS_1, \ldots, DS_l$, whose data models respectively are $M_1, \ldots, M_l$, is encoded as a relational query $enc(Q)$ over the dataset's relational encoding. $enc(Q)$ is centered around conjunctive queries, with extensions such as aggregates, UDFs, nesting, disjunction and negation.

The reformulation problem is thus reduced to a purely relational setting: given a relational query $enc(Q)$, a set of relational integrity constraints encoding the views, $enc(V_1) \cup \ldots \cup enc(V_n)$, and the set of relational constraints obtained by encoding the data models $M_1, \ldots, M_l$, find the queries RW_r^i expressed over the relational views, for some integer k and $1 \leq i \leq k$, such that each RW_r^i is equivalent to $enc(Q)$ under these constraints. The challenge here is to design a *faithful* encoding, i.e., one in which rewritings found by (*i*) encoding relationally, (*ii*) solving the resulting relational reformulation problem, and (*iii*) decoding each reformulation RW_r^i into a QBT^{XM} query $R = dec(RW_r^i)$ over the views in the polystore, correspond to rewritings found by solving the original problem.

The details of this encoding can be found in [1], which also shows that our technique can lead to performance savings of orders of magnitude, depending on the workload and the capabilities of the underlying systems, on two different polystore systems. An upcoming demonstration [2] adds to the relational, JSON, and key-value data models supported by ESTOCADA also the support for matrix operations such as those frequently encountered in Machine Learning workloads for data analytics.

3   The ConnectionLens Project: Heterogeneous Data Integration into Graphs

Information integration as envisioned in the 1990–2000 assumed a *sharing (or compatibility) intent*, that is: the owners or producers of data involved in an integration had common or compatible goals, and could be relied upon to interact and harmonize their views of an application domain, to make the data integration application work. At the current dataset production and sharing rate, this process cannot scale; the actors having designed or shared a dataset are not available to help integrating their data with other sources. The advent of the World Wide Web's RDF standard and associated stack of technologies (SPARQL for querying, ontology languages such as RDF Schema and OWL for modeling domain knowledge) provide a set of tools for building data integration applications following the Ontology-Based Data Access [10] paradigm. However, using this stack for data integration still requires time, resources, and relatively advanced technical skills.

In recent years, I have been fascinated by the challenges raised by *data management for journalism and fact-checking* [5,9,11]. In contrast with the usual enterprise data management systems, ve journalists in newsrooms: are usually not trained to think in terms of databases and queries; have limited IT resources at their disposal; have a hard time convincing their management of the interest to invest in building and maintaining complex information systems; and have to focus on varied and quick-changing topics. There is tremendous potential in making digital tools available to journalists, as they have the skills to select their sources, carry investigations online and in the real world, and return this to the general audience in a compelling form. But how to work with their data sources?

In data journalism scenarios, high-value, trusted data may come in any shape and form: it may be text (official statements or law), semistructured data (tweets which are JSON documents), open data (RDF knowledge bases) or relational databases (scientific readings data, CSV open data etc.) Further, *data sources must be considered first-class citizens*, that is: any piece of information, such as "France promised to cut its CO_2 emissions by 20% by 2020", should always be immediately *traceable to its source*. This is because the availability of a source (evidence) is the common standard of truth in both courts of law and schools of journalism, and to increase the public trust in results derived from analyzing a set of data sources.

No single query language can be used on such heterogeneous data; instead, in the ConnectionLens project [6], we query such a heterogeneous corpus by specifying some keywords and asking for all the connections that exist, in one or across several datasources, between these keywords. Since that proof-of-concept prototype, the system has been under intense (re)development. From a technical perspective, the main challenges are: (*i*) how to efficiently integrate heterogeneous data sources in a single graph, without requiring user input, and while preserving the identity of each input data source? (*ii*) how to efficiently find interesting answers to such imprecise queries? (*iii*) how to learn what makes a certain answer interesting? and (*iv*) how to allow enable users to explore and make sense of such heterogeneous integration graphs [4]?

Research along all these axes will continue in the next few years, as part of the SourcesSay AI Chair project. We hope it will help data management research serve more communities of users such as journalists, and other similar communities; more broadly, we hope it will improve the way we all analyze and think of the world, and help us converge to a common understanding thereof.

Acknowledgment. This research has been supported by the ANR projects ContentCheck (Content Management Techniques Content Management Techniques for Fact-Checking: Models, Algorithms, and Tools) and CQFD (Complex Ontological Queries over Federated and Heterogenous Data) and the ANR-DGA AI Chair Sources-Say (Intelligent Analysis and Interconnexion of Heterogeneous Data). We thank the journalists from Les Décodeurs, the fact-checking team of Le Monde, for sharing their insights into data journalism scenarios and needs.

References

1. Alotaibi, R., Bursztyn, D., Deutsch, A., Manolescu, I., Zampetakis, S.: Towards scalable hybrid stores: constraint-based rewriting to the rescue. In: SIGMOD (2019). https://hal.inria.fr/hal-02070827
2. Alotaibi, R., Cautis, B., Deutsch, A., Latrache, M., Manolescu, I., Yang, Y.: ESTO-CADA: towards scalable polystore systems (demonstration). In: PVLDB (2020)
3. Bugiotti, F., Bursztyn, D., Deutsch, A., Ileana, I., Manolescu, I.: Invisible glue: Scalable self-tunning multi-stores. In: CIDR 2015, Proceedings of Seventh Biennial Conference on Innovative Data Systems Research, Asilomar, CA, USA, 4–7 January 2015 (2015). http://cidrdb.org/cidr2015/Papers/CIDR15_Paper7.pdf
4. Burger, I., Manolescu, I., Pietriga, E., Suchanek, F.M.: Toward visual interactive exploration of heterogeneous graphs. In: SEAdata 2020 - Workshop on Searching, Exploring and Analyzing Heterogeneous Data in conjunction with EDBT/ICDT, Copenhagen, Denmark, March 2020. https://hal.inria.fr/hal-02468778
5. Cazalens, S., Lamarre, P., Leblay, J., Manolescu, I., Tannier, X.: A content management perspective on fact-checking. In: The Web Conference, "Journalism, Misinformation and Fact Checking" track (2018). https://hal.archives-ouvertes.fr/hal-01722666
6. Chanial, C., Dziri, R., Galhardas, H., Leblay, J., Le Nguyen, M.H., Manolescu, I.: ConnectionLens: finding connections across heterogeneous data sources (demonstration). PVLDB **11** (2018). https://doi.org/10.14778/3229863.3236252. https://hal.inria.fr/hal-01841009
7. Doan, A., Halevy, A.Y., Ives, Z.G.: Principles of Data Integration. Morgan Kaufmann, Burlington (2012). http://research.cs.wisc.edu/dibook/
8. Franklin, M.J., Halevy, A.Y., Maier, D.: From databases to dataspaces: a new abstraction for information management. SIGMOD Rec. **34**(4) (2005). https://doi.org/10.1145/1107499.1107502
9. Goasdoué, F., Karanasos, K., Katsis, Y., Leblay, J., Manolescu, I., Zampetakis, S.: Fact checking and analyzing the web (demonstration). In: SIGMOD (2013)
10. Lenzerini, M.: Ontology-based data management. In: CIKM (2011). https://doi.org/10.1145/2063576.2063582. http://doi.acm.org/10.1145/2063576.2063582

11. Manolescu, I.: Journalistic dataspaces: data management for journalism and fact-checking (keynote talk). In: EDBT/ICDT 2019 Joint Conference, March 2019. https://hal.inria.fr/hal-02081430
12. Wiederhold, G.: Mediators in the architecture of future information systems. IEEE Comput. **25**(3), 38–49 (1992). https://doi.org/10.1109/2.121508

Data Access and Database Performance

Upper Bound on the Size of FP-Tree

Nima Shahbazi[1(✉)] and Jarek Gryz[2(✉)]

[1] Mindle Inc., Toronto, Canada
nima@mindle.ai
[2] York University, Toronto, Canada
jarek@cse.yorku.ca

Abstract. Efficient tree structures known as FP-tree [3] are used to store a database in memory for mining frequent patterns. However, there has been no discussion on tight upper bound for the number of nodes in this tree. Instead, a very loose upper bound of 2^n (where n is the number of distinct items in the database) is used. In this paper, we provide a tighter upper bound for the number of nodes in a closed form solution. This result is illustrated in the context of various examples both in graphical and mathematical forms.

1 Introduction

Association rules, or more specifically, frequent itemsets have been around for more than twenty years. Given a data set of transactions (each containing a set of items), frequent itemset mining finds all the sets of items that satisfy the minimum support, a parameter provided by a user or an application. The value of this parameter determines the number of itemsets discovered by the mining algorithm. When dealing with large databases, the representation and storage of the data becomes a critical factor for the processing time of the mining algorithms. The existing techniques employ list-based [1,2,6] or tree based [3–5] structures to store data. The tree structure that is widely used is FP-tree [3]. However, no theoretical tight upper bound for the number of nodes in these trees exists. In the literature, the upper bound of 2^n [5], where n is the number of distinct items in the database, is used.

In this paper, we derive a formula for computing much tighter upper bound for FP-trees (we assume reader's familiarity with FP-trees). The size of the tree which we compute is much smaller than the loose upper bounds based on 2^n formula used so far. Table 1 shows a few examples of FP-trees for different number of items in a database. We assume there are 10^{11} transactions each containing 10 items on average (a reasonable assumption for a data warehouse). The second column shows the size of the tree based on the 2^n formula, the third column shows our results (we do not present the actual memory requirements for these two scenarios as they depend on data structures used to represent the trees. Various data structures like trees, arrays and graphs are studied in [7] and [8]).

The paper is organized in a straightforward way. After some preliminaries in Sect. 2, we derive the upper bound for FP-tree in Sect. 3 and conclude in Sect. 4.

© Springer Nature Switzerland AG 2020
J. Darmont et al. (Eds.): ADBIS 2020, LNCS 12245, pp. 23–33, 2020.
https://doi.org/10.1007/978-3-030-54832-2_4

Table 1. Upper bounds for FP-tree

n	Loose upper bound	Tight upper bound
10	2^{10}	2^{10}
20	2^{20}	1.048576×10^{6}
40	$2^{40} \approx 1.1 \times 10^{12}$	1.593597×10^{11}
100	$2^{100} \approx 1.2 \times 10^{30}$	6.771798×10^{11}
1000	$2^{1000} \approx 1.07 \times 10^{301}$	9.710737×10^{11}

2 Preliminaries

We start by setting up a formal framework for our paper.

Definition 1. *Let $A = \{a_1, a_2, ..., a_n\}$ be a set of distinct literals, called items.*
Set $P = \{a_{i_1}, ..., a_{i_k}\} \subseteq A$, where $i_k \in [1, n]$, is called a pattern *(or a k-itemset if it contains k items).*
A transaction $T = (tid, P)$ or $T_{tid} = P$ is a tuple where tid is a transaction-id and P is a pattern or itemset. A transaction $T = (tid, P)$ contains (or supports) an itemset X, if $X \subseteq P$.
We put a total order $<_x$ on the items in A, where x represents item ordering. A pattern $P = \{a_{i_1}, ..., a_{i_k}\}$ is ordered if we change it to sequence $\mathcal{P} = \langle a_{i_1}, ..., a_{i_k} \rangle$, and $\forall j \in [1, k-1]$, $a_{i_j} <_x a_{i_{j+1}}$.
Given two ordered patterns, $\mathcal{P}_1 = \langle a_{i_1}, ..., a_{i_m} \rangle$ and $\mathcal{P}_2 = \langle a_{j_1}, ..., a_{j_k} \rangle$, $m \leqslant k$, if $\forall s \in [1, m], a_{i_s} = a_{j_s}$, then $\mathcal{P}_1$ is called a prefix of $\mathcal{P}_2$.
An ordered transaction, $\mathcal{T}_{tid}$, is a transaction with an ordered pattern. For $\mathcal{T}_{tid} = \langle a_{i_1}, ..., a_{i_k} \rangle$, $size(\mathcal{T}_{tid}) = k$.

In this paper, we consider one order, the frequency order, $<_{\mathsf{Freq}}$, for FP-tree, defined in the next two definitions.

Definition 2. $\mathsf{Freq}_{\mathcal{D}}(a)$ *is the number of transactions that contain a in database $\mathcal{D}$ (we omit the subscription $\mathcal{D}$ when it is clear from the context):*

$$\mathsf{Freq}_{\mathcal{D}}(a) = \sum_{i=1}^{m} \mathsf{Acc}(a; \mathcal{T}_i) \text{ where } \mathcal{D} = \langle \mathcal{T}_1, ..., \mathcal{T}_m \rangle \text{ and}$$
$$\mathsf{Acc}(a; \mathcal{T}_i) = \begin{cases} 1 & a \in \mathcal{T}_i \\ 0 & a \notin \mathcal{T}_i \end{cases}$$

Definition 3. $<_{\mathsf{Freq}}$ *is item ordering in frequency descending order defined as follows:*
$$a <_{\mathsf{Freq}} b \text{ iff } (\mathsf{Freq}_{\mathcal{D}}(a) > \mathsf{Freq}_{\mathcal{D}}(b) \text{ or } (\mathsf{Freq}_{\mathcal{D}}(a) = \mathsf{Freq}_{\mathcal{D}}(b) \text{ and } a <_A b))$$

Without loss of generality we define a database to be a sequence (rather than a set) of transactions.

Definition 4. *Database $\mathcal{D}$ is a sequence of transactions: $\mathcal{D} = \langle \mathcal{T}_1, ..., \mathcal{T}_m \rangle$ and total count or $TC = \sum_{i=1}^{m} size(\mathcal{T}_i)$. Also adding transaction $\mathcal{T}_x$ to database $\mathcal{D}$ is shown as: $\mathcal{D}; \mathcal{T}_x = \langle \mathcal{T}_1, ..., \mathcal{T}_m, \mathcal{T}_x \rangle$.*

The following example illustrates some of the concepts from above.

Example 1. Suppose that the transaction database, DB, be the first two columns of Table 2. We have $N = 7$ distinct items $A = \{a, b, c, d, e, f, g\}$, and the database consists of 8 transactions. A scan of DB derives the Freq of each item as follows; $\mathsf{Freq}(b) = 8, \mathsf{Freq}(c) = 6, \mathsf{Freq}(a) = 3, \mathsf{Freq}(e) = 3, \mathsf{Freq}(d) = 2, \mathsf{Freq}(f) = 1$ and $\mathsf{Freq}(g) = 1$, with $TC = 24$. Hence, the FP-tree item ordering will be: $b <_{\mathsf{Freq}} c <_{\mathsf{Freq}} a <_{\mathsf{Freq}} e <_{\mathsf{Freq}} d <_{\mathsf{Freq}} f <_{\mathsf{Freq}} g$. For constructing a FP-tree, first we need to create ordered transactions based on $<_{\mathsf{Freq}}$, as shown in third column of Table 2 (i.e. $\{a, d, b, g, e, c\} \rightarrow <b, c, a, e, d, g>$) respectively. Constructing FP-tree from these ordered transactions is straightforward (the reader is referred to [4] and [3] for details). Note that each node has a field called node-count, and Freq for each item equals to the sum of all of it's node-counts. Figure 1 shows the FP-tree constructed from Table 2.

Table 2. Transaction database

tid	Content	$<_{\mathsf{Freq}}$ (FP-tree)
1	$\{a, d, b, g, e, c\}$	$\langle b, c, a, e, d, g \rangle$
2	$\{b, f, c, a, e\}$	$\langle b, c, a, e, f \rangle$
3	$\{b\}$	$\langle b \rangle$
4	$\{d, b\}$	$\langle b, d \rangle$
5	$\{a, c, b\}$	$\langle b, c, a \rangle$
6	$\{c, b, e\}$	$\langle b, c, e \rangle$
7	$\{b, c\}$	$\langle b, c \rangle$
8	$\{c, b\}$	$\langle b, c \rangle$

A set with n distinct items has 2^n subsets. Therefore, for a transaction database with n distinct items, the number of nodes in the tree representation with prefix-merging (which it is called prefix-tree) is bounded by 2^n [3]. The intuition behind it is that if A has n items then the transaction database which has *all subsets* of A (i.e., the power-set of A) has 2^n distinct transactions (including an empty transaction). Hence, when all these transactions are attached to the root of the tree (with prefix merging) then each one of them is represented as a path from the root to a particular node.[1] Since there are 2^n such paths each one ending in a distinct node, the tree will have 2^n nodes; we call it *complete prefix-tree*.

We start with the definition of FP-tree layout-tree.

Definition 5. *A FP-tree layout-tree ($\mathbb{T}_{Layout(A)}$ is a complete prefix-tree on A, where transactions are ordered by $<_{\mathsf{Freq}}$. For each node we keep a field called node-count with 0 value.*

---

[1] We assume no duplicate transactions.

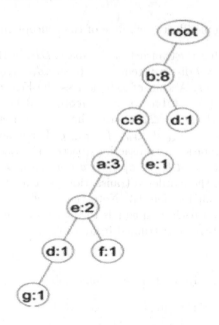

Fig. 1. Constructing FP-tree from Table 2

Figure 2 shows the layout-tree on $A = \{a, b, c, d, e\}$ (*node-count* fields are removed for simplicity) where we are assuming $a <_{\text{Freq}} b <_{\text{Freq}} c <_{\text{Freq}} d <_{\text{Freq}} e$ (note that by Definition 3, $a <_{\text{Freq}} b$ if a is *more* frequent than b).

3   FP-Tree Upper Bound

In this section, we derive a formula to compute an upper bound for the number of nodes in an FP-tree. We define our task as follows: given the number of items in a database, n, and the sum of sizes of all transactions, TC, find the largest FP-tree than can be constructed for these transactions.

As illustrated in Fig. 2, the number of nodes for item 'a' (most frequent item) is 2^0. The number of nodes for item 'b' (second most frequent item) is 2^1, the number of nodes for item 'c' is 2^2 and so on. Let us rename the nodes using the indices so that $a = a_1$, $b = a_2$, $c = a_3$, $d = a_4$ and $e = a_5$, such that $i < j \Leftrightarrow a_i <_{\text{Freq}} a_j$, etc. Therefore, the number of nodes for item a_i in the layout tree is 2^{i-1} as stated in the following Lemma.

Lemma 1. *Assume $A = \{a_1, \ldots, a_n\}$ such that $i < j$ iff $a_i <_{\text{Freq}} a_j$. Node a_i in $\mathbb{T}_{Layout(A)}$ appears 2^{i-1} times.*

Proof. By induction on n.

If $n = 1$ then $A = \{a_1\}$ and hence $\mathbb{T}_{Layout(A)}$ is a tree with root and just one child (2^{1-1}) labeled by a_1.

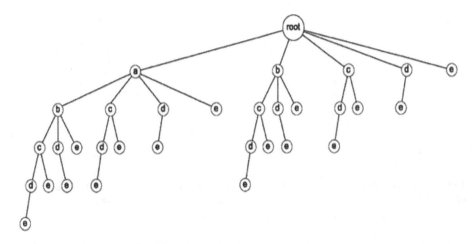

Fig. 2. FP layout-tree on $A = \{a, b, c, d, e\}$, where $a <_{\mathsf{Freq}} b <_{\mathsf{Freq}} c <_{\mathsf{Freq}} d <_{\mathsf{Freq}} e$ (fields with *node-count = 0* are removed for simplicity.)

Suppose that for $n = k$, a_k appears 2^{k-1}. We need to show that if $n = k+1$, then a_{k+1} appears 2^{k+1-1}. $\mathbb{T}_{Layout(A)}$ with $k + 1$ items is constructed from $\mathbb{T}_{Layout(A)}$ with k items, where the new node a_{k+1} is attached to all the nodes including root, so a_{k+1} appears:

$$1 + \sum_{i=1}^{k} 2^{i-1} = 1 + \sum_{i=0}^{k-1} 2^i = 1 + (2^k - 1) = 2^k = 2^{k+1-1}$$

Example 2. Suppose that $A = \{a_1, a_2, a_3\}$ and $i < j \Leftrightarrow a_i <_{\mathsf{Freq}} a_j$. Figure 3 shows layout tree on A. One can confirm that a_1 appears $2^{(1-1)}$ times, a_2 appears $2^{(2-1)}$ times and a_3 appears $2^{(3-1)}$ times in the tree. Figure 4 shows the previous layout tree with additional node a_4. This a_4 node is added to all the nodes with the total appearance of $2^{(4-1)}$.

The intuition behind the formula is illustrated by the following example.

Example 3. Let us find the upper bound for FP-tree if $n = 5$, $A = \{a, b, c, d, e\}$, and $TC = 15$ and suppose that the frequencies, Freq, of items, are as follows: $\mathsf{Freq}(a) = 5, \mathsf{Freq}(b) = 4, \mathsf{Freq}(c) = 3, \mathsf{Freq}(d) = 2$ and $\mathsf{Freq}(e) = 1$.

There are 2^4 nodes for item e in the layout-tree (shown in Fig. 2) but in our example, $\mathsf{Freq}(e) = 1$. Hence, $(2^4 - 1) = 15$ nodes of the layout-tree will not appear in the actual tree for this example (we call them *unused nodes* of the layout-tree). For item d, we have 2^3 nodes in the layout tree, but in this example $\mathsf{Freq}(b) = 2$, therefore $(2^3 - 2) = 6$ nodes of the layout-tree will not appear in the actual tree. For item c there are 2^2 nodes in the layout-tree, but in this example $\mathsf{Freq}(c) = 3$, thus $(2^2 - 3) = 1$ nodes will not appear in the tree. For item b there are 2^1 nodes in the layout tree and $\mathsf{Freq}(b) = 4$. In this case $(2^1 - 4) = -2$ is negative, so this item has no *unused nodes* (we cannot have more nodes than

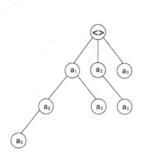

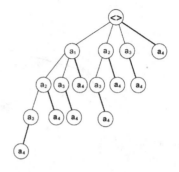

Fig. 3. Layout tree on A where each a_i appears $2^{(i-1)}$

Fig. 4. Adding a_4 with total appearance of $1 + \sum_{i=1}^{3} 2^{i-1} = 2^{4-1}$

those appearing in the layout-tree). In general, when the difference between the number of nodes in the layout-tree for some item and the actual frequency for that item becomes negative it means there are no *unused nodes* for that item. Similarly, for item a there are 2^0 nodes in the tree, but again Freq$(a) = 5$, and $(2^0 - 5) = -4$ is negative, therefore, there are no *unused nodes* for item a.

To generalize the calculation of the number of *unused nodes* for each item described above, we introduce an operator called cut-off subtraction:

$$\text{cut off subtraction:} \quad x \dotdiv y = \begin{cases} x - y & x \geqslant y \\ 0 & \text{otherwise} \end{cases} \tag{1}$$

As shown in Table 3, there are 22 *unused nodes* for Example 3.

Table 3. Unused nodes in FP-tree with cut off subtraction.

Item	Freq	Number of unused nodes
a	5	$2^0 \dotdiv 5 = 0$
b	4	$2^1 \dotdiv 4 = 0$
c	3	$2^2 \dotdiv 3 = 1$
d	2	$2^3 \dotdiv 2 = 6$
e	1	$2^4 \dotdiv 1 = 15$
		$Total = 0 + 0 + 1 + 6 + 15 = 22$

In order to compute the maximum number of nodes in the tree for Example 3, we simply need to subtract the number of unused nodes from the total number of nodes in the layout-tree. Hence, the upper bound, U, is $2^5 - 22 = 10$.

We use another example to show how to compute U based on just TC and n rather than the actual frequencies of the items.

Example 4. What is the U for FP-tree if $TC = 15$ and $n = 5$? We know that the upper bound, U, for the size of the tree is the size of the layout-tree minus the total number of unused nodes (NUN).

$$U = 2^5 - \text{NUN} \qquad (2)$$

$\text{NUN} = 2^0 \dot{-} \text{Freq}(a) + 2^1 \dot{-} \text{Freq}(b) + 2^2 \dot{-} \text{Freq}(c) + 2^3 \dot{-} \text{Freq}(d) + 2^4 \dot{-} \text{Freq}(e)$

Therefore,

$U = 2^5 - (2^0 \dot{-} \text{Freq}(a) + 2^1 \dot{-} \text{Freq}(b) + 2^2 \dot{-} \text{Freq}(c) + 2^3 \dot{-} \text{Freq}(d) + 2^4 \dot{-} \text{Freq}(e))$.

To maximize U, we need to **minimize the total number of unused nodes**, NUN, by manipulating item frequencies so that they satisfy the following constraints:

1. $\text{Freq}(a) \geqslant \text{Freq}(b) \geqslant \text{Freq}(c) \geqslant \text{Freq}(d) \geqslant \text{Freq}(e)$
1. $\text{Freq}(a) + \text{Freq}(b) + \text{Freq}(c) + \text{Freq}(d) + \text{Freq}(e) = 15$
2. $\text{Freq}(a) > 0, \text{Freq}(b) > 0, \text{Freq}(c) > 0, \text{Freq}(d) > 0, \text{Freq}(e) > 0$

We have a **total budget** of $TC = 15$ to be distributed among item frequencies. To satisfy Constraint No. 3, we need to assign frequency at least 1 for each distinct item. Hence, we start with assigning 1 for a, 1 for b, 1 for c, 1 for d and 1 for e. This already minimizes the first term in the formula for NUN, i.e., $(2^0 \dot{-} \text{Freq}(a))$. Our budget has been decreased by 5 and now $TC = 15 - 5 = 10$. To minimize NUN, we need to assign the most of our budget to e *(since the term for item e has the biggest value in cut-off subtraction, which is $2^4 \dot{-} \text{Freq}(e)$).* However, Constraint No. 1, prevents us from assigning a frequency to e before assigning it to the more frequent items. To best use the budget, we only add 1 to the more frequent items. We keep repeating this process until we exhaust the budget. Therefore we assign 1 for a, 1 for b, 1 for c, 1 for d and 1 for e, total 5 assigned, and now $TC = 10 - 5 = 5$. The remaining budget of 5 is also assigned in the same order from a to e. This means, to maximize U, TC should be evenly distributed among the items. We state this claim formally in Lemma 2.

Lemma 2. *Suppose $\mathcal{D}$ is a database on A and $\exists\, a, b \in A$ where $\text{Freq}_\mathcal{D}(a) > \text{Freq}_\mathcal{D}(b)$. Then there is a database $\mathcal{D}'$ such that by decreasing the Freq of a by 1 and adding 1 to Freq of b (such that the frequency ordering remains unchanged), may result in an **increase** in FP-tree size of the $\mathbb{T}_{\mathcal{D}'}$, that is:*

1. $\text{Freq}_{\mathcal{D}'}(a) = \text{Freq}_\mathcal{D}(a) - 1$
2. $\text{Freq}_{\mathcal{D}'}(b) = \text{Freq}_\mathcal{D}(b) + 1$
3. $\forall x (x \neq a \wedge x \neq b) \Rightarrow \text{Freq}_{\mathcal{D}'}(x) = \text{Freq}_\mathcal{D}(x)$
4. $\text{Freq}_{\mathcal{D}'}(a) > \text{Freq}_{\mathcal{D}'}(b)$
   and
5. $size(\mathbb{T}_{\mathcal{D}'}) \geqslant size(\mathbb{T}_\mathcal{D})$

Proof. We distinguish two cases:

1. There exist a node in $\mathbb{T}_\mathcal{D}$ such that $node - count$ of a is greater than one. Then decreasing Freq of a by 1, means that simply removing a from a transaction

on this path (tree size remain unchanged). Increasing Freq of b by 1 may result in a node of b in tree from $node - count = 0$ to $node - count = 1$, which means a *new* node is created (tree size increased). If a node of b with $node - count \neq 0$ increased, then no new node is created (tree size remain unchanged). Therefore,

$$\mathbb{T}_{\mathcal{D}'} \geqslant \mathbb{T}_{\mathcal{D}}$$

2. All nodes of a's have a $node - count$ equal to one. Since $\mathsf{Freq}_{\mathcal{D}}(a) > \mathsf{Freq}_{\mathcal{D}}(b)$, there exist a transaction $\mathcal{T}$ where $\mathsf{Acc}(a; \mathcal{T}) = 1$ but $\mathsf{Acc}(b; \mathcal{T}) = 0$. We can simply replace a by b in $\mathcal{T}$ to get $\mathcal{D}'$. Therefore, we ended up with the same tree size in $\mathcal{D}'$.

The following example better illustrates the lemma.

Example 5. Suppose that $\mathcal{D} = \{\mathcal{T}_1, \mathcal{T}_2, \mathcal{T}_3, \mathcal{T}_4 \, \mathcal{T}_5\}$, $\mathcal{T}_1 = \langle a \rangle$, $\mathcal{T}_2 = \langle a, b, c \rangle$, $\mathcal{T}_3 = \langle a \rangle$, $\mathcal{T}_4 = \langle a, b \rangle$ and $\mathcal{T}_5 = \langle a \rangle$. FP-tree $\mathbb{T}_{\mathcal{D}}$ (inscribed into a layout-tree) is shown in Fig. 5 where $\mathsf{Freq}(a) = 5$, $\mathsf{Freq}(b) = 2$, $\mathsf{Freq}(c) = 1$ and $size(\mathbb{T}_{\mathcal{D}}) = 4$.

By decreasing Freq a by 1 and increasing b's Freq by 1, we end up with two different trees as shown in Fig. 6 and Fig. 7 (affected nodes are bold). Figure 6 shows where increasing b's Freq leads to a new node and $size(\mathbb{T}_{\mathcal{D}'}) = size(\mathbb{T}_{\mathcal{D}})+1 = 5$. Figure 7 shows where increasing b's Freq does not create a new node and $size(\mathbb{T}_{\mathcal{D}'}) = size(\mathbb{T}_{\mathcal{D}})$.

The immediate consequence of Lemma 2 can be stated as the following result.

Lemma 3. *For a given A and $\mathcal{D}$, the largest size of $\mathbb{T}_{\mathcal{D}}$ requires that for any $a, b \in A$, $\mathsf{Freq}_{\mathcal{D}}(a) - \mathsf{Freq}_{\mathcal{D}}(b) \leqslant 1$.*

Proof. Suppose that for the sake of contradiction $\exists \, a, b \in A$ where $\mathsf{Freq}_{\mathcal{D}}(a) - \mathsf{Freq}_{\mathcal{D}}(b) \geqslant 2$. Then we can decrease Freq of a by 1 and increase Freq of b by 1 as described in Lemma 2 (notice that frequency ordering remains the same) and the resulting tree may increase in size, a contradiction.

Thus, to maximize U, all item frequencies must be equal or should differ by **at most** 1, that is, TC should be as evenly distributed among the items as possible.

Theorem 1. *Maximum size of FP-tree on $A = \{a_1, \ldots, a_n\}$ based on $\mathsf{Freq}_{\mathcal{D}}(a)$ for all $a \in A$, equals to:*

$$2^n - \sum_{i=1}^{n} (2^{i-1} \doteq \mathsf{Freq}_{\mathcal{D}}(a_i)). \tag{3}$$

Proof. $U = 2^n - $ *total number of unused nodes* and Lemma 1 says that ith element of A appears 2^{i-1} times in the layout tree. In addition, we know a_i occurs $\mathsf{Freq}_{\mathcal{D}}(a_i)$ times in $\mathbb{T}_{\mathcal{D}}$, hence the minimum number of unused nodes of a_i equals $2^{i-1} \doteq \mathsf{Freq}_{\mathcal{D}}(a_i)$. Adding this up for all n items, will result in the *total number of unused nodes* $= \sum_{i=1}^{n} (2^{i-1} \doteq \mathsf{Freq}_{\mathcal{D}}(a_i))$.

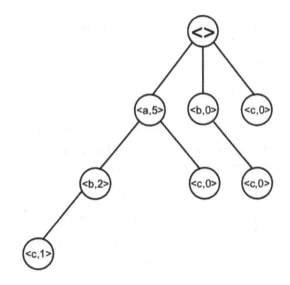

Fig. 5. FP-tree $\mathbb{T}_D$ for Example 2

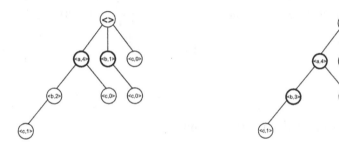

Fig. 6. Increasing b's Freq leads to a new node

Fig. 7. Increasing b's Freq do not create a new node

Finally, Theorem 2 provides a formula to compute the upper bound.

Theorem 2. *Upper bound for FP-tree, $U(n, TC)$ equals to:*

$$
\begin{cases}
2^n - \sum_{i=1}^{n}(2^{i-1} \dot{-} \frac{TC}{n}) & n \ divides \ TC \\
2^n - \sum_{i=1}^{n}\left(2^{i-1} \dot{-} \left(\left\lfloor \frac{TC}{n} \right\rfloor + \left((TC - \left\lfloor \frac{TC}{n} \right\rfloor \times n) \dot{-} (i-1)\right)\right)\right) & otherwise
\end{cases}
$$

$$(4)$$

Proof. The condition of Lemma 3 states that either all frequencies are equal or they differ by only 1 in size. To achieve this, if n divides TC then $\frac{TC}{n}$ is equally assigned for each item frequency. By plugging in $\frac{TC}{n}$ in Lemma 1's equation, *Upper bound* equals to $2^n - \sum_{i=1}^{n}(2^{i-1} \dot{-} \frac{TC}{n})$.

If TC is not divisible by n, first $\left\lfloor \dfrac{TC}{n} \right\rfloor$ is equally assigned for each item frequency. Then, we need another term to divide the *residual budget* $(TC - \left\lfloor \dfrac{TC}{n} \right\rfloor \times n)$ to items (1 for each item until the residual is finished), which is: $\left((TC - \left\lfloor \dfrac{TC}{n} \right\rfloor \times n) \div (i-1) \right)$. Note that the argument inside the function is positive or zero (so function will return either 0 or 1). In the latter case if the frequencies are not equal, it is guaranteed to differ only 1 in size.

We illustrate Theorem 2 with the following example.

Example 6. Suppose $n = 4$ and consider two TC values 12 and 15.

If $TC = 12$ then n divides TC and $\dfrac{12}{4} = 3$ is equally assigned for each item frequency. $U = 2^4 - \sum_{i=1}^{4}(2^{i-1} \div 3) = 10$.

If $TC = 15$ then TC is not divisible to n. First $\left\lfloor \dfrac{15}{4} \right\rfloor = 3$ is equally assigned for each item frequency, and the *residual budget* $(15 - \left\lfloor \dfrac{15}{4} \right\rfloor \times 4 = 3)$ split between a_1, a_2 and a_3 (1 for each). $U = 2^4 - \sum_{i=1}^{4} \left(2^{i-1} \div (\left\lfloor \dfrac{15}{4} \right\rfloor + \left((15 - \left\lfloor \dfrac{15}{4} \right\rfloor \times 4) \div (i-1) \right) \right) = 11$.

4 Conclusions and Future Work

FP-tree is a very popular data structure used for mining frequent patterns. Predicting the size of such tree - based on the number of stored transactions and items - is of utmost importance as it determines memory requirements for the mining process. However, until now, no tight upper bound existed for the size of FP-tree. In this paper, we have presented a formula that provides a much tighter upper bound than a naive and rather useless 2^n limit.

We are currently working on deriving an upper bound for another popular data structure for mining frequent patterns, the Can-tree. We have been able to construct an algorithm for computing the upper bound for this type of tree but finding a solution in a closed form has been elusive so far.

References

1. Deng, Z.-H., Lv, S.-L.: PrePost+: an efficient N-lists-based algorithm for mining frequent itemsets via children-parent equivalence pruning. Expert. Syst. Appl. **42**(13), 5424–5432 (2015)
2. Deng, Z.H., Wang, Z.H., Jiang, J.J.: A new algorithm for fast mining frequent itemsets using N-lists. Sci. China Inf. Sci. **55**(9), 2008–2030 (2012)

3. Han, J., Pei, J., Yin, Y.: Mining frequent patterns without candidate generation. ACM SIGMOD Rec. **29**, 1–12 (2000)
4. Leung, C.K.-S., Khan, Q.I., Li, Z., Hoque, T.: CanTree: a canonical-order tree for incremental frequent-pattern mining. Knowl. Inf. Syst. **11**(3), 287–311 (2007). https://doi.org/10.1007/s10115-006-0032-8
5. Liu, G., Lu, H., Yu, J.X.: CFP-tree: a compact disk-based structure for storing and querying frequent itemsets. Inf. Syst. **32**(2), 295–319 (2007)
6. Pei, J., Han, J., Lu, H., Nishio, S., Tang, S., Yang, D.: H-mine: hyper-structure mining of frequent patterns in large databases. In: Proceedings of ICDM, pp. 441–448. IEEE (2001)
7. Schlegel, B., Gemulla, R., Lehner, W.: Memory-efficient frequent-itemset mining. In: Proceedings of the 14th International Conference on Extending Database Technology, pp. 461–472 (2011)
8. Shahbazi, N., Soltani, R., Gryz, J.: Memory efficient frequent itemset mining. In: Perner, P. (ed.) MLDM 2018. LNCS (LNAI), vol. 10935, pp. 16–27. Springer, Cham (2018). https://doi.org/10.1007/978-3-319-96133-0_2

An Efficient Index for Reachability Queries in Public Transport Networks

Bezaye Tesfaye[1]($\boxtimes$), Nikolaus Augsten[1], Mateusz Pawlik[1], Michael H. Böhlen[2], and Christian S. Jensen[3]

[1] University of Salzburg, Salzburg, Austria
{bbelayneh,augsten,mpawlik}@cs.sbg.ac.at
[2] University of Zurich, Zürich, Switzerland
boehlen@ifi.uzh.ch
[3] Aalborg University, Aalborg, Denmark
csj@cs.aau.dk

Abstract. Computing path queries such as the shortest path in public transport networks is challenging because the path costs between nodes change over time. A reachability query from a node at a given start time on such a network retrieves all points of interest (POIs) that are reachable within a given cost budget. Reachability queries are essential building blocks in many applications, for example, group recommendations, ranking spatial queries, or geomarketing. We propose an efficient solution for reachability queries in public transport networks. Currently, there are two options to solve reachability queries. (1) Execute a modified version of Dijkstra's algorithm that supports time-dependent edge traversal costs; this solution is slow since it must expand edge by edge and does not use an index. (2) Issue a separate path query for each single POI, i.e., a single reachability query requires answering many path queries. None of these solutions scales to large networks with many POIs. We propose a novel and lightweight reachability index. The key idea is to partition the network into cells. Then, in contrast to other approaches, we expand the network cell by cell. Empirical evaluations on synthetic and real-world networks confirm the efficiency and the effectiveness of our index-based reachability query solution.

Keywords: Reachability queries · Public transport networks · Temporal graphs · Spatial network databases

1 Introduction

We study the problem of scalable and efficient reachability querying in public transport networks. A reachability query retrieves all points of interest (POIs) reachable from a given query node at a specific start time within a given time budget. The start time is required since the reachability result changes over time. Interesting applications of reachability queries include group recommendations, ranking spatial queries, urban planning, and geomarketing. We present two examples.

The original version of this chapter was revised: the paper has been made available open access at SpringerLink. The correction to this chapter is available at https://doi.org/10.1007/978-3-030-54832-2_17

© The Author(s) 2020, corrected publication 2020
J. Darmont et al. (Eds.): ADBIS 2020, LNCS 12245, pp. 34–48, 2020.
https://doi.org/10.1007/978-3-030-54832-2_5

Consider a platform that recommends events to a group of people such that the group members like to attend the event together [2,14]. Group members are query nodes and events are POIs. When the group is given, the events must be evaluated by various criteria to optimize the benefit to the group. One important aspect is the location of the event relative to the group members. The start time and the travel time budget to reach an event may differ for each member. Events too far away are unlikely to be successful. A single recommendation comprises multiple reachability queries, one for each group member.

Another example is a real estate website that ranks properties (query nodes) according to user preferences. The users may customize reachability criteria for different POIs (e.g., school, working place, train station). Thereby, the time budget for individual types of POIs may vary: a user may be willing to commute to work for an hour, while a school must be nearby. Ranking the results of a single user query requires the computation of multiple reachability queries: one for each property and parameter setting.

To support such applications, reachability queries must be computed efficiently. Achieving this goal in public transport networks is tricky since the shortest path between two nodes depends on the start time, and the time to traverse a path may vary greatly across time. In a public transport network, stations are nodes, and connections between stations are edges between nodes. An edge can only be traversed at specific points in time as given by a schedule. Therefore, computing an index for public transport networks is more complex than for networks with constant edge-traversal costs or networks in which an edge can be traversed at any time (like pedestrian networks or road networks).

Example 1. *Consider, the public transport network in Fig. 1a. The nodes v_1, v_2, ..., v_{12} represent stations, and the directed edges represent connections between the stations. Each connection has a pair (t_d, t_a) of departure and arrival times. For example, there is a connection leaving v_4 at time 10 and arriving at v_3 at time 11. The traversal cost between nodes is expressed in terms of time units. The cost of traversing the edge (v_4, v_3) at time 9 is 2, since we have a waiting time in addition to the edge traversal time. The shortest path from v_{10} to v_{11} at start time $t_s = 9$ has cost 2 (edge (v_{10}, v_{11})), while at $t_s = 10$, the cost of the shortest path is 3 (edges (v_{10}, v_{12}), (v_{12}, v_{11})). At start time $t_s = 9$, the nodes $\{v_8, v_9, v_{11}\}$ are reachable from v_{10} with budget $\Delta t = 2$; at $t_s = 10$ with the same budget, we can reach the nodes $\{v_9, v_{12}\}$.*

The state of the art in answering reachability queries in public transport networks includes two approaches. The first is based on a temporal version of Dijkstra's algorithm [10] that expands in the network until the budget is exhausted. Algorithms following this approach compute a so-called isochrone (the reachable region) and intersect it with the set of POIs [6,12]. Since all edges in the isochrone must be expanded, these algorithms do not scale to large networks. The second approach translates a single reachability query into a set of path queries (e.g., shortest path or earliest-arrival path [18,20,21]), one for each POI. Path queries require heavy index structures and do not scale to large numbers of POIs.

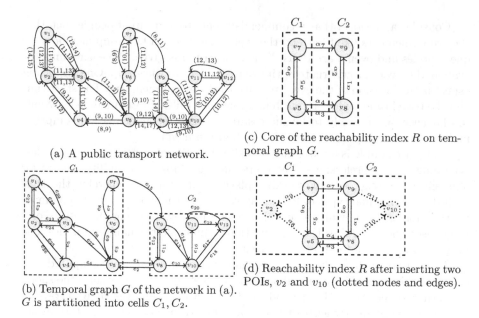

(a) A public transport network.

(c) Core of the reachability index R on temporal graph G.

(b) Temporal graph G of the network in (a). G is partitioned into cells C_1, C_2.

(d) Reachability index R after inserting two POIs, v_2 and v_{10} (dotted nodes and edges).

Fig. 1. Temporal graph of public transport network and reachability index.

We propose an index-based technique for reachability queries in public transport networks. Instead of expanding edge by edge, in a precomputation step, we partition the network into cells and construct a novel reachability index. At query time, the index is used to expand cell by cell. Each cell covers a region of the network and all POIs in that region. The precomputation effort for a specific cell is independent of the other cells such that the index scales to large networks. The index is small, even smaller than the original graph for some inputs. To the best of our knowledge, this is the first work that proposes an index for reachability queries in public transport networks.

The rest of the paper is structured as follows. In Sect. 2, we define the problem, and we give an overview of our solution in Sect. 3. We introduce our reachability index in Sect. 4 and discuss query processing using the index in Sect. 5. In Sect. 6, we review related work. In Sect. 7 we investigate experimentally the performance of our solution. We conclude in Sect. 8.

2   Preliminaries and Problem Definition

In a public transport network, stations are nodes and connections are edges. A connection has a departure time t_d and an arrival time t_a. We assume periodic schedules as is typically the case in public transport networks, e.g., schedules repeat daily or weekly.

A *temporal graph* $G = (V, E, c)$ is a directed graph with vertices V, edges $E \subseteq V \times V$, and a time-dependent cost function $c(e, t)$, $c : E \times \mathbb{R} \to \mathbb{R}_{\geq 0}$

that captures the cost of traversing edge e starting at time t. We represent public transport networks as temporal graphs with a specific cost function, which we derive from the schedule. Each station is a node in the graph, and there is an edge from node u to node v iff there is a direct connection (i.e., there are no intermediate stops) from the station of u to the station of v. The cost function is periodic with period Π, i.e., $c(e,t) = c(e, t + \Pi)$ and piecewise linear; all linear pieces have slope $k = -1$; the cost function is not continuous; all discontinuities are at departure times of some connections. For a single connection $s_i = (t_d, t_a)$ on an edge e, the cost in the period $(t_d - \Pi, t_d]$ is $c_i(e,t) = t_a - t$; if there are multiple connections $S = \{s_1, s_2, \ldots, s_i\}$ for edge e, the cost of e at time t is the minimum of all costs of the individual connections at time t, $c(e,t) = \min\{c_i(e,t) \mid c_i$ is the cost function of connection $s_i\}$. Our cost function is *consistent*, i.e., for any edge $e \in E$ and all start times $t_1 \leq t_2$: $t_1 + c(e, t_1) \leq t_2 + c(e, t_2)$. Intuitively, in a consistent cost function, it never pays off to wait. Consistency is required for the use with Dijkstra's shortest-path algorithm [17].

Example 2. *Consider the edge e_7 in Fig. 1b with connections $s_1 = (10, 11)$ and $s_2 = (11, 12)$. Then, for $\Pi = 12$, the cost function of s_1 is $c_1(e_7, t) = 11 - t$, $t \in (-2, 10]$ and for s_2 is $c_2(e_7, t) = 12 - t, t \in (-1, 11]$. The overall cost function $c(e_7, t)$ is the minimum of $c_1(e_7, t)$ and $c_2(e_7, t)$.*

A *path* p from u to v in a temporal graph $G = (V, E, c)$ is a sequence of edges $p = \langle e_1, e_2, \ldots, e_n \rangle$ such that $e_i \in E$, $e_i = (w_{i-1}, w_i)$, $w_0 = u$, and $w_n = v$; $P(u, v)$ is the *set of all paths* from node u to node v. The cost of a path is the fastest time to traverse the path at a given start time. Due to the consistency property of our cost function, the path cost is the sum of all edge costs. The *cost of path* $p = \langle e_1, e_2, \ldots, e_n \rangle$ at time t, is the cost sum of all edges in p: $c(p, t) = \sum_{1 \leq i \leq n} c(e_i, t_i)$, where $t_1 = t$ and $t_i = t_{i-1} + c(e_{i-1}, t_{i-1})$ for $i > 1$. The *shortest-path* cost from node u to node v at time t is the minimum cost of any path from u to v, $sp(u, v, t) = \min\{c(p, t) \mid p \in P(u, v)\}$. A path with the minimum cost is called the *shortest path*. A node v is *reachable* from a node u at time t within budget Δt iff there is a path $p \in P(u, v)$ such that the cost of p at time t is no larger than Δt, i.e., $c(p, t) \leq \Delta t$. The *reachability query*, $RQ(u, t, \Delta t) = \{v \in V \mid \exists p \in P(u, v), c(p, t) \leq \Delta t, v \in POI\}$, in a temporal graph $G = (V, E, c)$ with points of interst $POI \subseteq V$, returns all points of interest reachable from node u at time t within budget Δt.

Problem Definition. The goal of this work is to develop an efficient index-based solution for reachability queries that scales to large temporal graphs.

3 Solution Overview

We propose a novel index structure, the *reachability index*, to answer reachability queries. We introduce a bulk loading technique for our index, provide access methods for answering reachability queries, and discuss the incremental insertion and deletion of POIs in the index.

The reachability index is built in a precomputation step. To construct the index, we partition the temporal graph into disjoint cells. Any such partitioning yields correct results. The choice of cells, however, affects the effectiveness of the index. We define requirements for a good partitioning and propose a suitable partitioning technique.

The index is a temporal graph that contains only those nodes of the original graph that are POIs or directly connect different cells, called *border nodes*. Each POI belongs to a cell. POIs can be inserted into and deleted from the index at any time; the update cost is low and depends on a single cell. The index consists of the original edges between border nodes of neighboring cells and new edges between the border nodes within a cell. Further, an edge between each POI and the border nodes in its cell is introduced. The edge costs are the costs of shortest paths between the respective nodes in the original graph.

A high number of border nodes per cell increases the index size. Each POI adds as many edges to the index as there are border nodes in its cell.

A search query traverses the index cell by cell. The border nodes are used to cross cells and to reach neighboring cells. For each border node, we verify if any of the POIs in that cell is reachable.

4   The Reachability Index

The reachability index R is a temporal graph that is constructed from the original graph G as follows:

1. *Graph partitioning.* The nodes of graph G are split into disjoint *cells*. At query time, instead of expanding edge by edge in G, we expand cell by cell in the index.
2. *Constructing the index core.* Based on the graph partitioning, we insert nodes and edges into the initially empty index. This index core never changes.
3. *Computing the index cost function.* The edge cost is computed as a shortest-path cost for each departure time from a source node to a destination node.
4. *Inserting POIs.* Inserting a POI into a cell adds a new node and an edge to each border node of the cell. POIs that are not *border nodes* can be inserted and deleted dynamically without modifying the rest of the index.

We detail each step of the index construction next. Additionally, we discuss the factors that affect the size of the reachability index and present a compaction technique to reduce the number of connections.

4.1   Graph Partitioning

We partition the nodes of a temporal graph $G = (V, E, c)$ into a set of disjoint cells $C = \{C_1, C_2, \ldots, C_n\}$, such that each node of G belongs to exactly one cell C_i, i.e., $C_i \cap C_j = \emptyset$ for any pair of cells with $i \neq j$, and $\bigcup_{1 \leq i \leq n} C_i = V$. Each disconnected component of the graph should be partitioned into at least two cells. Within each cell C_i, we distinguish *border nodes* B_i. A node $v \in C_i$ is a border node if it has an edge to or from another cell, i.e., there is a node $w \in V, w \notin C_i$, and an edge $(v, w) \in E$ or an edge $(w, v) \in E$. For example, the temporal graph G in Fig. 1b of our example public transport network (Fig. 1a) can be partitioned into two cells (dashed boxes): C_1 with border nodes v_5 and v_7, and C_2 with border nodes v_8 and v_9.

The cells define the structure of the reachability index. The index will be expanded cell by cell to answer reachability queries. A good partitioning should satisfy the following properties:

1. *Well connected inside.* A cell comprises highly-linked nodes with many edges and connections inside the cell.
2. *Loosely connected outside.* The number of border nodes per cell is small.
3. *Large distance between cells.* Crossing cell borders is expensive: the number of connections between cells is small and their cost is high.

Finding a good partitioning that satisfies our requirements is not straightforward. In our scenario, the number of partitions or their sizes is not known up front, which renders many partitioning techniques inapplicable. We propose to use the Louvain method for community detection [7], which produces good partitions in our experiments. This technique efficiently finds communities in a network. It partitions the graph into communities of strongly connected nodes; nodes from different communities are loosely connected. The quality of the partitions is the so-called modularity that measures the density of links inside a community as compared to links between communities. Louvain iteratively finds good communities by increasing the modularity value. It starts with each node being in a different community and improves by moving nodes between communities. It supports a custom weight function for the links between nodes. We chose the number of connections between nodes for the weight function, i.e., how many times, according to the schedule, one can cross a direct edge between two nodes. Such a weight results in cells that are well connected inside and are loosely connected to other cells.

Exploring alternative weight functions and partitioning techniques is certainly a worthwhile effort. A possible weight refinement uses edge costs and assigns higher weights to edges with lower traversal cost. Interesting alternative graph partitionings include METIS [16] and the Merging-Algorithm [11].

4.2   Constructing the Index Core

Given a temporal graph $G = (V, E, c)$ and a partitioning C of G, we construct the core of our reachability index. The index core is independent of POIs and never changes. The reachability index is a temporal graph $R = (V_R, E_R, c_R)$ with nodes $V_R \subset V$, edges $E_R \subseteq V_R \times V_R$, and cost function $c_R(e, t)$ on the edges $e \in E_R$. For an edge $e = (u, v) \in E_R$, c_R returns the shortest-path cost from u to v at time t, i.e., $c_R(e, t) = sp(u, v, t)$.

Index Nodes. For each cell $C_i \in C$, we insert all its *border nodes* B_i into the node set V_R of the index. Thus, the nodes of the index $V_R = \bigcup_{1 \leq i \leq |C|} B_i$. Figure 1c shows the index core of the temporal graph (Fig. 1b) with cells $C_1 = \{v_5, v_7\}$ and $C_2 = \{v_8, v_9\}$.

Index Edges. The edges of the index core are $E_R = BB \cup BC$. BB is all edges between border nodes of neighboring cells. For each edge $(u, v) \in E$ between two border nodes of different cells in C, $u \in C_i, v \in C_j, i \neq j$, insert a new edge between the respective nodes into the index, $E_R = E_R \cup \{(u, v)\}$. BC is edges between pairs of border nodes within a cell. For each pair $u, v \in B_i$, insert two new edges (u, v) and (v, u) into the index, $E_R = E_R \cup \{(u, v), (v, u)\}$. For example, $BB = \{\alpha_3, \alpha_4, \alpha_7\}$ and $BC = \{\alpha_1, \alpha_2, \alpha_5, \alpha_6\}$ in Fig. 1c.

4.3   Computing the Index Cost Function

The cost function c_R of an edge $e = (u, v) \in E_R$ in index R is defined as the shortest-path cost from u to v at time t in graph G, i.e., $c_R(e, t) = sp(u, v, t)$. For computing the values of the cost function c_R, we execute Dijkstra's single-source shortest-path algorithm once for every border node $b \in B_i$ and every departure time at b. The expansion stops when all other border nodes in the cell and all direct neighbors of b (i.e., nodes reachable from b via a BB edge) are visited. Since the cells are small compared to the overall graph, typically only a small number of nodes needs to be considered for each execution of Dijkstra's algorithm. BC and BP edges may connect nodes that are not reachable in the original temporal graph. If a node is not reached during one of the shortest-path computations, we assign infinite cost to the respective edges. Cost examples for the index core in Fig. 1c are: $c_R(\alpha_3, 14) = 3$, $c_R(\alpha_4, 9) = 3$, $c_R(\alpha_7, 8) = 3$, $c_R(\alpha_1, 9) = 2$, $c_R(\alpha_2, 11) = 3$, $c_R(\alpha_5, 9) = 2$, $c_R(\alpha_6, 8) = 2$.

4.4   Points of Interest

POIs can be inserted and deleted at any time, also after index construction. This is beneficial because POIs may change over time. A POI $v \in V$ may be any node in the original temporal graph. If v is a border node, no action is required because such a node is in the index core already. Otherwise, similarly to border nodes, inserting v into the index involves three steps. (1) We add v to the index nodes ($V_R = V_R \cup \{v\}$). (2) We add an edge from each border node of $v's$ cell to v (we call such edges BP edges). (3) The cost function based on shortest paths (like for all other edges) is computed. Deleting a POI from the index removes the POI node and all its incoming edges. For example, consider inserting two POIs, v_2, v_{10}, into the index in Fig. 1d. We add edges $BP = \{\alpha_8, \alpha_9, \alpha_{10}, \alpha_{11}\}$ with cost examples $c_R(\alpha_8, 9) = 3$, $c_R(\alpha_9, 8) = 7$, $c_R(\alpha_{10}, 9) = 1$, and $c_R(\alpha_{11}, 11) = 1$.

4.5   Index Size

The index consists of border nodes and POIs. Thus, the number of index nodes is at most the number of nodes in the temporal graph. We introduce three types of edges into the index. BB edges connect border nodes between different cells, and they are a subset of the temporal graph edges. BC edges connect border nodes in a single cell, and their cardinality is at most quadratic in the number of border nodes. Each POI adds as many BP edges as border nodes in a cell. The numbers of BC and BP edges depend only on the subset of temporal graph nodes that are in a single cell. The numbers do not depend on the graph size. In sparse graphs, where many nodes have only a few edges, the reachability index may grow larger than the temporal graph: we can remove only a small number of original edges but need to insert new BC and BP edges.

Each edge has as many edge cost values as there are departure times from a node. The edge costs are computed for each single cell in isolation, making parallel computation possible. In particular, the edge cost of a specific border node at a specific departure time is independent of all other edge costs.

4.6   Index Compaction

The index size, as well as the size of the temporal graph, is dominated by the size of the schedule, i.e., the number of edge connections. After computing the edge costs in the index, we observe that many different departure times have the same arrival time at the destination. It is enough to keep only one connection per arrival time, namely the one with the maximum departure time. We leverage that and compact the index by reducing the number of connections as follows. Consider an edge $e(u, v) \in E_R$ and set S of departure–arrival connection pairs (d, a) on that edge. We compact S to $S' \subseteq S$, such that $S' = \{(d, a) \in S : \nexists_{(d_i, a_i) \in S} a_i = a \wedge d_i > d\}$. Experiments show that this compaction technique is highly effective and reduces the index size by up to 73% (cf. Sect. 7). For example, the set of all connections on edge α_8 in Fig. 1d, $\{(8, 12), (9, 12), (11, 15)\}$, is compacted into $\{(9, 12), (11, 15)\}$.

5   Answering Reachability Queries

The core idea of our reachability algorithm is to expand cell by cell rather than edge by edge. The BB edges between border nodes of different cells allow us to expand to the neighboring cells; the BC edges between border nodes of the same cell reflect the time to cross a cell; the direct BP edges from border nodes to POIs allow for a quick evaluation of which POIs can be reached. In addition, we discuss a heuristic to avoid unnecessary edge expansions and processing of query nodes that are non-border nodes.

The Reachability Algorithm. Algorithm 1, takes as an input the reachability index $R = (V_R, E_R, c_R)$, query node q, start time t_s, and the cost budget Δt. The expansion proceeds like in Dijkstra's algorithm and returns the set N of reachable

---

Algorithm 1: $RQ(R, q, t_s, \Delta t)$

---

1 M: min-heap ordered by time from q; $M[q] = 0$; $M[v] = \infty, v \in V_R \setminus \{q\}$
2 $N \leftarrow \{\}$
3 **while** M *is not empty* **do**
4 $\quad$ pop (v, w) from M $\qquad\qquad\qquad$ // $v \in V_R$, $w = sp(q, v, t_s)$
5 $\quad$ **if** $w > \Delta t$ **then break**; $\qquad\qquad$ // *no more reachable nodes*
6 $\quad$ $O \leftarrow$ outgoing edges from v
7 $\quad$ **if** v *is flagged* **then** $O \leftarrow \{$edges BB at $v\}$; $\qquad$ // *avoid expansions*
8 $\quad$ **foreach** $(v, u) \in O$ **do**
9 $\quad\quad$ $w' \leftarrow w + c_R((v, u), t_s + w)$ $\qquad$ // *binary search in list of edge costs*
10 $\quad\quad$ **if** $w' \leq \Delta t \land w' < M[u]$ **then**
11 $\quad\quad\quad$ $M[u] \leftarrow w'$
12 $\quad\quad\quad$ **if** u *in cell of* v **then** flag v **else** remove flag from v
13 $\quad$ $N \leftarrow N \cup \{v\}$
14 **return** N

POIs in R. Nodes and their costs from q are stored in a min-heap M initialized to $M[q] = 0$, and $M[v] = \infty$ for all other nodes v (line 1). The closest node v to q is popped from the min-heap (line 4), and the costs for nodes adjacent to v are updated if smaller (lines 9–11). To retrieve the correct edge cost, we do a binary search in the list of edge costs sorted by departure time (line 9). Each node is traversed only once. The algorithm terminates when no more nodes with cost lower than the budget are in the heap (line 5). Consider the reachability index in Fig. 1d. Here, $RQ(R, v_5, 8, 6) = \{v_2, v_{10}\}$ because $sp(v_5, v_2, t) = 4$ (through α_8) and $sp(v_5, v_{10}, t) = 5$ (through α_4 and α_{10}). $RQ(R, v_5, 6, 6) = \{v_2\}$ because $sp(v_5, v_2, t) = 6$ (through α_8) but $sp(v_5, v_{10}, t) = 7$ (through α_4 and α_{10}).

Avoiding Unnecessary Expansions. Regarding the edges within a cell, we observe the following. Consider Algorithm 1 processing a border node b of a cell C_i. Then, the costs of the other nodes, $v_j \in C_i$, are updated w.r.t. the cost of reaching them from b. When we pop a node v_j in a later round, and if v_j was last updated by b, there is no point in following the edges from v_j to the other nodes in the cell. The cost of accessing the other nodes in the cell through v_j cannot be smaller than the cost of accessing these nodes directly from b since all edge costs are shortest paths. If, however, v_j was updated through an edge from a neighboring cell, the edges to the other nodes in the cell need to be followed. We exploit this observation to avoid following edges inside a cell that cannot lead to an update and thus do not affect the solution. We flag the nodes whenever their cost was updated by processing a node from within a cell, and we remove the flag, otherwise (line 12). The outgoing edges that must be expanded are selected based on the flag (line 7).

Note that the number of edges within a cell is quadratic in the number of border nodes of that cell. Thanks to the use of flags we avoid unnecessary expansions. In particular, if the cheapest way to reach all nodes in a cell is through k border nodes, we only expand $k(w-1)$ edges per cell, where w is the number of all border nodes and POIs in a cell. The value of k is expected to be small and will often be 1 (i.e., the shortest path from a query node q to all nodes in the cell crosses the border node that is closest to q).

Non-border Query Nodes. The reachability index does not contain all nodes of the original graph. If the query node q in cell C_i is not a border node, the algorithm starts the expansion from q in the temporal graph. All POIs reached in cell C_i are part of the result. Once a border node $b' \in B_i$ is reached, the expansion continues in the index at time $t_s + sp(q, b', t_s)$.

Correctness. We show that the shortest-path costs in the index and the original temporal graph are identical. Let $u, w \in V_R$ be two index nodes and $p = \langle (v_0, v_1), (v_1, v_2), \ldots, (v_{n-1}, v_n) \rangle$ be the corresponding shortest path in the temporal graph, i.e., $u = v_0, w = v_n$. If there is a direct edge between u and w in the index, the shortest-path cost is the cost of that edge: this cost is precomputed using Dijkstra's algorithm for each departure time in the original temporal graph; since our cost function is consistent (cf. Sect. 2), the edge cost is correct [17]. Otherwise, u and w are not in the same cell (all nodes in a cell are connected with an edge). So, there must be a path along index nodes $u_1, u_2, \ldots u_k \subseteq v_1, \ldots v_{n-1}$ that are all on path p since cells can be exited only through border nodes. We show that the cost of the index path is indeed the shortest path. Assume a node u_i exists such that $sp(v_0, v_n, t) < sp(u, u_i, t) + sp(u_i, w, t) + sp(u, u_i, t)$. On a path of length two, the costs of edges (u, u_1) and (u_1, w) are precomputed shortest-path costs, and they are therefore correct. The assumption, however, implies that one of the edge costs could be decreased, i.e., the assumption is incorrect. This argument can be extended edge by edge to paths of arbitrary length.

6 Related Work

Shortest-path and reachability queries on road networks, i.e., graphs with constant edge cost, have been studied extensively. Unfortunately, these works cannot be applied readily to public transport networks [3]. An evaluation by Bast et al. [4] shows a large performance gap between the two types of networks. This is due to the time-dependent edge costs of public transport networks, which makes the precomputation efforts of many algorithms infeasible.

Current solutions for public transport networks either rely on Dijkstra's algorithm [10] or require heavy precomputations. Dijkstra-based approaches include isochrone algorithms for multimodal networks [6,12]. They expand from a query point using Dijkstra's algorithm and compute a so-called isochrone, which is the reachable portion of the network at a given point in time. Since all edges in the isochrone must be expanded, this approach does not scale to large networks.

Many works fall into the category of labeling approaches. The earliest work, 2-hop labeling [9], is designed for weighted graphs and is based on 2-hop covers of shortest paths. Recent works strive to decrease the index size and construction time [8,15], which are bottlenecks of 2-hop labeling and prevent application to

large graphs. Time Table Labeling (TTL) [20] and Top Chain [21] adapt 2-hop
labeling to public transport networks; they support shortest-path and point-to-
point reachability queries. In TTL, the main idea is to precompute label sets
for each node v containing reachable nodes from and to v. Top Chain creates
a directed acyclic graph (DAG), where each node represents a departure time,
and decomposes the DAG to create the label sets. Creating label sets in both
techniques requires high precomputation costs and large index sizes. To decrease
the index size, Top Chain only stores K label sets, called chains. The index size
of Top Chain for small K values is smaller than that of TTL, but there is no
guarantee that the query results can be found using the index.

Non-labeling techniques include Scalable Transfer Patterns [5], Connection Scan Algorithm (CSA) [19], and Contraction Hierarchy for Timetables
(CHT) [13]. Transfer Patterns require an expensive profile search from each
node to find the optimal paths to all other nodes. CSA organizes a schedule as
two sequences of edges. The first sequence contains sorted edges based on arrival
times, and the second sorts edges based on departure times. These approaches
involve expensive precomputations or large index sizes, which limits their scalability.

To compute reachability queries as defined in this paper, all techniques based
on point-to-point queries require the computation of shortest paths from a given
query node to every POI, which does not scale to large number of POIs.

Table 1. Statistics of our datasets

Dataset	#Nodes	#Edges	#Conn	#Part	#B-nodes		Part. size			#POIs	
					sum	avg	avg	min	max	sum	avg
Zurich	2,508	5,630	555,713	45	315	7.0	55	2	157	99	2.20
Berlin	12,984	34,791	1,348,070	50	1,241	24.8	259	2	921	567	11.34
Synthetic	145,188	433,272	31,042,468	44	1,245	28.3	3,299	831	4,037	7,176	163.00

7 Experiments

We experimentally evaluate our solution, RQ, and compare it with two competitors, a no-index solution, NI, and a fully-indexed solution, SP. We report on the
index size and efficiency of the algorithms w.r.t. the number of expanded edges,
which is the work that an algorithm has to do to find reachable nodes. The
algorithms are implemented in Python 3 and executed on a Intel Xeon server
(E5-2630 v3 2.40 GHz, 2 CPUs of 8 cores, 96 GB RAM, Debian 9.12).

Competitors. The no-index solution, NI, operates on the original temporal graph
and does not build an index. The reachability is computed with a modified version of Dijkstra's algorithm that supports our cost function (cf. Sect. 5). The
fully-indexed solution, SP, stores all shortest paths from every node in the temporal graph to all POIs at every departure time. SP represents the collection of
works that index the shortest paths between pairs of nodes (cf. Sect. 6).

Datasets. We use two real-world public transport networks represented as temporal graphs, *Zurich* and *Berlin* [1], and one synthetic graph, *Synthetic*. *Zurich* and *Berlin* are obtained in GTFS format that is further processed. For these graphs, we chose all transport modes and all connections operating on Mondays. *Synthetic* is a 6 × 6 grid of equally-sized spider-web subgraphs. Each spider-web subgraph has one edge to every neighboring subgraph (to its left, right, top, and bottom). This graph simulates loosely connected cities that are densely connected inside. Table 1 shows the statistics. Here, #Conn is the number of all connections (departure-arrival pairs) that can be used to cross an edge. We report the details of partitioning the data graphs using the Louvain method (with maximum partition sizes): number of partitions, number of border nodes (sum and average per partition), partition sizes (avg, min, and max). We also show the number of POIs (sum and average per partition). POIs are chosen randomly as 5% of the nodes of each partition (at least one per partition).

Index Size. RQ and SP precompute certain shortest paths and build an index structure that is sufficient to answer reachability queries. If the index of SP is stored as a graph, its number of nodes equals #Nodes (POIs are nodes of the graph), its number of edges equals #Nodes × #POIs (shortest paths from every node to every POI are computed), and the number of connection equals #Conn × #POIs (a shortest path at every departure time to every POI is computed); #Nodes, #POIs, and #Conn are of the original temporal graph. Although *NI* does not require precomputation, the input graph has to be kept in memory. In Table 2, we compare the index sizes (*RQ*, *SP*) to the input graph size (*NI*). The values that increase the index size are the number of nodes and edges, and the number of connections. The index size of *RQ* is always smaller than that of *SP* (up to four orders of magnitude). *RQ* is also significantly smaller than the original *Zurich* and *Synthetic* graphs (*NI*). For *Berlin*, despite it having significantly fewer nodes, the numbers of edges and connections in *RQ* are larger than in the original graph. This is caused by the sparsity of *Berlin* (cf. Sect. 4.5). Finally, #Connections is the number of edge connections stored. For *RQ*, we list

Table 2. Index details

Dataset	Algorithm	#Nodes	#Edges	#Connections
Zurich	*RQ*	414	4,021	421,268
	SP	2,508	248,292	55,015,587
	NI	2,508	5,630	555,713
Berlin	*RQ*	1,808	53,543	2,533,940
	SP	12,984	7,361,928	764,355,690
	NI	12,984	34,791	1,348,070
Synthetic	*RQ*	8,421	212,564	18,018,811
	SP	145,188	1,041,869,088	222,760,750,368
	NI	145,188	433,272	31,042,468

the absolute number of connections after the compaction. The reduction rate of compaction varies from 67% in *Synthetic* to 73% in *Zurich* and *Berlin*.

Number of Expanded Edges. To evaluate the efficiency, we compare the number of edges that an algorithm has to process in order to find all reachable POIs (Fig. 2). One data point in the figure (scatter plot) is a single reachability query. Data points are sorted along the x-axis by the number of expanded edges. The number of expanded edges (y-axis) is displayed in log scale. We execute one reachability query starting at every border node in our index. We do so at five different start times (8:00, 12:00, 16:00, 18:00, 22:00) and for two time budgets (60 and 120 min). Thus, the number of data points is 10× #Border nodes. The budgets are large enough to force RQ to traverse multiple edges. Since the edge costs of large cells in the RQ index are often above 15 min (and above 30 min in about half of the cases), budgets near these values provide little insight. Since SP precomputes the path to each POI, it always evaluates one edge per POI. This is a lower bound on the cost of any point-to-point index. Although the index of SP is orders of magnitude larger, RQ expands significantly fewer edges for many of the data points. We observe the largest differences for the budget of 120 min. On *Synthetic*, the number of edges expanded by RQ is up to three orders of magnitude lower than that of SP, and it is up to one order of magnitude lower than that of NI. RQ always expands fewer edges than NI. Values equal to zero indicate that an algorithm cannot expand due to high connection costs. We also performed similar experiment with an increased percentage of POIs (more than 5%): the difference in the number of expanded edges between RQ and NI decreases. This is to be expected since RQ can leverage the sparsity of POIs, while NI cannot.

Overall, our experiments show that dispite its small size, RQ substantially reduces the number of edges (by about an order of magnitude in realistic settings) and therefore speeds up reachability queries in public transport networks.

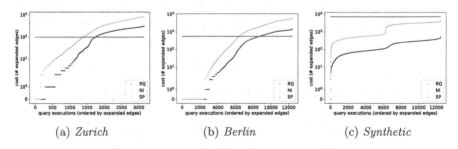

| (a) *Zurich* | (b) *Berlin* | (c) *Synthetic* |

Fig. 2. Number of expanded edges (y-axis in log scale).

8 Conclusion

The paper offers improved support for reachability queries in temporal graphs that retrieve all reachable points of interest (POIs) from a given query node at a specific start time within a given time budget. We observe that current solutions do not scale to large network (solutions based on Dijkstra's algorithm without a pre-computed index) or to networks with many POIs (solutions based on an index for single-path queries that must be executed for each POI separately). We propose a solution based on a novel access structure, the reachability index. This index partitions the original temporal graph into cells, thus enabling us to expand the graph cell by cell rather than edge by edge. We report on experiments that suggest that our technique is both effective and efficient.

Acknowledgments. This work was supported by Austrian Science Fund (FWF): W1237. We wish to thank Christine Gfrerer for her valuable suggestions, as well as Alfred Egger and Manuel Kocher for their help with the experiments.

References

1. Zurich and Berlin GTFS. https://data.stadt-zuerich.ch/dataset/vbz_fahrplandat en_gtfs, https://daten.berlin.de/datensaetze/vbb-fahrplandaten-gtfs. Accessed 31 Jan 2020
2. Amer-Yahia, S., Roy, S.B., Chawlat, A., Das, G., Yu, C.: Group recommendation: semantics and efficiency. Proc. VLDB Endow. **2**(1), 754–765 (2009). https://doi.org/10.14778/1687627.1687713
3. Bast, H.: Car or public transport - two worlds. In: Efficient Algorithms: Essays Dedicated to Kurt Mehlhorn on the Occasion of His 60th Birthday, pp. 355–367 (2009). https://doi.org/10.1007/978-3-642-03456-5_24
4. Bast, H., et al.: Route planning in transportation networks. In: Kliemann, L., Sanders, P. (eds.) Algorithm Engineering. LNCS, vol. 9220, pp. 19–80. Springer, Cham (2016). https://doi.org/10.1007/978-3-319-49487-6_2
5. Bast, H., Hertel, M., Storandt, S.: Scalable transfer patterns. In: Proceedings of the Meeting on Algorithm Engineering and Experiments (ALENEX), pp. 15–29 (2016). https://doi.org/10.1137/1.9781611974317.2
6. Bauer, V., Gamper, J., Loperfido, R., Profanter, S., Putzer, S., Timko, I.: Computing isochrones in multi-modal, schedule-based transport networks. In: Proceedings of the ACM SIGSPATIAL International Conference on Advances in Geographic Information Systems (2008). https://doi.org/10.1145/1463434.1463524
7. Blondel, V.D., Guillaume, J.L., Lambiotte, R., Lefebvre, E.: Fast unfolding of communities in large networks. J. Stat. Mech. Theory Exp. **2008**(10) (2008). https://doi.org/10.1088/1742-5468/2008/10/p10008
8. Cheng, J., Huang, S., Wu, H., Fu, A.W.: TF-label: a topological-folding labeling scheme for reachability querying in a large graph. In: Proceedings of the ACM SIGMOD International Conference on Management of Data, pp. 193–204 (2013). https://doi.org/10.1145/2463676.2465286
9. Cohen, E., Halperin, E., Kaplan, H., Zwick, U.: Reachability and distance queries via 2-hop labels. SIAM J. Comput. **32**(5), 1338–1355 (2003). https://doi.org/10.1137/S0097539702403098
10. Dijkstra, E.W.: A note on two problems in connexion with graphs. Numerische Mathematik **1**, 269–271 (1959). https://doi.org/10.1007/BF01386390
11. Flinsenberg, I., van der Horst, M., Lukkien, J., Verriet, J.: Creating graph partitions for fast optimum route planning. WSEAS Trans. Comput. **3**(3), 569–574 (2004)
12. Gamper, J., Böhlen, M., Cometti, W., Innerebner, M.: Defining isochrones in multimodal spatial networks. In: Proceedings of the ACM International Conference on Information and Knowledge Management (CIKM), pp. 2381–2384 (2011). https://doi.org/10.1145/2063576.2063972

13. Geisberger, R.: Contraction of timetable networks with realistic transfers. In: Proceedings of the International Symposium on Experimental Algorithms, pp. 71–82 (2010). https://doi.org/10.1007/978-3-642-13193-6_7
14. Jameson, A., Smyth, B.: Recommendation to groups. In: The Adaptive Web: Methods and Strategies of Web Personalization, pp. 596–627 (2007). https://doi.org/10.1007/978-3-540-72079-9_20
15. Jin, R., Wang, G.: Simple, fast, and scalable reachability oracle. Proc. VLDB Endow. **6**(14), 1978–1989 (2013). https://doi.org/10.14778/2556549.2556578
16. Karypis, G., Kumar, V.: A fast and high quality multilevel scheme for partitioning irregular graphs. SIAM J. Sci. Comput. **20**(1), 359–392 (1998). https://doi.org/10.1137/S1064827595287997
17. Kaufmann, D.E., Smith, R.L.: Fastest paths in time-dependent networks for intelligent vehicle-highway systems application. J. Intell. Transp. Syst. **1**(1), 1–11 (1993). https://doi.org/10.1080/10248079308903779
18. Seufert, S., Anand, A., Bedathur, S.J., Weikum, G.: FERRARI: flexible and efficient reachability range assignment for graph indexing. In: Proceedings of the IEEE International Conference on Data Engineering (ICDE), pp. 1009–1020 (2013). https://doi.org/10.1109/ICDE.2013.6544893
19. Strasser, B.: Intriguingly simple and efficient time-dependent routing in road networks. CoRR abs/1606.06636 (2016). http://arxiv.org/abs/1606.06636
20. Wang, S., Lin, W., Yang, Y., Xiao, X., Zhou, S.: Efficient route planning on public transportation networks: a labelling approach. In: Proceedings of the ACM SIGMOD International Conference on Management of Data, pp. 967–982 (2015). https://doi.org/10.1145/2723372.2749456
21. Wu, H., Huang, Y., Cheng, J., Li, J., Ke, Y.: Reachability and time-based path queries in temporal graphs. In: Proceedings of the IEEE International Conference on Data Engineering (ICDE), pp. 145–156 (2016). https://doi.org/10.1109/ICDE.2016.7498236

Context-Free Path Querying by Kronecker Product

Egor Orachev[1], Ilya Epelbaum[1], Rustam Azimov[1,2(✉)],
and Semyon Grigorev[1,2]

[1] St. Petersburg State University, 7/9 Universitetskaya nab.,
St. Petersburg 199034, Russia
egor.orachev@gmail.com, iliyepelbaun@gmail.com,
rustam.azimov19021995@gmail.com, s.v.grigoriev@spbu.ru
[2] JetBrains Research, Primorskiy prospekt 68-70, Building 1,
St. Petersburg 197374, Russia
semyon.grigorev@jetbrains.com

Abstract. Context-free path queries (CFPQ) extend the regular path queries (RPQ) by allowing context-free grammars to be used as constraints for paths. Algorithms for CFPQ are actively developed, but J. Kuijpers et al. have recently concluded, that existing algorithms are not performant enough to be used in real-world applications. Thus the development of new algorithms for CFPQ is justified. In this paper, we provide a new CFPQ algorithm which is based on such linear algebra operations as Kronecker product and transitive closure and handles grammars presented as recursive state machines. Thus, the proposed algorithm can be implemented by using high-performance libraries and modern parallel hardware. Moreover, it avoids grammar growth which provides the possibility for queries optimization.

Keywords: Context-free path querying · Graph database · Context-free grammars · CFPQ · Kronecker product · Recursive state machines

1 Introduction

Language-constrained path querying [3], and particularly context-free path querying (CFPQ) [13], allows one to express constraints for paths in a graph in terms of context-free grammars. A path in a graph is included in a query result only if the labels along this path form a word that belongs to the language, generated by the query grammar. CFPQ is widely used in bioinformatics [12], graph databases querying [5,9,10], and RDF analysis [14].

CFPQ algorithms are actively developed but still suffer from poor performance [9]. The algorithm proposed by Rustam Azimov [2] is one of the most promising. This algorithm makes it possible to offload computational intensive

The research was supported by the Russian Science Foundation, grant №18-11-00100.

J. Darmont et al. (Eds.): ADBIS 2020, LNCS 12245, pp. 49–59, 2020.
https://doi.org/10.1007/978-3-030-54832-2_6

parts to high-performance libraries for linear algebra, this way one can utilize modern parallel hardware for CFPQ. One disadvantage of this algorithm is that a query grammar should be converted to a Chomsky Normal Form (CNF) which significantly increases its size. The performance of the algorithm depends on the grammar size, thus it is desirable to create the algorithm which does not modify the query grammar.

In this work, we propose a new algorithm for CFPQ which can be expressed in terms of matrix operations and does not require grammar transformation. This algorithm can be efficiently implemented on modern parallel hardware and it provides ways to optimize queries. The main contribution of this paper could be summarized as follows.

1. We introduce a new algorithm for CFPQ, which is based on the intersection of recursive state machines and can be expressed in terms of Kronecker product and transitive closure.
2. We provide a step-by-step example of the algorithm.
3. We provide an evaluation of the presented algorithm and its comparison with the matrix-based algorithm. The presented algorithm outperforms the previous matrix-based algorithm in the worst-case scenario, but further optimizations are required to make it applicable for real-world cases.

2 Recursive State Machines

In this section, we introduce recursive state machines (RSM) [1]. This kind of computational machine extends the definition of finite state machines and increases the computational capabilities of this formalism.

A recursive state machine R over a finite alphabet Σ is defined as a tuple of elements $(M, m, \{C_i\}_{i \in M})$, where:

- M is a finite set of labels of boxes.
- $m \in M$ is an initial box label.
- Set of *component state machines* or *boxes*, where $C_i = (\Sigma \cup M, Q_i, q_i^0, F_i, \delta_i)$:
  - $\Sigma \cup M$ is a set of symbols, $\Sigma \cap M = \emptyset$
  - Q_i is a finite set of states, where $Q_i \cap Q_j = \emptyset, \forall i \neq j$
  - q_i^0 is an initial state for the component state machine C_i
  - F_i is a set of final states for C_i, where $F_i \subseteq Q_i$
  - δ_i is a transition function for C_i, where $\delta_i : Q_i \times (\Sigma \cup M) \to Q_i$

RSM behaves as a set of finite state machines (or FSM). Each FSM is called a *box* or a *component state machine* [1]. A box works almost the same as a classical FSM, but it also handles additional *recursive calls* and employs an implicit *call stack* to *call* one component from another and then return execution flow back.

The execution of an RSM could be defined as a sequence of the configuration transitions, which are done on input symbols reading. The pair (q_i, S), where q_i is current state for box C_i and S is stack of *return states*, describes execution configurations.

The RSM execution starts form configuration $(q_m^0, \langle\rangle)$. The following list of rules defines the machine transition from configuration (q_i, S) to (q', S') on some input symbol a from the input sequence, which is read as usual for FSA:

- $q' \leftarrow q_i^t, S' \leftarrow S$, where $q_i^t = \delta_i(q_i^k, a), q_i^k = q$
- $q' \leftarrow q_j^0, S' \leftarrow q_i^t \circ S$, where $q_i^t = \delta_i(q_i^k, j), q_i^k = q, j \in M$
- $q' \leftarrow q_i^t, S' \leftarrow S_{tail}$, where $S = q_i^t \circ S_{tail}, q_j^k = q, q_j^k \in F_j$

Some input sequence of the symbols $a_1...a_n$, which forms some input word, accepted, if machine reaches configuration $(q, \langle\rangle)$, where $q \in F_m$. It is also worth noting that the RSM makes not deterministic transitions, without reading the input character when it *calls* some component or makes a *return*.

According to [1], recursive state machines are equivalent to pushdown systems. Since pushdown systems are capable of accepting context-free languages [7], it is clear that RSMs are equivalent to context-free languages. Thus RSMs suit to encode query grammars. Any CFG can be easily converted to an RSM with one box per nonterminal. The box which corresponds to a nonterminal A is constructed using the right-hand side of each rule for A. An example of such RSM R constructed for the grammar G with rules $S \rightarrow aSb \mid ab$ is provided in Fig. 1.

Since R is a set of FSMs, it is useful to represent R as an adjacency matrix for the graph where vertices are states from $\bigcup_{i \in M} Q_i$ and edges are transitions between q_i^a and q_i^b with label $l \in \Sigma \cup M$, if $\delta_i(q_i^a, l) = q_i^b$. An example of such adjacency matrix M_R for the machine R is provided in Sect. 4.1.

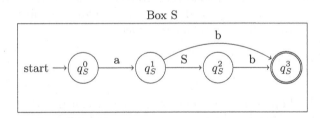

Fig. 1. The recursive state machine R for grammar G

3   Kronecker Product

In this section, we introduce the Kronecker product definition and its relation to the RSM and a directed graph intersection.

A directed labeled graph could be interpreted as an FSM, where transitions correspond to the labeled edges between vertices of the graph. As initial and final states could be chosen all vertices of the graph since this formal decision does not affect the algorithm idea. As shown in the Sect. 2, an RSM is composed of a set of component state machines, which behave as a normal FSM. Notice, that these component machines are structurally independent, and actual communications are done only on *recursive calls* in time of the machine execution. It makes an intuition that one could apply automata theory to intersect an RSM with a directed graph.

The classical intersection algorithm of two deterministic FSMs is presented in [7]. The idea behind this algorithm is to create new FSM, which imitates the parallel work of both machines through an increase in the number of states and transitions. For any given FSMs $C_1 = (\Sigma \cup M, Q_1, q_1^0, F_1, \delta_1)$ and $C_2 = (\Sigma \cup M, Q_2, q_2^0, F_2, \delta_2)$ the intersection machine C defines as follows:
$C = (\Sigma \cup M, Q, q^0, F, \delta)$, where:

- States $Q = \{(q_1, q_2) \ : \ q_1 \in Q_1, q_2 \in Q_2\}$
- Final states $F = \{(q_1, q_2) \ : \ q_1 \in F_1, q_2 \in F_2\}$
- Initial state $q = (q_1^0, q_2^0)$
- Transition function $\delta((q_1, q_2), a) \rightarrow (\delta_1(q_1, a), \delta_2(q_2, a))$, where $a \in \Sigma \cup M$, only if ($\delta_1(q_1, a)$ and $\delta_2(q_2, a)$) are present.

A structurally similar procedure for constructing an intersection machine can be implemented using the Kronecker product for the corresponding transition matrices for FSMs if we provide a satisfying operation of elementwise multiplication, which allows further use of high-performance math libraries for intersection computation.

Since an RSM transitions matrix is composed as a blocked matrix of component state machines adjacency matrices, and a directed labeled graph could be presented as an adjacency matrix, it is convenient to implement the intersection of such objects via Kronecker product of the corresponding matrices. As an elementwise operation for one can employ the following function $\bullet : \Sigma \cup M \times \Sigma \cup M \rightarrow Boolean$, defined as follows:

- $A_1 \bullet A_2 = true$, if $A_1 \cap A_2 \neq \emptyset$
- $A_1 \bullet A_2 = false$, otherwise

An example of applying the Kronecker product is illustrated in the Sect. 4.1.

The operation defined in this way allows us to construct an adjacency Boolean matrix for some directed graph, where a path between two vertices exists only if corresponding paths exist in some component state machine of the RSM and in source graph at the same time. This fact with transitive closure could be employed in order to extract all the path and components labels from M for context-free reachability problem-solving.

4   Kronecker Product Based CFPQ Algorithm

In this section, we introduce the algorithm for the computation of context-free reachability in a graph $\mathcal{G}$. The algorithm determines the existence of a path, which forms a sentence of the language defined by the input RSM R, between each pair of vertices in the graph $\mathcal{G}$. The algorithm is based on the generalization of the FSM intersection for an RSM, and an input graph. The idea of using the Kronecker product for the intersection of an RSM and a directed input graph is presented in the Sect. 3.

Listing 1 shows the main steps of the algorithm. The algorithm accepts context-free grammar $G = (\Sigma, N, P)$ and graph $\mathcal{G} = (V, E, L)$ as an input. An RSM R is created from the grammar G. Note, that R must have no ε-transitions. M_1 and M_2 are the adjacency matrices for the machine R and the graph $\mathcal{G}$ correspondingly.

Then for each vertex i of the graph $\mathcal{G}$, the algorithm adds loops with non-terminals, which allows deriving ε-word. Here the following rule is implied: each vertex of the graph is reachable by itself through an ε-transition. Since the machine R does not have any ε-transitions, the ε-word could be derived only if a state s in the box B of the R is both initial and final. This data is queried by the $getNonterminals()$ function for each state s.

The algorithm terminates when the matrix M_2 stops changing. Kronecker product of matrices M_1 and M_2 is evaluated for each iteration. The result is stored in M_3 as a Boolean matrix. For the given M_3 a C_3 matrix is evaluated by the $transitiveClosure()$ function call. The M_3 could be interpreted as an adjacency matrix for a directed graph with no labels, used to evaluate transitive closure in terms of classical graph definition of this operation. Then the algorithm iterates over cells of the C_3. For the pair of indices (i, j), it computes s and f—the initial and final states in the recursive automata R which relate to the concrete $C_3[i, j]$ of the closure matrix. If the given s and f belong to the same box B of R, $s = q_B^0$, and $f \in F_B$, then $getNonterminals()$ returns the respective non-terminal. If the condition holds then the algorithm adds the computed non-terminals to the respective cell of the adjacency matrix M_2 of the graph.

The functions $getStates$ and $getCoordinates$ (see Listing 2) are used to map indices between Kronecker product arguments and the result matrix. The Implementation appeals to the blocked structure of the matrix C_3, where each block corresponds to some automata and graph edge.

The algorithm returns the updated matrix M_2 which contains the initial graph $\mathcal{G}$ data as well as non-terminals from N. If a cell $M_2[i, j]$ for any valid indices i and j contains symbol $S \in N$, then vertex j is reachable from vertex i in grammar G for non-terminal S.

4.1   Example

This section provides a step-by-step demonstration of the presented algorithm. We consider the theoretical worst case for CFPQ time complexity, proposed by J. Hellings [5] as an example: the graph $\mathcal{G}$ is presented in Fig. 2a and the context-free grammar G for a language $\{a^n b^n \mid n \geq 1\}$ is $S \rightarrow aSb \mid ab$.

Since the proposed algorithm processes grammar in the form of a recursive machine, we first provide RSM R in Fig. 1. The initial box of the R is S, the initial state q_S^0 is (0), the set of final states $F_S = \{(3)\}$.

Listing 1. Kronecker product based CFPQ

```
1: function CONTEXTFREEPATHQUERYING(G, 𝒢)
2:     R ← Recursive automata for G
3:     M₁ ← Adjacency matrix for R
4:     M₂ ← Adjacency matrix for 𝒢
5:     for s ∈ 0..dim(M₁) − 1 do
6:         for i ∈ 0..dim(M₂) − 1 do
7:             M₂[i, i] ← M₂[i, i] ∪ getNonterminals(R, s, s)
8:     while Matrix M₂ is changing do
9:         M₃ ← M₁ ⊗ M₂                          ▷ Evaluate Kronecker product
10:        C₃ ← transitiveClosure(M₃)
11:        n ← dim(M₃)                           ▷ Matrix M₃ size = n × n
12:        for i ∈ 0..n − 1 do
13:            for j ∈ 0..n − 1 do
14:                if C₃[i, j] then
15:                    s, f ← getStates(C₃, i, j)
16:                    if getNonterminals(R, s, f) ≠ ∅ then
17:                        x, y ← getCoordinates(C₃, i, j)
18:                        M₂[x, y] ← M₂[x, y] ∪ getNonterminals(R, s, f)
19:    return M₂
```

Listing 2. Help functions for Kronecker product based CFPQ

```
1: function GETSTATES(C, i, j)
2:     r ← dim(M₁)                    ▷ M₁ is adjacency matrix for automata R
3:     return ⌊i/r⌋, ⌊j/r⌋
4: function GETCOORDINATES(C, i, j)
5:     n ← dim(M₂)                    ▷ M₂ is adjacency matrix for graph 𝒢
6:     return i mod n, j mod n
```

Adjacency matrices M_1 and M_2 for automata R and graph $\mathcal{G}$ respectively are initialized as follows:

$$M_1 = \begin{pmatrix} \cdot & \{a\} & \cdot & \cdot \\ \cdot & \cdot & \{S\} & \{b\} \\ \cdot & \cdot & \cdot & \{b\} \\ \cdot & \cdot & \cdot & \cdot \end{pmatrix}, \quad M_2^0 = \begin{pmatrix} \cdot & \{a\} & \cdot & \cdot \\ \cdot & \cdot & \{a\} & \cdot \\ \{a\} & \cdot & \cdot & \{b\} \\ \cdot & \cdot & \{b\} & \cdot \end{pmatrix}.$$

After the initialization in lines **2–4**, the algorithm handles ε-case. Because the machine R does not have ε-transitions and ε-word is not included in the language, lines **5–7** of the algorithm do not affect the input data.

Then the algorithm enters the while loop and iterates while matrix M_2 is changing. We provide both the values of the matrices M_3, C_3 at each algorithm step as well as how the matrix M_2 is updated. The current loop iteration number is provided in the superscript for each matrix. The first iteration is indexed as 1.

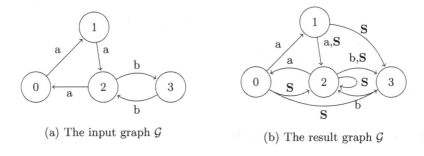

(a) The input graph $\mathcal{G}$

(b) The result graph $\mathcal{G}$

Fig. 2. The input and result graphs for example

During the first iteration the Kronecker product $M_3^1 = M_1 \otimes M_2^0$ and transitive closure C_3^1 are the following:

$$M_3^1 = \begin{pmatrix} & & & & & & & & & & & \\ & & & & & & & & & & & \end{pmatrix}, \quad C_3^1 = \begin{pmatrix} & & & & & & & & & & & \\ & & & & & & & & & & & \end{pmatrix}.$$

After the transitive closure evaluation $C_3^1[1, 15]$ contains a non-zero value. It means that the vertex with index 15 is accessible from the vertex with index 1 in the graph, represented by the adjacency matrix M_3^1.

Then the lines **14–18** are executed: the algorithm adds non-terminals to the graph matrix M_2^1. Because this step is additive we are only interested in the newly appeared values in the matrix C_3^1, such as value $C_3^1[1, 15]$, for which we get the following:

- Indices of the automata vertices $s = 0$ and $f = 3$, because value $C_3^1[1, 15]$ is located in the upper right matrix block $(0, 3)$.
- Indices of the graph vertices $x = 1$ and $y = 3$ are evaluated as the value $C_3^1[1, 15]$ indices relatively to its block $(0, 3)$.
- The function $getNonterminals()$ returns $\{S\}$ since this is the only non-terminal which could be derived in path from vertex 0 to 3 in the box S.

Thus we can conclude that the vertex with $id = 3$ is reachable from the vertex with $id = 1$ by the path derivable from S. As a result, S is added to the $M_2^1[1, 3]$. The updated matrix and graph after the first iteration are presented in Fig. 3.

For the second iteration matrices M_3^2 and C_3^2 are evaluated as follows:

$$M_3^2 = \begin{pmatrix} & & & & & & & & & & & \\ & & & & & & & & & & & \end{pmatrix}, \quad C_3^2 = \begin{pmatrix} & & & & & & & & & & & \\ & & & & & & & & & & & \end{pmatrix}.$$

$$M_2^1 = \begin{pmatrix} \cdot & \{a\} & \cdot & \cdot \\ \cdot & \cdot & \{a\} & \{\mathbf{S}\} \\ \{a\} & \cdot & \cdot & \{b\} \\ \cdot & \cdot & \{b\} & \cdot \end{pmatrix}$$

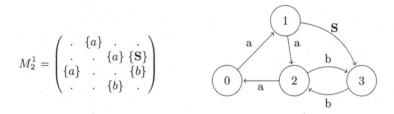

Fig. 3. Example: the updated matrix M_2^1 and graph $\mathcal{G}$ after first loop iteration

New non-zero values in the matrix C_3^2 have appeared during this iteration in cells with indices $[0, 11]$, $[0, 14]$ and $[5, 14]$. Because only the cell value with index $[0, 14]$ corresponds to the automata path with not empty non-terminal set $\{S\}$ its data affects the adjacency matrix M_2. The updated matrix and graph $\mathcal{G}$ are shown in Fig. 4.

$$M_2^2 = \begin{pmatrix} \cdot & \{a\} & \{\mathbf{S}\} & \cdot \\ \cdot & \cdot & \{a\} & \{S\} \\ \{a\} & \cdot & \cdot & \{b\} \\ \cdot & \cdot & \{b\} & \cdot \end{pmatrix}$$

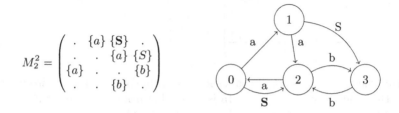

Fig. 4. Example: the updated matrix M_2^2 and graph $\mathcal{G}$ after second loop iteration

The remaining matrices C_3 and M_2 for the algorithm's main loop execution are listed in the Fig. 5 and Fig. 6 correspondingly. The evaluated matrices M_3 are not included because its computation is straightforward. The last loop iteration is 7. Although the matrix M_2^6 is updated with the new non-terminal S for the cell $[2, 2]$ after the transitive closure evaluation, the new values are not added to the matrix M_2. Therefore matrix M_2 has stopped changing and the algorithm has finished. The graph $\mathcal{G}$ with the new edges is presented in the Fig. 2b.

5   Evaluation

We implement the proposed algorithm by using SuiteSparse[1] [4]: the implementation of GraphBlas API [8]. GraphBlas API specifies a set of linear algebra primitives and operations which allows one to formulate graph algorithms using linear algebra over custom semirings.

---

[1] SuteSparse is a sparse matrix software which incudes GraphBLAS API implementation. Project web page: http://faculty.cse.tamu.edu/davis/suitesparse.html. Access date: 12.03.2020.

$$C_3^3 = \qquad C_3^4 =$$

$$C_3^5 = \qquad C_3^6 =$$

Fig. 5. Transitive closure for loop iterations $3 - 6$ for example query

$$M_2^3 = \begin{pmatrix} . & \{a\} & \{S\} & . \\ . & . & \{a\} & \{S\} \\ \{a\} & . & . & \{b,\mathbf{S}\} \\ . & . & \{b\} & . \end{pmatrix} M_2^4 = \begin{pmatrix} . & \{a\} & \{S\} & . \\ . & . & \{a,\mathbf{S}\} & \{S\} \\ \{a\} & . & . & \{b,S\} \\ . & . & \{b\} & . \end{pmatrix}$$

$$M_2^5 = \begin{pmatrix} . & \{a\} & \{S\} & \{\mathbf{S}\} \\ . & . & \{a,S\} & \{S\} \\ \{a\} & . & . & \{b,S\} \\ . & . & \{b\} & . \end{pmatrix} M_2^6 = \begin{pmatrix} . & \{a\} & \{S\} & \{S\} \\ . & . & \{a,S\} & \{S\} \\ \{a\} & . & \{\mathbf{S}\} & \{b,S\} \\ . & . & \{b\} & . \end{pmatrix}$$

Fig. 6. The updated matrix M_2 for loop iterations $3 - 6$ for example query

We compare our implementation with the results provided in [11]. We use the dataset described in this article which consists of **RDF**, **Worst case**, and **Full** subsets. For RDF querying we use same-generation query G_4 from [11].

For the evaluation, we use a PC with Ubuntu 18.04 installed. It has Intel(R) Core(TM) i7-4790 CPU @ 3.60 GHz CPU, DDR4 32 Gb RAM.

The results of the evaluation are summarized in the Table 1. Time is measured in seconds, t_1 is the execution time for the proposed algorithm, and t_2 is the time for M4RI-based implementation—the best CPU version form [11]. The time measurements are averaged over 10 runs. We exclude the time required to load data from the input file. The time required for the data transfer and its conversion is included.

We can see, that while RDF querying time is better for M4RI in general, in some cases execution times are comparable: for graphs *generations, travel, unv-bnch, skos*. Our algorithm demonstrates poor performance for the **Full** data set because SuiteSparse is based on sparse matrix representation, and in this case, the density of the matrices changes aggressively from very sparse to full. At the same time, we can see that in the **Worst case** our algorithms up to 4 times faster than M4RI (graph WC_5).

To sum up, our prototype implementation of the described algorithm is not performant enough to be used for real-world applications but it outperforms the matrix-based algorithm on the **Worst case** dataset and is comparable with it

Table 1. Evaluation results: t_1—proposed algorithm; t_2—matrix-based algorithm

	Graph	#V	#E	t_1	t_2		Graph	#V	#E	t_1	t_2
RDF	atm-prim	291	685	0.24	0.02	RDF	core	1323	8684	0.28	0.12
	biomed	341	711	0.24	0.05		wine	733	2450	1.71	0.06
	foaf	256	815	0.07	0.02	Worst case	WC_1	64	65	0.03	0.04
	funding	778	1480	0.43	0.07		WC_2	128	129	0.16	0.23
	generations	129	351	0.04	0.03		WC_3	256	257	0.96	1.99
	people_pets	337	834	0.18	0.03		WC_4	512	513	7.14	23.21
	pizza	671	2604	1.14	0.08		WC_5	1024	1025	121.99	528.52
	skos	144	323	0.02	0.04	Full	F_1	100	100	0.17	0.02
	travel	131	397	0.05	0.05		F_2	200	200	1.04	0.03
	unv-bnch	179	413	0.05	0.04		F_3	500	500	18.86	0.03
	pathways	6238	37196	4.88	0.18		F_4	1000	1000	554.22	0.07

on some graphs from the **RDF** dataset. We conclude that we should improve our implementation to achieve better performance, while the algorithm idea is viable.

6   Conclusion

We presented a new algorithm for CFPQ which is based on Kronecker product and transitive closure. It can be implemented by using high-performance libraries for linear algebra. Also, our algorithm avoids grammar growth by handling queries represented as recursive state machines.

We implement the proposed algorithm by using SuiteSparse and evaluate it on several graphs and queries. We show that in some cases our algorithm outperforms the matrix-based algorithm, but in the future, we should improve our implementation for it to be applicable for real-world graphs analysis.

Also in the future, we should investigate such formal properties of the proposed algorithm as time and space complexity. Moreover, we plan to analyze how the behavior depends on the query type and its form. Namely, we should analyze regular path queries evaluation and context-free path queries in the form of extended context-free grammars (ECFG) [6]. The utilization of ECFGs may provide a way to optimize queries by minimization of both the right-hand sides of productions and the whole result RSM.

Finally, it is necessary to compare our algorithm with the matrix-based one in cases when the size difference between Chomsky Normal Form and ECFG representation of the query is significant.

References

1. Alur, R., Etessami, K., Yannakakis, M.: Analysis of recursive state machines. In: Berry, G., Comon, H., Finkel, A. (eds.) CAV 2001. LNCS, vol. 2102, pp. 207–220. Springer, Heidelberg (2001). https://doi.org/10.1007/3-540-44585-4_18

2. Azimov, R., Grigorev, S.: Context-free path querying by matrix multiplication. In: Proceedings of the 1st ACM SIGMOD Joint International Workshop on Graph Data Management Experiences & Systems (GRADES) and Network Data Analytics (NDA), GRADES-NDA 2018, pp. 5:1–5:10. ACM, New York (2018). http://doi.acm.org/10.1145/3210259.3210264

3. Barrett, C., Jacob, R., Marathe, M.: Formal-language-constrained path problems. SIAM J. Comput. **30**(3), 809–837 (2000). https://doi.org/10.1137/S0097539798337716

4. Davis, T.A.: Algorithm 9xx: SuiteSparse: GraphBLAS: graph algorithms in the language of sparse linear algebra (2018)

5. Hellings, J.: Querying for paths in graphs using context-free path queries. arXiv preprint arXiv:1502.02242 (2015)

6. Hemerik, K.: Towards a taxonomy for ECFG and RRPG parsing. In: Dediu, A.H., Ionescu, A.M., Martín-Vide, C. (eds.) LATA 2009. LNCS, vol. 5457, pp. 410–421. Springer, Heidelberg (2009). https://doi.org/10.1007/978-3-642-00982-2_35

7. Hopcroft, J.E., Motwani, R., Ullman, J.D.: Introduction to Automata Theory, Languages, and Computation, 3rd edn. Addison-Wesley Longman Publishing Co., Inc., Boston (2006)

8. Kepner, J., et al.: Mathematical foundations of the GraphBLAS. In: 2016 IEEE High Performance Extreme Computing Conference (HPEC), pp. 1–9, September 2016. https://doi.org/10.1109/HPEC.2016.7761646

9. Kuijpers, J., Fletcher, G., Yakovets, N., Lindaaker, T.: An experimental study of context-free path query evaluation methods. In: Proceedings of the 31st International Conference on Scientific and Statistical Database Management, SSDBM 2019, pp. 121–132. Association for Computing Machinery, New York (2019). https://doi.org/10.1145/3335783.3335791

10. Medeiros, C.M., Musicante, M.A., Costa, U.S.: Efficient evaluation of context-free path queries for graph databases. In: Proceedings of the 33rd Annual ACM Symposium on Applied Computing, SAC 2018, pp. 1230–1237. ACM, New York (2018). https://doi.org/10.1145/3167132.3167265. http://doi.acm.org/10.1145/3167132.3167265

11. Mishin, N., et al.: Evaluation of the context-free path querying algorithm based on matrix multiplication. In: Proceedings of the 2nd Joint International Workshop on Graph Data Management Experiences & Systems (GRADES) and Network Data Analytics (NDA), GRADES-NDA 2019. Association for Computing Machinery, New York (2019). https://doi.org/10.1145/3327964.3328503

12. Sevon, P., Eronen, L.: Subgraph queries by context-free grammars. J. Integr. Bioinform. **5**(2), 100 (2008)

13. Yannakakis, M.: Graph-theoretic methods in database theory. In: Proceedings of the Ninth ACM SIGACT-SIGMOD-SIGART Symposium on Principles of Database Systems, PODS 1990, pp. 230–242. ACM, New York (1990). http://doi.acm.org/10.1145/298514.298576

14. Zhang, X., Feng, Z., Wang, X., Rao, G., Wu, W.: Context-free path queries on RDF graphs. In: Groth, P., et al. (eds.) ISWC 2016. LNCS, vol. 9981, pp. 632–648. Springer, Cham (2016). https://doi.org/10.1007/978-3-319-46523-4_38

Pattern Sampling in Distributed Databases

Lamine Diop[1,2], Cheikh Talibouya Diop[2], Arnaud Giacometti[1], and Arnaud Soulet[1(✉)]

[1] Université de Tours, Tours, France
{arnaud.giacometti,arnaud.soulet}@univ-tours.fr
[2] Université Gaston Berger de Saint-Louis, Saint-Louis, Senegal
{diop.lamine3,cheikh-talibouya.diop}@ugb.edu.sn

Abstract. Many applications rely on distributed databases. However, only few discovery methods exist to extract patterns without centralizing the data. In fact, this centralization is often less expensive than the communication of extracted patterns from the different nodes. To circumvent this difficulty, this paper revisits the problem of pattern mining in distributed databases by benefiting from pattern sampling. Specifically, we propose the algorithm DDSAMPLING that randomly draws a pattern from a distributed database with a probability proportional to its interest. We demonstrate the soundness of DDSAMPLING and analyze its time complexity. Finally, experiments on benchmark datasets highlight its low communication cost and its robustness. We also illustrate its interest on real-world data from the Semantic Web for detecting outlier entities in DBpedia and Wikidata.

1 Introduction

Many applications require storage and manipulation of distributed databases [14] like large-scale wireless sensor networks [15] or the Semantic Web [2]. In most cases, the centralization of data is very costly, in particular when the databases evolve continuously. Sometimes legal constraints also prevent this centralization [6]. Thus, [16] underlines the importance of extending knowledge discovery to distributed databases. In the context of the Semantic Web, Table 1 illustrates an example of Resource Description Framework (RDF) data distributed over four triplestores $\mathcal{P} = \{\mathcal{D}_1, \mathcal{D}_2, \mathcal{D}_3, \mathcal{D}_4\}$ accessible via SPARQL queries. In this context, the properties describing the entity identified by TId 1 (e.g., the singer "Youssou N'Dour") are spread over several fragments (i.e., *DBpedia* $\mathcal{D}_1$ with the property A, and *Wikidata* $\mathcal{D}_2$ with the properties B and C). There exist federated systems to execute SPARQL queries on multiple triplestores [9]. Unfortunately, SPARQL is not expressive enough to directly extract patterns like frequent itemsets. By relying on a basic communication model, this paper aims at extracting patterns from a distributed database $\mathcal{P}$ (including RDF data) as if the data were centralized (see $\mathcal{P}^*$ in Table 1).

© Springer Nature Switzerland AG 2020
J. Darmont et al. (Eds.): ADBIS 2020, LNCS 12245, pp. 60–74, 2020.
https://doi.org/10.1007/978-3-030-54832-2_7

Table 1. Example of a distributed database $\mathcal{P} = \{\mathcal{D}_1, \mathcal{D}_2, \mathcal{D}_3, \mathcal{D}_4\}$

$\mathcal{P}$

$\mathcal{D}_1$		$\mathcal{D}_2$		$\mathcal{D}_3$		$\mathcal{D}_4$	
TId	Trans.	TId	Trans.	TId	Trans.	TId	Trans.
1	A	1	B C	2	D	2	A
4	B E	2	F G	4	F G	3	D E F
5	B C	5	D				

$\rightarrow$

$\mathcal{P}^*$

TId	Trans.
1	A B C
2	A D F G
3	D E F
4	B E F G
5	B C D

Few works in the literature [4,10,11,13] are dedicated to pattern mining in distributed databases. Unfortunately, they suffer from three major limitations. First, they exclusively address horizontally partitioned data (i.e, unlike the example $\mathcal{P}$ in Table 1, a transaction cannot be split into two fragments). Second, as these proposals focused on an *exhaustive extraction* of patterns, the volume of data exchanged between the different fragments can be very high. Finally, these proposals need computing capacity on each fragment for locally mining patterns, which is often impossible (for example, in the case of the SPARQL endpoints of the Semantic Web). To overcome these limitations, we propose to benefit from *pattern sampling* [1,3]. Pattern sampling consists in randomly drawing a collection of patterns with a probability proportional to their interest. This technique has a low computational cost, but it is also useful in many tasks such as classification [3], outlier detection [8] or interactive data mining [7].

In this paper, we show how to sample patterns from a distributed database that can be partitioned both horizontally and vertically, without using the computing capacity of the different fragments. Our main contributions are as follows:

- We propose a generic algorithm called Distributed Database Sampling (DDSAMPLING) which randomly draws a pattern from a distributed database proportionally to an interestingness measure combining frequency and length-based utility functions (including length constraints).
- We demonstrate that DDSAMPLING performs an *exact* sampling and analyze its complexity on average. Experiments show that DDSAMPLING is very fast and that the communication cost of our proposal is much lower than that of data centralization for drawing a few thousand patterns. We also show that in the context of distributed databases, DDSAMPLING is a fault-resistant algorithm against network and node failures.
- We illustrate the interest of DDSAMPLING on a use case by detecting outliers in two real-world triplestores: *DBpedia* and *Wikidata*. These experiments show the importance of using a maximum length constraint and that *output space* sampling is more efficient than *input space* sampling.

This paper is structured as follows. After the related work in Sect. 2, Sect. 3 introduces basic definitions and formalizes the problem of pattern sampling in distributed databases. We detail the algorithm DDSAMPLING in Sect. 4 that exactly draws patterns as if the distributed database was centralized. Section 5 evaluates its performance on benchmarks datasets and illustrates the interest of pattern sampling to detect outliers in the Semantic Web.

2   Related Work

Several approaches in the literature focused on frequent pattern mining in distributed databases. This task is complex because whatever the minimum frequency threshold user-specified on the distributed database (global frequency), it is not possible to constrain the local frequency on each fragment without communicating information between sites. In this context, [4] proposes the first method to extract all the globally frequent patterns by identifying the sites where the patterns are the most frequent and thus, reducing communication costs. More drastically, [13] proposes to save communication costs by limiting themselves to the collection of the maximal frequent patterns. To prevent each fragment from enumerating all its patterns, [10] imposes a minimum local frequency threshold on each fragment. From the different local extractions, [11] builds an approximate global collection of frequent patterns. A centralized pruning proposed by [18] is based on the construction of a tree containing for each pattern all its occurrences (i.e., fragment/transaction pairs), which still requires a considerable volume of communications. More recently, [17] implements a decentralized pruning technique within the extraction on each fragment by exchanging Bloom filters. This approach significantly reduces computation time but the cost of communications remains too large. Indeed, for low support threshold, the volume of extracted patterns invariably generates an enormous communication cost much higher than that of data centralization. In addition, all these frequent pattern mining approaches are limited to horizontal partitioning of data, i.e. the same transaction cannot be distributed on two separate fragments. Finally, all the existing proposals require a computation capacity on each fragment, which is not always possible. For instance, the Semantic Web provides access to distributed data via SPARQL endpoints, but it is not possible to execute a pattern mining routine on these endpoints. For all these reasons, we propose to revisit the discovery of patterns in distributed databases in the light of pattern sampling. We will see that our approach does not require computation capacity on the fragments and reduces the communication costs because all the patterns are not extracted.

Output space sampling methods [1,3] aim at drawing patterns with a probability distribution proportional to their interest. Most sampling techniques fall into two broad categories: stochastic methods [1] and multi-step methods [3]. In order to randomly walk from a pattern X to another, stochastic methods require to consider the global interest of all the neighboring patterns of X. For example, in the case of frequency, it would be necessary to know the global frequency of all the subsets and supersets of X, which would generate many communications. For this reason, we prefer to adopt a multi-step random method. This type of method has already been used for several interestingness measures (e.g., support or area [3] or exceptional measure [12]) and several data types like sequential data [5]. Nevertheless, the context of distributed databases is an orthogonal challenge. In particular, we determine minimal information that the fragments must communicate to make an unbiased draw of patterns.

3   Problem Formulation

3.1   Pattern Language and Distributed Databases

Given a set $\mathcal{I}$ of distinct literals called *items*, an itemset (or pattern) is a subset of $\mathcal{I}$. The language of itemsets corresponds to $\mathcal{L} = 2^{\mathcal{I}}$, and the size or length of an itemset $X \in \mathcal{L}$, denoted by $|X|$, is its cardinality. In our approach, a transactional database $\mathcal{D}$ is a set of pairs (j, X) where j is the unique identifier of a transaction and X is an itemset in $\mathcal{L}$, i.e. $\mathcal{D} \subseteq \mathbb{N} \times \mathcal{L}$. In the following, given a transactional database $\mathcal{D}$, for every integer $j \in \mathbb{N}$, $\mathcal{D}[j]$ represents the itemset of transaction j, i.e. $\mathcal{D}[j] = X$ if $(j, X) \in \mathcal{D}$ (otherwise, we consider that $\mathcal{D}[j] = \emptyset$). Moreover, $|\mathcal{D}|$ is the number of transactions in $\mathcal{D}$ and $||\mathcal{D}|| = \sum_{j \in \mathbb{N}} |\mathcal{D}[j]|$ defines the size of the transactional database $\mathcal{D}$. For example, in Table 1, the transactional database $\mathcal{D}_1$ contains 3 transactions of identifiers 1, 4 and 5. Besides, we have $\mathcal{D}_1[1] = A$, $\mathcal{D}_1[4] = BE$ and $\mathcal{D}_1[5] = BC$. Thus, we have $||\mathcal{D}_1|| = 1 + 2 + 2 = 5$.

Intuitively, a *(transactional) distributed database* is a set of transactional databases, also called *fragments*, where transactions do not overlap. More formally, a distributed database is defined as follows:

Definition 1 (Transactional distributed and centralized databases). *A (transactional) distributed database* $\mathcal{P} = \{\mathcal{D}_1, \ldots, \mathcal{D}_K\}$ *is a set of transactional databases* $\mathcal{D}_k$ *($k \in [1..K]$) such that for each* $j \in \mathbb{N}$, *we have* $\mathcal{D}_k[j] \cap \mathcal{D}_l[j] = \emptyset$ *if* $k \neq l$. *Then, the* centralized version *of* $\mathcal{P}$, *denoted by* $\mathcal{P}^*$, *is the transactional database defined by:* $\mathcal{P}^* = \{(j, X) : X = \bigcup_{k=1}^{K} \mathcal{D}_k[j] \wedge X \neq \emptyset\}$.

For example, in Table 1, it is easy to see that $\mathcal{P}^*$ is the centralized version of the distributed database $\mathcal{P} = \{\mathcal{D}_1, \ldots, \mathcal{D}_4\}$. In the following, we also say that $\mathcal{P}$ is a partitioning of the centralized database $\mathcal{P}^*$. In general, different types of partitioning are distinguished. On the one hand, a distributed database is a *horizontal partitioning* if every transaction is described in only one fragment, i.e. if for every $j \in \mathbb{N}$, $\mathcal{D}_k[j] \neq \emptyset$ and $\mathcal{D}_l[j] \neq \emptyset$ implies that $k = l$. On the other hand, a distributed database is a *vertical partitioning* if every item is present in only one fragment, i.e. if for every $x \in \mathcal{I}$, $x \in \bigcup_{j \in \mathbb{N}} \mathcal{D}_k[j]$ and $x \in \bigcup_{j \in \mathbb{N}} \mathcal{D}_l[j]$ implies that $k = l$. Finally, a partitioning is said to be *hybrid* if it is neither *horizontal* nor *vertical*. For example, in Table 1, $\mathcal{P}$ is a hybrid partitioning of $\mathcal{P}^*$. Indeed, the transaction 2 is described both in the fragments $\mathcal{D}_2$, $\mathcal{D}_3$ et $\mathcal{D}_4$ and the item A is both present in fragments $\mathcal{D}_1$ and $\mathcal{D}_4$. We consider that only two forms of query can be sent to the fragment:

1. `lengthOf` **primitive:** Given a transaction identifier j and a fragment $\mathcal{D}_k$, the query `lengthOf`$(j, \mathcal{D}_k)$ returns the length of the transaction j in fragment k, i.e. `lengthOf`$(j, \mathcal{D}_k) = |\mathcal{D}_k[j]|$. In our example, we have `lengthOf`$(4, \mathcal{D}_1) = 2$ since $|\mathcal{D}_1[4]| = |BE| = 2$.

2. `itemAt` **primitive:** Given a position i, a transaction j and a fragment $\mathcal{D}_k$, the query `itemAt`$(i, j, \mathcal{D}_k)$ returns the i-th item of the transaction j in fragment $\mathcal{D}_k$ (assuming an arbitrary order over the set of items $\mathcal{I}$). In our example, considering the lexicographic order over $\mathcal{I}$, we have `itemAt`$(2, 4, \mathcal{D}_1) = E$.

Our communication model is generic since more complex queries can be reduced to these two basic primitives for describing the exchanges. For instance, advanced queries may directly obtain a transaction of ℓ items from a fragment corresponding to ℓ `itemAt` primitives. For the Semantic Web, for the primitive `lengthOf`, the SPARQL query `SELECT (COUNT(DISTINCT ?p) AS ?length)` `WHERE {wd:Q210734 ?p ?o}` returns the length of Youssou N'Dour's transaction (`wd:Q210734`) from *Wikidata* SPARQL endpoint (here, the length is 143 items). In the same way, the query `SELECT DISTINCT ?p WHERE {wd:Q210734 ?p ?o} OFFSET 2 LIMIT 1` gives the second item of the transaction. Of course, it is possible to use the query `SELECT DISTINCT ?p WHERE {wd:Q210734 ?p ?o}` for having the entire transaction instead of using 143 `itemAt` queries. Unlike the two primitives that have 1 as communication cost, the communication cost of this query is 143.

3.2   Class of Interestingness Measures

Pattern discovery is based on interestingness measures that evaluate the quality of a pattern. One of the most popular interestingness measure is the frequency which is intuitive for experts and is an atomic element to build many other interestingness measures (like area or discriminative measures). The frequency of an itemset $X \in \mathcal{L}$ in the transactional database $\mathcal{D}$, denoted by $freq(X, \mathcal{D})$, is defined by: $freq(X, \mathcal{D}) = |\{(j, T) \in \mathcal{D} : X \subseteq T\}|$. In Table 1, we have $freq(DF, \mathcal{P}^*) = 2$ since the itemset DF is included in transactions 2 and 3.

It is also common to associate a utility to an itemset, and to combine the frequency of an itemset with its utility. For example, if we consider the utility function $u(X) = |X|$, we obtain the area measure: $freq(X, \mathcal{D}) \times |X|$. More generally, we consider the class of interestingness measures of the form $freq(X, \mathcal{D}) \times u(X)$ where u exclusively depends on the length of itemsets:

Definition 2 (Length-based utilities and measures). *A utility u defined from $\mathcal{L}$ to $\mathbb{R}$ is called a length-based utility if there exists a function f_u from $\mathbb{N}$ to $\mathbb{R}$ such that $u(X) = f_u(|X|)$ for each $X \in \mathcal{L}$. Given the set $\mathcal{U}$ of length-based utilities, $\mathcal{M}_\mathcal{U}$ is the set of interestingness measures m_u such that for every pattern X and database $\mathcal{D}$, $m_u(X, \mathcal{D}) = freq(X, \mathcal{D}) \times u(X)$ with $u \in \mathcal{U}$.*

We already see that the utility function defined for every pattern $X \in \mathcal{L}$ by $u_{area}(X) = |X|$ allows us to consider the area measure $freq(X, \mathcal{D}) \times |X|$. Obviously, let us notice that the utility function defined by $u_{freq}(X) = 1$ enables us to consider the frequency as interestingness measure. Besides, the utility function defined by $u_{\leq M}(X) = 1$ iff $|X| \leq M$ (0 otherwise) simulates a maximum length constraint. Indeed, with the induced interestingness measure $freq(X, \mathcal{D}) \times u_{\leq M}(X)$, an itemset with a cardinality strictly greater than M is judged useless (whatever its frequency). Dually, the utility function defined by $u_{\geq m}(X) = 1$ iff $|X| \geq m$ (0 otherwise) simulates a minimum length constraint. Finally, the utility function defined by $u_{decay}(X) = \alpha^{|X|}$ with $\alpha \in]0,1[$, named exponential decay, is useful for penalizing large itemsets but in a smooth way in comparison with $u_{\leq M}$.

3.3   Pattern Sampling in a Distributed Database

A pattern sampling method aims at randomly drawing a pattern X from a language $\mathcal{L}$ according to an interestingness measure f. $X \sim \pi(\mathcal{L})$ denotes such a pattern where $\pi(.) = f(.)/Z$ is a probability distribution over $\mathcal{L}$ (with Z as normalizing constant). In this paper, our goal is to randomly draw patterns in a distributed database according to an interestingness measure in $\mathcal{M}_\mathcal{U}$:

Given a distributed database $\mathcal{P}$, an interestingness measure $m \in \mathcal{M}_\mathcal{U}$, we aim at randomly drawing a pattern $X \in \mathcal{L}$ with a probability distribution π proportional to its interestingness measure m i.e., $\pi(X) = \frac{m(X, \mathcal{P}^*)}{Z}$ where $\mathcal{P}^*$ is the centralized version of $\mathcal{P}$ and $Z = \sum_{X \in \mathcal{L}} m(X, \mathcal{P}^*)$ is a normalizing constant.

A naive approach could apply the classical two-step random procedure [3] after having centralized all the fragments of the distributed database $\mathcal{P}$ for building $\mathcal{P}^*$ (using `itemAt` queries). The communication cost of this preliminary centralization would be very high. Indeed, it would be proportional to the size of $\mathcal{P}^*$, i.e. $||\mathcal{P}^*|| = \sum_{k=1}^{K} ||\mathcal{D}_k||$. Next section shows that it is only necessary to centralize the lengths of the transaction parts stored in the different fragments of $\mathcal{P}$ in order to draw an exact sample of patterns.

4   Decentralized Pattern Sampling

4.1   DDSAMPLING Algorithm

This section presents our algorithm called DDSAMPLING (for Distributed Database Sampling), which randomly draws a pattern from a distributed database $\mathcal{P}$ proportionally to an interestingness measure $m \in \mathcal{M}_\mathcal{U}$.

The key idea of our proposal is first to centralize only the lengths of the transaction parts contained in the different fragments. Indeed, this information requires a low communication cost and it enables us to draw a transaction identifier j according to its weight $\omega(j)$ and an itemset length ℓ proportionally to $\omega_\ell(j)$. Finally, we show how to emulate a decentralized sampling of a subset of $\mathcal{D}[j]$ of length ℓ without centralizing all the items of $\mathcal{D}[j]$.

Preprocessing Phase. In this phase (see lines 1–2 of Algorithm 1), we first compute and store locally a matrix M that contains for every transaction j and every fragment $\mathcal{D}_k$ of $\mathcal{P}$, the length of the transaction j in $\mathcal{D}_k$.

Definition 3 (Weight matrix). *Given a distributed database $\mathcal{P} = \{\mathcal{D}_1, \ldots, \mathcal{D}_K\}$, let $M \in \mathbb{R}^{|\mathcal{P}^*| \times |\mathcal{P}|}$ be the matrix defined for every $j \in [1..|\mathcal{P}^*|]$ and $k \in [1..K]$ by $M_{jk} = \text{lengthOf}(j, \mathcal{D}_k)$.*

In practice, it is important to note that the matrix M is computed offline before the drawing phase. In the following, $M_{j\bullet}$ denotes the sum $M_{j\bullet} = \sum_{k=1}^{K} M_{jk}$. It is easy to see that $M_{j\bullet}$ represents the length of the transaction j in $\mathcal{P}^*$, i.e. $M_{j\bullet} = |\mathcal{P}^*[j]|$. For example, Table 2 presents the weight matrix M of the distributed database of Table 1. We can also check that $M_{1\bullet} = 1 + 2 = |\mathcal{P}^*[1]|$.

Table 2. Weight matrix M and transaction drawing weights

j	M	$M_{j\bullet}$	$\sum_{\ell=0}^{M_{j\bullet}} \omega_{\ell}^{freq}(j) =$	$\omega^{freq}(j)$	$\omega^{area}(j)$	$\omega^{\leq 2}(j)$	$\omega^{decay}(j)$
1	1 2 0 0	3	$1 + 3 + 3 + 1 =$	8	12	7	1.331
2	0 2 1 1	4	$1 + 6 + 4 + 4 + 1 =$	16	32	11	1.6441
3	0 0 0 3	3	$1 + 3 + 3 + 1 =$	8	12	7	1.331
4	2 0 2 0	4	$1 + 6 + 4 + 4 + 1 =$	16	32	11	1.6441
5	2 1 0 0	3	$1 + 3 + 3 + 1 =$	8	12	7	1.331

Algorithm 1. DDSAMPLING

Input: A distributed database $\mathcal{P} = \{\mathcal{D}_1, \cdots, \mathcal{D}_K\}$ and a length-based utility $u \in \mathcal{U}$
Output: An itemset $X \in \mathcal{L}$ randomly drawn w.r.t. $freq(X, \mathcal{P}^*) \times u(X)$
    // **Preprocessing Phase**
1: Compute M defined by $M_{jk} := \texttt{lengthOf}(j, \mathcal{D}_k)$ for $j \in [1..|\mathcal{P}^*|]$ and $k \in [1..K]$
2: Compute the weights ω defined by $\omega(j) := \sum_{\ell=0}^{M_{j\bullet}} \binom{M_{j\bullet}}{\ell} \times f_u(\ell)$ for $j \in [1..|\mathcal{P}^*|]$
    // **Drawing Phase – Step 1**: *sampling of a transaction*
3: Draw a transaction identifier $j \in [1..|\mathcal{P}^*|]$ proportionally to ω: $j \sim \omega(\mathcal{P}^*)$
    // **Drawing Phase – Step 2**: *decentralized sampling of an itemset*
4: Compute the weights defined by $\omega_{\ell}(j) := \binom{M_{j\bullet}}{\ell} \times f_u(\ell)$ for every $\ell \in [0..M_{j\bullet}]$
5: Draw a length ℓ proportionally to $\omega_{\ell}(j)$: $\ell \sim \omega_{[0..M_{j\bullet}]}(j)$
6: $\vartheta := \emptyset$ and $X := \emptyset$
7: **while** $|X| < \ell$ **do**
8:     $i \sim u([1..M_{j\bullet}] \setminus \vartheta)$
9:     $k := \min\{p \in [1..K] : i \leq \sum_{m=1}^{p} M_{jm}\}$
10:    $i' := \sum_{m=1}^{k} M_{jm} - i + 1$ and $x := \texttt{itemAt}(i', j, \mathcal{D}_k)$
11:    $X := X \cup \{x\}$
12:    $\vartheta := \vartheta \cup \{i\}$
13: **od**
14: **return** X

Given a distributed database $\mathcal{P}$ and its associated weight matrix M, Property 1 shows how the weights $\omega(j)$ and $\omega_{\ell}(j)$ can be computed for each transaction j and length ℓ for any length-based utility function $u \in \mathcal{U}$:

Property 1. Let $\mathcal{P} = \{\mathcal{D}_1, \ldots, \mathcal{D}_K\}$ be a distributed database and $u \in \mathcal{U}$ a length-based utility. Given the weight matrix M associated with $\mathcal{P}$, for each transaction $j \in [1..|\mathcal{P}^*|]$ and $\ell \in [1..M_{j\bullet}]$, we have: $\omega_{\ell}(j) = \sum_{X \subseteq \mathcal{P}^*[j] \wedge |X|=\ell} u(X) = \binom{M_{j\bullet}}{\ell} \times f_u(\ell)$. Moreover, we have $\omega(j) = \sum_{\ell=0}^{M_{j\bullet}} \omega_{\ell}(j)$.

Due to space limitation, the proofs have been omitted. Intuitively, this property is valid because all the itemsets of length ℓ in a transaction j have the same utility. In Algorithm 1, this property is used during the preprocessing phase to compute the weights of all the transactions. This preprocessing phase is illustrated in Table 2 with four length-based utility functions: u_{freq}, u_{area}, $u_{\leq 2}$ and u_{decay} (with $\alpha = 0.1$). For example, because $u_{freq}(X) = 1$ for every $X \in \mathcal{L}$, we have $w^{freq}(1) = \sum_{\ell=0}^{3} \binom{3}{\ell} = 1 + 3 + 3 + 1 = 8 = 2^3$. Considering the area utility function u_{area}, we have $w^{area}(1) = \sum_{\ell=0}^{3} \binom{3}{\ell} \times \ell = (1 \cdot 0) + (3 \cdot 1) + (3 \cdot 2) + (1 \cdot 3) = 3 + 6 + 3 = 12$ since $u_{area}(X) = \ell$ for every pattern X of length ℓ. With the maximum length constraint, it is easy to see that $w^{\leq 2}(1) = \sum_{\ell=0}^{2} \binom{3}{\ell} = 1 + 3 + 3 = 7$. Finally, with the decay utility function u_{decay} and $\alpha = 0.1$, we have $w^{decay}(1) = \sum_{\ell=0}^{3} \binom{3}{\ell} \times 0.1^{\ell} = (1 \cdot 0.1^0) + (3 \cdot 0.1^1) + (3 \cdot 0.1^2) + (1 \cdot 0.1^3) = 1 + 0.3 + 0.03 + 0.001 = 1.331$.

Drawing Phase. In this phase, we can apply a direct generalization of the two-step random procedure proposed in [3] to draw itemsets with a probability proportional to their interest in the manner of the area measure. We start by drawing in Step 1 a transaction identifier j with a probability proportional to its weight $w(j)$ (see line 3 of Algorithm 1). The only difference is that the weights $w(j)$ are computed during the preprocessing phase using the weight matrix M and Property 1.

In Step 2, as the weights $w_\ell(j)$ of the transaction j are not stored during the preprocessing phase to reduce the storage cost, line 4 computes them for any length ℓ. After drawing the length ℓ of the itemset that will be returned (lines 4–5), DDSAMPLING draws an itemset of length ℓ from the different fragments of $\mathcal{P}$. At each iteration of the while loop (lines 7–13), the key idea is to draw *without replacement* the position i of an item in the transaction j (line 8) and to search the fragment $\mathcal{D}_k$ that contains this item (line 9). Then, we compute the position i' of this item in the fragment $\mathcal{D}_k$ before querying the corresponding item x (see line 10). Finally, the item x is added to the itemset X (line 11) that will be returned (line 14) and the position i is added to the set ϑ (line 12) in order to avoid sampling the same position (and item) twice (see line 8). This process is repeated ℓ times in order to return an itemset X of length ℓ. For example, considering the toy example in Table 2, if we draw the position $i = 2$ in the transaction $j = 1$, we find that the involved fragment is $\mathcal{D}_2$ since $2 > M_{11} = 1$ whereas $2 \leq M_{11} + M_{12} = 3$. Then, we compute $i' = 2 - 1 = 1$ and the item $\texttt{itemAt}(1, 1, \mathcal{D}_2) = B$ is added to the itemset X.

4.2   Theoretical Analysis of the Method

The following property states that DDSAMPLING returns an exact sample of itemsets without centralizing the distributed database:

Property 2 (Correction). Given a distributed database $\mathcal{P} = \{D_1, ..., D_K\}$ and a length-based utility function $u \in \mathcal{U}$, Algorithm 1 draws an itemset X according to a distribution proportional to $m_u(X, \mathcal{D}) = freq(X, \mathcal{D}) \times u(X)$ where $\mathcal{D} = \mathcal{P}^*$.

This follows from the fact that the three different draws (i.e., transaction j, length ℓ and the sampled itemset) take into account the number of itemsets occurring in each transaction weighted by the utility function. We now study the complexity of our method by distinguishing the two main phases: the preprocessing phase (where the matrix M is computed) and the drawing phase of itemsets. For each phase, we evaluate the complexity in time and in communication.

Time and Space Complexity. In the preprocessing phase, the weight matrix M is first computed with a complexity in time $O(|\mathcal{P}^*| \cdot |\mathcal{P}|)$. Then, the weight $\omega(j)$ of all transactions $j \in [1..|\mathcal{P}^*|]$ is computed in time $O(|\mathcal{P}^*| \cdot |\mathcal{I}|)$ due to the use of the binomial function. Thus, the preprocessing phase is performed in time $O(|\mathcal{P}^*| \cdot (|\mathcal{P}| + |\mathcal{I}|))$. The draw of an itemset is less expensive. First, the draw of a transaction identifier can be achieved in $O(log(|\mathcal{P}^*|))$. Then, the drawing of an itemset from this transaction is done in time $O(|\mathcal{I}|)$. Therefore, the drawing complexity of an itemset is in $O(log(|\mathcal{P}^*|) + |\mathcal{I}|)$. Besides, the space complexity only depends on the weight matrix dimension and it is in $O(|\mathcal{P}^*| \cdot |\mathcal{P}|)$. As this storage cost is really low in practice, we store the matrix in memory. In an extreme case, the matrix could be stored in a database with a B-tree index to have quick access to the rows.

Communication Complexity. In order to evaluate the communication cost, we simply count the number of queries `lengthOf` and `itemAt` required for the two main phases. First, it is easy to see that for the preprocessing phase, the construction of the weight matrix M requires $O(|\mathcal{D}_1| + \cdots + |\mathcal{D}_K|)$ exchanges (using `lengthOf` queries), which is in general significantly lower than the cost of a complete centralization of $\mathcal{P}$ in $O(||\mathcal{D}_1|| + \cdots + ||\mathcal{D}_K||) = O(||\mathcal{P}^*||)$ exchanges (using `itemAt` queries). For the drawing of an itemset of length ℓ, it is clear that ℓ `itemAt` queries are necessary to return an itemset. Therefore, the average communication cost to draw an itemset is equal to the average length $E[L]$ of an itemset returned by DDSAMPLING. Given a distributed database $\mathcal{P}$, we can easily see that $E[L]$ is equal to $\sum_{\ell=1}^{+\infty} P(\ell) \times \ell$ where $P(\ell) = \frac{\sum_{j \in [1..|\mathcal{P}^*|]} \omega_\ell(j)}{\sum_{j \in [1..|\mathcal{P}^*|]} \omega(j)}$ is the probability to draw an itemset of length ℓ. Considering our toy example in Table 2 and the maximum length utility function $u_{\leq 2}$, we have $P(L = 1) = \frac{3+6+3+6+3}{7+11+7+11+7} = \frac{21}{43}$ and $P(L = 2) = \frac{3+4+3+4+3}{7+11+7+11+7} = \frac{17}{43}$. Thus, the average communication cost for drawing an itemset is equal to $E[L] = (\frac{21}{43} \cdot 1) + (\frac{17}{43} \cdot 2) \approx 1.28$. Note that without length constraint (using u_{freq} utility function), this cost is higher and equal to $E[L] = (\frac{21}{56} \cdot 1) + (\frac{17}{56} \cdot 2) + (\frac{11}{56} \cdot 3) + (\frac{2}{56} \cdot 4) \approx 1.71$.

Rejection Rate. Two main problems arise in distributed databases: network communication errors (*network failure*) and node inaccessibility (*node failure*). These phenomena induce a bias in the performed drawings because we have to reject a pattern X as soon as an `itemAt` query fails during its drawing. In the case of *network failure*, let ϵ_{net} be the probability that an `itemAt` query failed. Assuming that the failures are independent, we can show that $\mathbf{P}(\text{reject}) = \sum_\ell P(\ell) \cdot (1 - (1 - \epsilon_{net})^\ell)$. Thus, if ϵ_{net} is a small number, we have $\mathbf{P}(\text{reject}) \approx \epsilon_{net} \cdot E[L]$ (where $E[L]$ is the average length of a sampled itemset). Now, in the case of *node failure*, let ϵ_{node} be the probability that a node is down. If the distributed database is an horizontal partitioning of a centralized database, it is clear that $\mathbf{P}(\text{reject}) = \epsilon_{node}$. Otherwise, if the distributed database is a vertical or hybrid partitioning of $\mathcal{P}^*$, assuming that the items are uniformly distributed over the nodes, we can show that $\mathbf{P}(\text{reject}) = \sum_{\ell} P(\ell) \cdot \left(1 - (1 - \epsilon_{node})^{\ell}\right)$. Thus, if ϵ_{node} is a small number, we have $\mathbf{P}(\text{reject}) \approx \epsilon_{node} \cdot E[L]$. Nowadays, ϵ_{net} and ϵ_{node} are very small. Therefore, it follows that the rejection rates are negligible.

5 Experimental Evaluation

In this section, we evaluate the efficiency of our approach compared to a centralized solution (see Sect. 5.1) and its interest to find outliers in knowledge bases of the Semantic Web (see Sect. 5.2). Note that our prototype is implemented in Java and is available at https://github.com/DDSamplingRDF/ddsampling.git. All experiments are conducted on a 3.5 GHz 2 core processor with the Windows 10 operating system and 16 GB of RAM.

5.1 Efficiency and Robustness of DDSAMPLING

In our first experiments, we use 4 UCI datasets that we uniformly partition into $K = 10$ fragments to simulate distributed databases. In the case of horizontal partitioning (resp. vertical partitioning), each transaction (reps. each item) is randomly placed to a fragment with the same probability $1/K$; in the case of hybrid partitioning, all the items of a transaction are randomly placed to a fragment (with the same probability $1/K$). The first columns of Table 3 show statistical information about all datasets. In all experiments, we use length constraints $u_{\geq 1}$ and $u_{\leq M}$ (with $M = \{3,5\}$). This choice avoids drawing too much infrequent patterns, in particular for datasets containing long transactions.

Execution Times and Communication Costs. Table 3 indicates the execution times of our method by distinguishing the preprocessing and drawing phase, only in the case of vertical partitioning for $M = 3$. As expected, the preprocessing time (which can be prepared offline) increases with the size of the dataset. However, it is very small (less than 3 s). Regarding the drawing phase, whatever the dataset, it is always under 0.02 ms (per pattern). For the communication costs, we consider the three types of partitionings. In the preprocessing phase, the communication cost corresponds to the number of lengthOf calls for constructing the weight matrix. This cost is naturally higher for hybrid and vertical partitionings since the items of a transaction may not be in the same fragment. In the drawing phase, the communication cost corresponds to the number of itemAt calls, and Table 3 shows the mean number of calls for drawing a pattern. This cost does not depend on the type of partitioning, but on the maximum length ($M \in \{3,5\}$). Finally, we compare the communication cost between distributed and centralized approaches by evaluating the number N_{max} of drawn patterns in the worst case (when $M = 5$ for vertical partitioning) that are necessary for the sampling approach to be as costly as data centralization. For all datasets, we can see that DDSAMPLING can draw a few thousand patterns with a communication cost lower than that of a data centralization.

Robustness. As seen in Sect. 4.2, network or node failures induce the rejection of some patterns. In this context, we evaluate the mean rejection rate by drawing 10,000 patterns by varying p and z. We repeat 100 times each experiment by randomly generating the dataset partition and changing down nodes. As rejection rates are independent of datasets, Fig. 1 plots the average rejection rate and the standard deviation computed by averaging the results from the 4 UCI datasets. For network failures, the average rejection rate does not depend on a particular partitioning type and Fig. 1 (left) presents the evolution of the average rejection rates according to p for $M \in \{1, 2, 3, 4, 5\}$. In accordance with the theoretical analysis, for a given p, we see that the rejection rate increases with M since $E[L]$ increases with M. Moreover, for a given M, we see that the increase of the rejection rate is sub-linear because $E[L]$ decreases with p. Nevertheless, it remains inferior to 50% if p is inferior to 0.1, which already is a level of network failure much higher than what is observed in practice. Figure 1 (right) presents the average rejection rates with the proportion of down nodes. First, as proved in Sect. 4.2, we observe that the average rejection rate is lower for horizontal partitioning than for hybrid or vertical partitioning (since $E[L] \geq 1$). Second, the standard deviation of vertical partitioning is higher than that of other partitioning. Indeed, with vertical partitioning, the average rejection rate

Table 3. Communication costs and execution times for 4 UCI partitioned datasets

| | | | | Nb of `lengthOf` calls | | | #`itemAt` | | | Vertical | |
| | Centralized databases | | | Distributed databases | | | Distributed | | N_{max} | Time (s) | |
$\mathcal{D}$	$|\mathcal{I}|$	$|\mathcal{D}|$	$||\mathcal{D}||$	Hor.	Hybrid	Vertical	M=3	M=5	vertical	Prep.	Sampl.
Chess	75	3,196	118k	3,196	31,312	31,427	2.91	4.83	17,976	0.13	$1\cdot10^{-5}$
Connect	129	67,557	2,905k	67,557	668,296	668,547	2.92	4.86	460,165	2.59	$2\cdot10^{-5}$
Mush.	119	8,124	187k	8,124	74,036	74,180	2.85	4.70	23,973	0.21	$1\cdot10^{-5}$
Wave.	67	5,000	110k	5,000	45,081	45,324	2.84	4.68	13,820	0.16	$1\cdot10^{-5}$

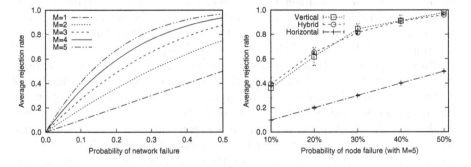

Fig. 1. Average rejection rates with failures

can be very low or very high depending on whether the most frequent items are placed or not into down nodes. However, as for network failures, we note that the rejection rate remains acceptable.

Table 4. Statistics and execution times for classes *Person* and *Organisation*

$\mathcal{D}$	$|\mathcal{D}|$	$|\mathcal{I}|_{DBpedia}$	$|\mathcal{I}|_{Wikidata}$	$|t|_{min}$	$|t|_{max}$	$|t|_{avg}$	Time (s) Prep.	Sampl
Person	772,432	13,142	6,213	8	552		50.02	8,400.80	0.34
Organisation	338,402	19,022	5,504	8	328		36.22	1,847.88	0.27

5.2 Outlier Detection in Transactional Distributed Databases

This section aims at detecting outliers in knowledge bases of the Semantic Web by approximating Frequent Pattern Outlier Factor (FPOF) with sampled patterns. More precisely, we use this measure for identifying misclassified entities from two classes (*Person* and *Organisation*) described in *DBpedia* and *Wikidata*. In this context, each entity of a class C is a transaction distributed over *DBpedia* and *Wikidata* where each property p from a RDF triple (x, p, y) is an item. Table 4 provides some statistics about the two classes. Execution times are longer than that for UCI benchmarks because we use public SPARQL endpoints.

Long Tail Problem and Norm Constraints. The exact FPOF of a transaction can be approximated using pattern sampling [8]. More precisely, given a database $\mathcal{D}$ and a sample $\mathcal{S}$, the approximated FPOF of a transaction $t \in \mathcal{D}$ is defined by $\widetilde{fpof}_{\mathcal{S}}(t, \mathcal{D}) = \frac{|\{X \in \mathcal{S} : X \subseteq t\}|}{max_{u \in \mathcal{D}}(|\{X \in \mathcal{S} : X \subseteq u\}|)}$. Given a maximum length constraint M, we can show that $\widetilde{fpof}_{\mathcal{S}}(t, \mathcal{D})$ tends to the exact FPOF $fpof_{\leq M}(t, \mathcal{D}) = \frac{\sum_{X \subseteq t, |X| \leq M} freq(X, \mathcal{D})}{max_{u \in \mathcal{D}}(\sum_{X \subseteq u, |X| \leq M} freq(X, \mathcal{D}))}$ when the size of $\mathcal{S}$ tends to infinity and $\mathcal{S}$ is sampled according to $m(X, \mathcal{D}) = freq(X, \mathcal{D}) \times u_{\leq M}(X)$. Figure 2 depicts the FPOF distributions of all entities for *Person* and *Organisation* without constraint ($M = \infty$) or with a maximum length constraint $M \in \{1, 2, 3, 4, 5, 10\}$. We see that without constraint or with a large value for M (≥ 5), a large majority of FPOF values are equal to zero, which implies that it is impossible to distinguish outliers from normal entities. Indeed, without constraint, FPOF suffers from the long tail problem [5]. Therefore, the use of a maximum length constraint is crucial for detecting outliers by means of FPOF. Consequently, we use $M = 3$ in the following experiments.

Output Space vs. Input Space Sampling. This experiment compares input and output space sampling to determine which method is the best for the same budget (same number of patterns, same communication cost). For a pattern budget k, we start by drawing a sample $\mathcal{S}_{out}$ of k patterns with DDSAMPLING and we calculate its communication cost $Cost_{out}$. Then, we draw a sample of transactions $\tilde{\mathcal{D}}$ requiring the same communication cost: $Cost_{in} = Cost_{out}$. Finally, we

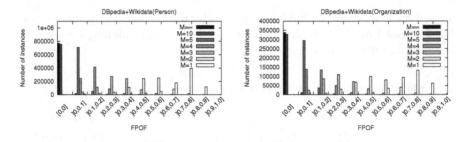

Fig. 2. Long tail problem of the FPOF distributions

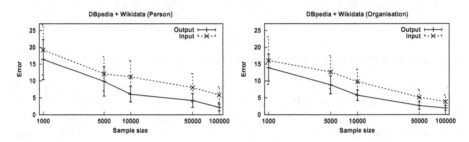

Fig. 3. Evolution of the Euclidean norm error for input/output space sampling

draw a sample $\mathcal{S}_{in}$ of k patterns from $\tilde{\mathcal{D}}$. Given a sample $\mathcal{S}$, we evaluate the quality of its approximated FPOF by using the Euclidean distance $\epsilon(\mathcal{S}, \mathcal{D})$ as error: $\epsilon(\mathcal{S}, \mathcal{D}) = \sqrt{\sum_{t \in \mathcal{D}} (\widetilde{fpofs}(t, \mathcal{D}) - fpof_{\leq M}(t, \mathcal{D}))^2}$. Figure 3 reports $\epsilon(\mathcal{S}_{out}, \mathcal{D})$ and $\epsilon(\mathcal{S}_{in}, \mathcal{D})$ w.r.t. the pattern budget (each measure is the arithmetic mean of 100 repeated samples with its standard deviation). Of course, both errors tend to zero when the sample size tends to infinity. But, it is clear that the convergence is faster and more stable with output space sampling (e.g., the FPOF quality of $\mathcal{S}_{out}$ with 10k patterns equals that of $\mathcal{S}_{in}$ with 100k patterns). This experience shows that output space sampling is more efficient at equal budget.

Qualitative Evaluation. We manually analyze the 50 best and worse entities of *Person* according to the FPOF. It is interesting to note that all entities with the highest FPOF are real persons, and not outliers. On the contrary, only 36% of the entities with the lowest FPOF are real persons, and 64% of them can be considered as outliers. Indeed, 44% of entities are fictional characters and more importantly, 8% of them should be classified in *Organisation* (a sibling class of *Person*), and 12% of them should be classified in another class (e.g., *Event*).

6 Conclusion

This paper proposes the first pattern sampling method in a transactional distributed database. It allows to consider different interestingness measures and interestingly, hybrid or vertical partitioning. As only transaction lengths are centralized, the communication costs of DDSAMPLING are low because the exchange of items is done only when the patterns are drawn. The experimental study emphasizes this low communication cost on several benchmark datasets whatever the partitioning. We also illustrate the interest of the sampled patterns in RDF data for detecting abnormal entities among persons and organizations without centralizing all the data. In future work, we plan to replace the exact drawing of transactions with a stochastic method so that we do not have to centralize the lengths of all transactions for each fragment.

Acknowledgements. This work has been partly supported by CEAMITIC (Centre d'Excellence Africain en Mathématiques, Informatique et TIC).

References

1. Al Hasan, M., Zaki, M.J.: Output space sampling for graph patterns. Proc. VLDB Endow. **2**(1), 730–741 (2009)
2. Berners-Lee, T., Hendler, J., Lassila, O., et al.: The semantic web. Sci. Am. **284**(5), 28–37 (2001)
3. Boley, M., Lucchese, C., Paurat, D., Gärtner, T.: Direct local pattern sampling by efficient two-step random procedures. In: Proceedings of KDD, pp. 582–590 (2011)
4. Cheung, D.W., Ng, V.T., Fu, A.W., Fu, Y.: Efficient mining of association rules in distributed databases. IEEE Trans. Knowl. Data Eng. **8**(6), 911–922 (1996)
5. Diop, L., Diop, C.T., Giacometti, A., Haoyuan, D.L., Soulet, A.: Sequential pattern sampling with norm constraints. In: Proceedings of ICDM 2018 (2018)
6. Domadiya, N., Rao, U.P.: Privacy preserving distributed association rule mining approach on vertically partitioned healthcare data. Proc. Comput. Sci. **148**, 303–312 (2019)
7. Dzyuba, V., van Leeuwen, M.: Learning what matters – sampling interesting patterns. In: Kim, J., Shim, K., Cao, L., Lee, J.-G., Lin, X., Moon, Y.-S. (eds.) PAKDD 2017. LNCS (LNAI), vol. 10234, pp. 534–546. Springer, Cham (2017). https://doi.org/10.1007/978-3-319-57454-7_42
8. Giacometti, A., Soulet, A.: Anytime algorithm for frequent pattern outlier detection. Int. J. Data Sci. Anal. **2**(3–4), 119–130 (2016)
9. Gombos, G., Kiss, A.: Federated query evaluation supported by SPARQL recommendation. In: Yamamoto, S. (ed.) HIMI 2016. LNCS, vol. 9734, pp. 263–274. Springer, Cham (2016). https://doi.org/10.1007/978-3-319-40349-6_25
10. Jin, R., Agrawal, G.: Systematic approach for optimizing complex mining tasks on multiple databases. In: Proceedings of ICDE, pp. 17, April 2006
11. Kum, H.C., Chang, J.H., Wang, W.: Sequential pattern mining in multi-databases via multiple alignment. DMKD J. **12**(2–3), 151–180 (2006)
12. Moens, S., Boley, M.: Instant exceptional model mining using weighted controlled pattern sampling. In: Blockeel, H., van Leeuwen, M., Vinciotti, V. (eds.) IDA 2014. LNCS, vol. 8819, pp. 203–214. Springer, Cham (2014). https://doi.org/10.1007/978-3-319-12571-8_18
13. Otey, M.E., Wang, C., Parthasarathy, S., Veloso, A., Meira, W.: Mining frequent itemsets in distributed and dynamic databases. In: Proceedings of ICDM 2003, pp. 617–620. IEEE (2003)

14. Özsu, M.T., Valduriez, P.: Principles of Distributed Database Systems. Springer, Switzerland (2011). https://doi.org/10.1007/978-3-030-26253-2
15. Shen, H., Zhao, L., Li, Z.: A distributed spatial-temporal similarity data storage scheme in wireless sensor networks. IEEE Trans. Mob. Comput. **10**(7), 982–996 (2011)
16. Zhang, S., Zaki, M.J.: Mining multiple data sources: local pattern analysis. DMKD J. **12**(2–3), 121–125 (2006)
17. Zhu, X., Li, B., Wu, X., He, D., Zhang, C.: CLAP: collaborative pattern mining for distributed information systems. Decis. Support Syst. **52**(1), 40–51 (2011)
18. Zhu, X., Wu, X.: Discovering relational patterns across multiple databases. In: Proceedings of ICDE, pp. 726–735. IEEE (2007)

Can We Probabilistically Generate Uniformly Distributed Relation Instances Efficiently?

Joachim Biskup[(✉)] and Marcel Preuß

Fakultät für Informatik, Technische Universität Dortmund, Dortmund, Germany
{joachim.biskup,marcel.preuss}@cs.tu-dortmund.de

Abstract. Software engineering includes the runtime evaluation of a prototype by experiments with carefully selected sample inputs. For the development of software intended to operate on relation instances for a given relational schema with a functional dependency, we are then challenged to generate appropriate sample instances of increasing size. Moreover, studying the impact of varying the sizes of the attribute domains might be important. We focus on seeing uniformly distributed collections of sample instances to be appropriate. Based on a combinatorial analysis and exploiting an algorithm for restricted integer partitions, we develop a sophisticated probabilistic procedure of high computational complexity for generating any element of such a collection with equal probability. Moreover, we demonstrate that simpler approaches based on uniform local selections fail to achieve global uniformity.

Keywords: Combinatorial analysis · Database relation · Domain cardinality · Duplicate-freeness · Functional dependency · Integer partition · Random instance · Uniform probability distribution

1 Introduction

The engineering of software to operate on database instances has to deal with many aspects, ranging from functional correctness with respect to an abstract specification over worst or average case complexity analysis to practical feasibility in terms of acceptable execution times observed for a prototype implementation and later on for a final optimized product. In particular the latter aspect of practical feasibility—but to a lesser extent also, e.g., testing the correctness or determining the average case complexity—require to evaluate the actual execution behavior of implemented code applied to carefully selected sample inputs.

In the database situation, such sample inputs have to be instances of a database schema that describes the possibly maintained data by means of data formats and integrity constraints as invariants. Restricting to a *relational schema* for just one table, such a description basically consists of three parts: a set of *attributes* denoting columns of the table; for each of these attributes a *domain*

© Springer Nature Switzerland AG 2020
J. Darmont et al. (Eds.): ADBIS 2020, LNCS 12245, pp. 75–89, 2020.
https://doi.org/10.1007/978-3-030-54832-2_8

as a finite set of possible values; and a set of database dependencies, in most cases only *functional dependencies* including keys. In more advanced cases we might also have general equality-generating and tuple-generating dependencies. We leave these cases for future work, just as for generalizing the current investigations for just *one* functional dependency to any number of them.

Accordingly, for a given relational schema any sample input selected for a software evaluation should be an *instance* of the schema, i.e., a finite *duplicate-free* set of tuples over the specified attributes such that each single tuple has values according to the specified domains and all tuples together satisfy the given functional dependency. Regarding the values, we argue that for many situations the *sizes of the domains* are most crucial, rather than the actual concrete elements of the domains. Moreover, the wanted *size of the samples* is significant.

Depending on the applications we have in mind, we further have to determine which collections of sample inputs we consider as appropriate to reflect the anticipated work load of the software. Ideally, we might dispose on some statistical assumption or even insight about which formally accepted instances will actually occur with which likelihood "in real life". For example, some probability distribution over the set of all possible instances could appear to be reasonable, or all samples should somehow be derived from some already known application data. Often, however, additional knowledge of this kind is not available or, at least, not reliable enough. Then applying an instance generator with *uniformly distributed* outputs might be the best option: each of the possible instances will be selected with equal probability, thus avoiding any bias that has not been made explicit by the schema.

We will develop and analyze such an instance generator under the restrictions mentioned above, more specifically aiming at the following requirements:

- **Inputs:**
  1. relational schema $(R(\mathcal{U}), \mathcal{SC})$ with attribute set $\mathcal{U} = \{A_1, \ldots, A_l\}$ and database dependencies $\mathcal{SC}$, consisting of just *one functional dependency*;
  2. for each attribute $att \in \mathcal{U}$, the domain dom_{att} of att with size $k_{att} \geq 2$ such that, w.l.o.g., $dom_{att} = \{1, 2, \ldots, k_{att}\}$;
  3. required size $n > 0$ of the relation instances to be generated.
- **Output:**
  a (duplicate-free, typed) relation instance of the schema $(R(\mathcal{U}), \mathcal{SC})$ with constants taken from the domains dom_{att} for $att \in \mathcal{U}$, having n tuples.
- **Assurances:**
  1. *termination* under the weakest precondition for the existence of an output of the required kind;
  2. *uniform probability distribution* of possible outputs.

In the remainder we selectively survey related work in Section 2. In Sect. 3, as our first main contribution, we develop a method to count the number of different instances. Based on that method and exploiting an algorithm for restricted integer partitions, in Sect. 4, as our second main contribution, we define and verify a somehow sophisticated probabilistic generation procedure of high computational complexity for uniformly random instances. In Sect. 5, for additionally justifying our generation procedure, we explain by means of examples why simpler approaches based on only local uniform selections fail to achieve global uniformity. In Sect. 6, we summarize our achievements and discuss directions of future work, in particular for answering our question.

2 Related Work

The need for generating appropriate test data is a well-known issue and, accordingly, there is a long history of efforts to provide tools for generating sample database instances under various kinds of interests. Such tools are also part of publicly available benchmark facilities as provided by the Transaction Processing Performance Council, TPC, since more than three decades [28].

Over the time, in particular by [2,4–9,14,16,17,19,22,27], the following major dimensions of algorithmic approaches to sample instance generation have been treated in varying combinations:

- *Abstract data types*: underlying data structures (single relation (table), collection of relations, XML, RDF, . . .); database operations to be tested (query evaluation, query optimization, updates, transactions, . . .).
- *Concrete data characteristics*: database dependencies declared in the schema (primary keys, functional dependencies, foreign keys, inclusion dependencies, . . .); schema restrictions (snowflake schema, . . .); declared domain types, in particular their sizes; required cardinality constraints on results of queries (select, join-select, project, . . .); required instance sizes; and data correlations within an instance (intra-column, intra-relational, inter-relational, . . .).
- *Generator properties*: expected satisfaction of requirements (probabilistically approximate, always guaranteed, . . .); instance data used (purely artificial, extracted from real life reference data, . . .); wanted probability distribution over all possibly generated instances; generation method (constraint satisfaction programming, linear integer programming, . . .); (worst case) computational complexity of formalized problem definition (requirement satisfiability, . . .); practical scaling (heuristics, approximation, . . .).

Besides practical engineering, several other aspects of instance data have been explored from a mainly fundamental point of view, often more inclined to understand the structure of a single sample instance or the properties of some declaratively specified class of instances rather than to actually generate samples for testing. In particular, the model-theoretic and combinatorial analysis of database dependencies has gathered much insight. Important contributions include studies about the maximal and the average number of keys, e.g., [10,11,23] and on Armstrong relations, e.g., [3,18,24]. A recent example of considering the impact of domain sizes can be found in [1]. Moreover, a recent study [15] on the notions of dependence and independence provides a fresh view on functional dependencies and the implied multivalued dependencies seen as a conditional independence assertion.

The practical tools and the theoretical insight can be understood as specialized investigations of the broader topic of the combinatorial analysis and the generation of finite structures, see, e.g., [12,13,20]. Indeed, the well-known problem of integer partitions, see in particular [25,26], having been studied by Leonhard Euler already in 1741, has turned out to be important for our task.

Despite all these rich works, to the best of our knowledge, the specific problem specified in the introduction has not been dealt with in the literature.

3   Counting the Number of Instances

We start by considering a somehow representative case. On the one hand, we have one functional dependency between two attributes. On the other hand, we have an additional attribute such that besides *dependency satisfaction* we have to take care about the *absence of duplicates*. In this case, the left-hand side of the functional dependency does not form a (minimal) key by itself but only together with the additional attribute. Accordingly, caring about the absence of duplicate tuples needs to consider both of the key attributes, whereas under each of the key attributes alone some values might occur repeatedly.

3.1   The Single-FD Scenario

Let $(R(\mathcal{U}), \mathcal{SC})$ be a relational *schema* with attribute set $\mathcal{U} = \{A, B, C\}$ and database dependencies $\mathcal{SC} = \{A \to B\}$, consisting of just one nonkey *functional dependency*. Then $\{A, C\}$ forms a (minimal) key which is even unique. Moreover, the functional dependency $A \to B$ implies the multivalued dependency $A \twoheadrightarrow B|C$. As will become clear, both the key and the multivalued dependency require an appropriate diversity on the attribute C. We want to generate a (nonempty) random *relation instance* of a given size $n > 0$. Moreover, for each of the attributes *att* the domain dom_{att} is required to be of some size $k_{att} = \|dom_{att}\| \geq 2$ of interest. Though, as usually, a relation instance is treated as an (unordered) set, the generation procedure should store the output as an array $r[tup, att]$ with the index range $tup = 1, \dots, n$ for lines, representing tuples, and the index range $att = A, B, C$ for columns, representing attributes. Notably, one relation instance of size n has $n!$ many array representations.

Example 1. Table 1 lists all (duplicate-free and dependency-satisfying) *relation instances* of size $n = 2$ with uniform domain sizes of 2, as represented by arrays. In total there are $4 + 16 = 20$ such instances, as can be seen by suitably combining the arguments for the satisfaction of the functional dependency and for the absences of duplicates. We will first consider the consequences of dependency satisfaction for duplicate-freeness and then, the other way round, the consequences of duplicate-freeness for the dependency satisfaction.

The first four instances shown in Table 1 have a unique value for attribute A, i.e., either 1 or 2 occurs twice. Accordingly by the *functional dependency*, in each case the assigned value for attribute B has to be unique as well—either 1 or 2. Moreover, since then the two subtuples are identical for the attributes A and B, the associated values under attribute C have to be different in order to achieve duplicate-freeness.

In the remaining sixteen instances each of the values 1 and 2 occurs only once under the attribute A and thus the *functional dependency* is trivially satisfied for any combination with the two possible values under the attribute B. Each of the four resulting cases can be associated with any of the four possible combinations of values under the attribute C, since duplicate-freeness is already ensured by the distinct values under attribute A.

Table 1. The collection of all (duplicate-free) relation instances over attributes $\{A, B, C\}$ with uniform domains $\{1, 2\}$, having $n = 2$ (different) tuples and satisfying the functional dependency $A \to B$.

instance no.	A	B	C
5	1	1	1
	2	1	1
6	1	1	2
	2	1	2
7	1	1	1
	2	1	2
8	1	1	2
	2	1	1
9	1	2	1
	2	2	1
10	1	2	2
	2	2	2
11	1	2	1
	2	2	2
12	1	2	2
	2	2	1

instance no.	A	B	C
13	1	1	1
	2	2	1
14	1	1	2
	2	2	2
15	1	1	1
	2	2	2
16	1	1	2
	2	1	1
17	1	2	1
	2	1	1
18	1	2	2
	2	1	2
19	1	2	1
	2	1	2
20	1	2	2
	2	1	1

instance no.	A	B	C
1	1	1	1
	1	1	2
2	1	2	1
	1	2	2
3	2	1	1
	2	1	2
4	2	2	1
	2	2	2

Starting with the requirement of *duplicate-freeness*, we observe that there are $k_A \cdot k_C = 2 \cdot 2 = 4$ different key values, from which two different ones are selected for an instance of size $n = 2$. Accordingly, there are $\binom{4}{2} = 6$ possibilities for such a selection. Two of the selections have a *unique value* under the attribute A (either 1 or 2) and, thus, need a unique value under attribute B (again either 1 or 2) for satisfying the functional dependency; the four possible cases are shown as the instances with no. 1–4. Four of the selections have *different values* under the attribute A (namely 1 and 2) and, thus, these values can be arbitrarily combined with values under the attribute B (either (1 and 1) or (2 and 2) or (1 and 2) or (2 and 1)); the sixteen possible cases are shown as the instances with no. 5–20.

3.2   A Systematic Counting Method

For the given functional dependency $A \to B$, each relation instance r of size n defines a function $f : act_A \longrightarrow act_B$ from the *active domain* $act_A := \pi_A(r) \subseteq dom_A$ of attribute A onto the active domain $act_B := \pi_B(r) \subseteq dom_B$ of attribute B. Such a function implies that $\|act_A\| \geq \|act_B\|$, and it induces a partition of act_A according to the equivalence relation $a_1 \sim_f a_2$:iff $f(a_1) = f(a_2)$. Furthermore, we also consider the partition into singletons of act_B according to the equality relation $b_1 \sim_= b_2$:iff $b_1 = b_2$. Regarding the array for r, which allows duplicates for tuples as well as for homogeneous subtuples, i.e., within one or more columns, there are two related partitions of the index range $\{1, \ldots, n\}$ for tuples, $tup_1 \sim_{r.B} tup_2$:iff $r[tup_1, B] = r[tup_2, B]$ and $tup_1 \sim_{r.A} tup_2$:iff $r[tup_1, A] = r[tup_2, A]$, where $\sim_{r.A}$ is a refinement of $\sim_{r.B}$, due to the functional dependency $A \to B$.

Each block of $\sim_{r.B}$ gets assigned a unique constant out of the domain dom_B of the attribute B and thus, under a suitable sorting of r, defines a "B-uniqueness area" in the column of B. Accordingly, there are $\|act_B\|$ many $\sim_{r.B}$-blocks and as many B-uniqueness areas. Each block of $\sim_{r.A}$ has a unique constant out of the domain dom_A of the attribute A and thus, under a suitable sorting of r, defines an "A-uniqueness area" in the column of A. Accordingly, there are $\|act_A\|$ many $\sim_{r.A}$-blocks and as many A-uniqueness areas. Finally, for a block of $\sim_{r.A}$ with

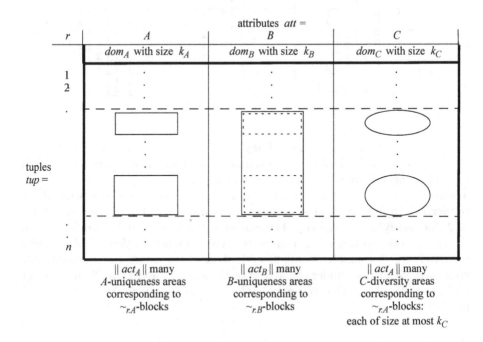

Fig. 1. Uniqueness and diversity areas of a relation instance r with n tuples over attributes A, B and C with given domains and satisfying the functional dependency $A \to B$, according to the partition blocks of $\sim_{r.A}$ and $\sim_{r.B}$, respectively.

size j—sharing both a constant $a \in dom_A$ and the assigned constant $b \in dom_B$—the associated constants out of the domain dom_C of the attribute C must be j pairwise different elements, forming a "C-diversity area", since the instance r does not contain duplicates. Accordingly, we have $j \leq \|dom_C\|$.

Figure 1 visualizes the structure of the instance r with its uniqueness and diversity areas described above. This structure immediately implies the following assertion about the possible sizes n of an instance for the simple case.

Proposition 1 (Single-FD instance existence). *Let $R(\{A, B, C\}, \{A \rightarrow B\})$ be a relational schema with domain sizes $k_{att} = \|dom_{att}\|$ for att $\in \{A, B, C\}$. Then there exists a nonempty relation instance of size n satisfying the given functional dependency and complying with the given domains iff $1 \leq n \leq k_A \cdot k_C$.*

Proof. The given functional dependency implies that $\{A, C\}$ is a (minimal) key. Each of the $k_A \cdot k_C$ many different key values (a, c) with $a \in dom_A$ and $c \in dom_C$ can occur at most once in a relation instance. If we take any element $b \in dom_B$ and combine it with each of the possible key values as the value under the attribute B, thus trivially satisfying the given functional dependency, we obtain an instance of maximum size $k_A \cdot k_C$. Moreover, any nonempty subset of this instance is an instance again. □

Theorem 1 (Single-FD instance count). *Let $R(\{A, B, C\}, \{A \rightarrow B\})$ be a relational schema with domain sizes $k_{att} = \|dom_{att}\|$ for att $\in \{A, B, C\}$, and let $1 \leq n \leq k_A \cdot k_C$ be the required instance size. Then the number of relation instances of size n satisfying the given functional dependency and complying with the given domains is equal to*

$$\sum_{\lceil \frac{n}{k_C} \rceil \leq ak_A \leq \min(k_A, n)} \sum_{\substack{1 \leq k \leq n, \\ (s_1, m_1), \ldots, (s_i, m_i), \ldots, (s_k, m_k): \\ 1 \leq s_i < s_{i+1} \leq k_C; \\ 1 \leq m_i \leq n; \\ n = \sum_{i=1}^{k} s_i \cdot m_i; \\ ak_A = \sum_{i=1}^{k} m_i}} \tag{1}$$

$$\left[\prod_{i=1}^{k} \binom{k_A - \sum_{1 \leq j < i} m_j}{m_i} \cdot k_B^{ak_A} \cdot \prod_{i=1}^{k} m_i \cdot \binom{k_C}{s_i} \right]. \tag{2}$$

Proof. We first explain the two summations shown in part (1) of the formula.

For any relation r meeting all requirements, the two key columns define a selection of exactly n different key values. There are $\binom{k_A \cdot k_C}{n}$ different *key value selections*, each of which defines the *active domain* $act_A = \pi_A(r)$ of the attribute A in the instance r. To enable C-diversity areas and to comply with size restrictions, its *cardinality* $ak_A = \|act_A\|$ is bounded by

$$\left\lceil \frac{n}{k_C} \right\rceil \leq ak_A \leq \min(k_A, n), \tag{3}$$

and ak_A is equal to the number of $\sim_{r.A}$-blocks in an array for r.

The required instance size n, a possible cardinality ak_A and the given domain size k_C together determine the options for the multiplicities and the sizes of the A-uniqueness areas of a relation instance, as they are illustrated in Figure 1:

- $1 \leq k \leq n$
  is the number of different sizes of actually occurring A-uniqueness areas;
- $(s_1, m_1), \ldots, (s_i, m_i), \ldots, (s_k, m_k)$
  is a sequence of such sizes with their multiplicity of occurrences;
- $1 \leq s_i < s_{i+1} \leq k_C$
  imposes a strict order on the sizes, which are bounded by the cardinality of dom_C according to the needed C-diversity areas;
- $1 \leq m_i \leq n$
  states that multiplicities are bounded by the overall required size n;
- $n = \sum_{i=1}^{k} s_i \cdot m_i$
  requires that the multiplied sizes sum up to the overall required size n;
- $ak_A = \sum_{i=1}^{k} m_i$
  requires that the multiplicities sum up to the size ak_A of the considered active A-domain, implying that there are ak_A many A-uniqueness areas.

For a given combination of the two summation terms, further on called an n-ak_A-k_C-representation S, we now explain the three main factors shown in part (2) of the formula.

- To fill the ak_A many A-uniqueness areas defined by S, in total we have to select ak_A many *different* values $act_A = \{a_1, \ldots, a_{ak_A}\}$ out of dom_A such that m_i many of them are placed in areas of size s_i, for each i not caring about the order. The number of different choices for that filling is given by

$$\prod_{i=1}^{k} \binom{k_A - \sum_{1 \leq j < i} m_j}{m_i} = \frac{k_A \cdot \ldots \cdot (k_A - (ak_A - 1))}{m_1! \cdot \ldots \cdot m_k!}. \tag{4}$$

- To fill the *partial* B-uniqueness areas corresponding to the A-uniqueness areas defined by S, for each of the ak_A many selected a_l, by the functional dependency, we have to independently select some unique value $b_l \in dom_B$. The number of different combinations with the selected A-values is

$$k_B^{ak_A}. \tag{5}$$

- To fill the C-diversity areas corresponding to the A-uniqueness areas and the corresponding partial B-uniqueness areas defined by S, for each of the ak_A many selected A-values a_l—each being combined with a unique b_l—by the duplicate-freeness, we have to independently select as many *different* values out of dom_C as there are occurrences of a_l. There are m_j many A-values that occur s_j often. In total the number of possibilities is given by

$$\prod_{i=1}^{k} m_i \cdot \binom{k_C}{s_i}. \tag{6}$$

Finally, *any two instances are different* if and only if they differ in at least one of the following features:

- the *cardinality* ak_A of the active domain of A, according to (3);
- the *n-ak_A-k_C-representation* S, as described in the second sum of (1);
- the actual selection of the *active domain* act_A of A, according to (4);
- the *B-combinations*, according to (5);
- the *C-associations*, according to (6). □

Example 2. Resuming Example 1 with Table 1, we evaluate the counting expression (1-2) for $n = k_A = k_B = k_C = 2$. Then the outer summation ranges over the values 1 and 2 for ak_A, since $\lceil \frac{2}{2} \rceil = 1 \le ak_A \le \min(2, 2) = 2$.

First, considering the term for $ak_A = 1$, there is just one 2-1-2-representation, namely $(2, 1)$, and we have $\binom{2}{1} = 2$ A-selections, $2^1 = 2$ B-selections, and $1 \cdot \binom{2}{2} = 1$ C-associations. In total, the term for $ak_A = 1$ contributes $2 \cdot 2 \cdot 1 = 4$.

Second, considering the term for $ak_A = 2$, there is again just one 2-2-2-representation, this time $(1, 2)$, and we have $\binom{2}{2} = 1$ A-selections, $2^2 = 4$ B-selections, and $2 \cdot \binom{2}{1} = 4$ C-associations. In total, the term for $ak_A = 2$ contributes $1 \cdot 4 \cdot 4 = 16$. Thus, overall there are $4 + 16 = 20$ different instances.

The general case of any relational schema with just one functional dependency (supposed to have a minimal left-hand side) can straightforwardly be derived from the considerations of the special case treated above. First, instead of three attributes having the three different roles of left-hand side, right-hand side and further attribute, respectively, we might have three mutual disjoint sets of attributes, having corresponding roles. Then we have to treat a subtuple for such a set like a single constant for an attribute. Second, the set corresponding to the role of the attribute C in the special case might be empty. Then the attribute A alone forms a key and, thus $ak_A = n$ is the only choice. Accordingly, the counting expression (1-2) reduces to either $\binom{k_A}{n} \cdot k_B^n$ or just $\binom{k_A}{n}$, depending on whether the role of the attribute B is non-empty or empty, respectively.

4   Probabilistic Generation of Random Instances

Under the representative assumptions of Theorem 1, and closely following the counting expression (1-2), we now define our

Probabilistic Generation Procedure for Random Instances:
I. Preprocessing: Listing All Possible Sizes act_A and All Possible n-ak_A-k_C-Representations with Required Probabilities

1. determine and list all possible sizes ak_A of an active domain act_A for attribute A according to the first part of (1) and (3);
2. for each listed ak_A: determine and list all possible n-ak_A-k_C-representations S according to the second part of (1);
3. for each listed ak_A, for each listed n-ak_A-k_C-representation S: calculate and keep the number $Inst(ak_A, S)$ of complying instances according to (2);

4. for each listed ak_A: calculate and keep the number $Inst(ak_A)$ of complying instances, by summing up the numbers $Inst(ak_A, S)$ for all pertinent S;
5. determine and keep the number $Inst$ of all instances, by summing up the numbers $Inst(ak_A)$ for all pertinent ak_A;
6. annotate each listed size ak_A and each listed n-ak_A-k_C-representation S with probabilities $Inst(ak_A)/Inst$ and $Inst(ak_A, S)/Inst(ak_A)$, respectively, as required in Part II.

II. Instance Generation from Listed Domains and Preprocessed Lists

1. *select with probability $Inst(ak_A)/Inst$ a listed active domain size ak_A;*
2. *select with probability $Inst(ak_A, S)/Inst(ak_A)$ a listed n-ak_A-k_C-representation S;*
3. **do in parallel**
   - fill each of the A-uniqueness areas with *uniformly selected* pairwise *different A-values*;
   - fill each of the partial B-uniqueness areas, independently from each other and thus (potentially) in parallel, with *uniformly selected B-values*;
   - fill each of the C-diversity areas, independently from each other and thus (potentially) in parallel, with *uniformly selected* pairwise *different C-values*.

Theorem 2 (Uniform distribution by generation procedure). *Under the assumption of an ideal underlying random number generator, each relation instance occurs as an output of the probabilistic generation procedure with equal probability, defined by the number of possible instances.*

Proof. On the one hand, let $R(k_A, k_B, k_C, n)$ be the set of relation instances as described by Theorem 1. On the other hand, let $E(k_A, k_B, k_C, n)$ be the set of possible executions of the Probabilistic Generation Procedure. Each such execution is uniquely determined by the sequence of probabilistic selections. Thus we can form a probability space over $E(k_A, k_B, k_C, n)$ by identifying executions with their respective sequences of probabilistic selections.

According to Part II, the sequences of probabilistic selections choose (i) an active domain size ak_A, (ii) an n-ak_A-k_C-representation S and (iii) appropriate values for filling the uniqueness areas and diversity areas determined by S.

The underlying (conditional) probability spaces are given by (i) the set of all possible active domain sizes ak_A, (ii) depending on ak_A, the set of all possible n-ak_A-k_C-representations S, and (iii) depending on ak_A and S, the set of all possible fillings according to S, equivalently the set of all possible relation instances r complying with S, respectively.

The (conditional) probabilities for a specific sequence of choices ak_A, S and r are then given by (i) $Inst(ak_A)/Inst$ by Step II.1 and the preprocessing, (ii) $Inst(ak_A, S)/Inst(ak_A)$ by Step II.2 and preprocessing, and (iii) $1/Inst(ak_A, S)$ by Step II.3 and preprocessing, respectively.

Hence, each specific relation instance appears with probability

$$Inst(ak_A)/Inst \cdot Inst(ak_A, S)/Inst(ak_A) \cdot 1/Inst(ak_A, S) = 1/Inst.$$

$\square$

An actual implementation of the probabilistic generation procedure would be challenging regarding the selections with the required probabilities and the overall practical feasibility. An implementation of Part I could be based on a tool for solving the *restricted integer partition problem* [12,25,26] that is essentially identical with the task of determining all n-ak_A-k_C-representations, the number of which grows exponentially (in the required instance size n) in general. But for fixed input parameters the preprocessing has to be performed only once.

An implementation of Part II could be based on a standard pseudo-random generator from which then further tools are derived, see, e.g., [21]. In particular we need the *give-next-element* operation, consuming approximately constant time, and the *shuffle* operation, consuming approximately (in the domain sizes) linear time. In each case, we have to suitably adapt the pseudo-randomness to a current set of options, in general requiring some additional time and summed up to at most a linear amount. Whenever a *selection of different values* is required, we could employ the following alternatives:

- repeat the give-next-element operation on a collision;
- shuffle an array representation of the pertinent set of options, and extract.

Accordingly, Part II requires at most (in the domain sizes) quadratic time (plus the time for adapting the pseudo-random generator) but could be optimized such that it is expected to run reasonably fast for inputs leading to few collisions.

5   Failure of Simpler Approaches

The combinatorially based generation procedure proposed in the preceding section might appear to be unnecessary complicated. One might hope that simpler approaches performing suitable local uniformly random selections will somehow "automatically" lead to a global uniform probability distribution. We will inspect two seemingly promising alternative approaches and show their failure.

The first approach does not explicitly impose the structural properties expressed by the first part (1) of the counting formula but instead, in the spirit of part (2) of the counting formula, somehow directly proceeds to select values under the attributes A, B and C in turn:

1. *Selecting independent left-hand side elements under size restriction*:
   Regarding attribute A, for each line (tuple) $tup = 1, \ldots n$ probabilistically select an element a out of the domain dom_A and set $r[tup, A] := a$, such that each selected $a \in dom_A$ occurs at most $\|dom_C\|$ often.
2. For each value $a \in dom_A$ occurring in the column A, mutually independently, determine $\Sigma_{A=a} = \{ tup \mid r[tup, A] = a \} = \{tup_1^a, \ldots, tup_{\|\Sigma_{A=a}\|}^a\}$ and
   (a) *Enforcing the functional dependency*:
       regarding attribute B (the right hand side of the functional dependency), probabilistically select an element b out of the domain dom_B for B, allowing arbitrary repetitions, and set $r[tup, B] := b$ for all $tup \in \Sigma_{A=a}$;

(b) *Assuring duplicate-freeness*:

regarding attribute C (the additional key attribute), probabilistically select $\|\Sigma_{A=a}\|$ many different elements $c_1^a, \ldots, c_{\|\Sigma_{A=a}\|}^a$ out of the domain dom_C for C, and set $r[tup_j^a, C] := c_j^a$ for all $tup_j^a \in \Sigma_{A=a}$.

By this approach, for our example shown in Table 1 each of the four instances 1–4 is generated with probability 1/8, while each of the remaining sixteen instances 5–20 appears with probability 1/32. Essentially, this failure is caused by neglecting that the former instances satisfy the 2-1-2-representation ($s_1 = 2, m_1 = 1$), and the latter ones the 2-2-2-representation ($s_1 = 1, m_1 = 2$). Figure 2 visualizes more details about the difference between the two cases.

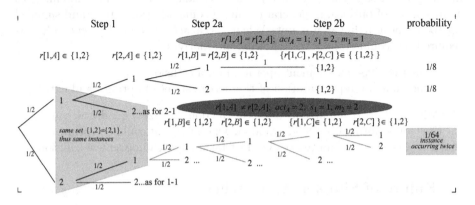

Fig. 2. Some selection sequences leading to relation instances shown in Table 1.

A second approach uses a list of still possible tuples, initialized by the Cartesian product of the domains, and just stepwise first randomly selects a further still possible tuple and then cancels all tuples in the list that are no longer possible, since leading to a violation of the functional dependency or the requirement of duplicate-freeness.

The following example again shows a failure of achieving uniformity. We now suppose that $dom_A = \{1, 2, 3\}$ while still $dom_B = dom_C = \{1, 2\}$ and we require a size $n = 3$. Assume that we get the tuples $(1, 1, 1)$, $(2, 2, 2)$ and $(3, 2, 2)$. Then the selections of the next tuple have been performed with probabilities 1/12, 1/9 and 1/6, respectively, and this holds for each of the six different sequences for these three selections. In total, this instance will be generated with probability $6 \cdot (1/12 \cdot 1/9 \cdot 1/6)$. Observe that we have $ak_A = 3$ and 3-3-2-representation ($s_1 = 1, m_1 = 3$).

In contrast, if we get the tuples $(1, 1, 1)$, $(1, 1, 2)$ and $(2, 2, 2)$ in this sequence—or with the first two tuples exchanged—then the selections of the next tuple have been performed with probabilities 1/12, 1/9 and 1/8, respectively. However, for the same tuples in the sequence $(1, 1, 1)$, $(2, 2, 2)$ and $(1, 1, 2)$ the probabilities are 1/12, 1/9 and 1/6, respectively, and this also holds if we exchange either the first two selections or the first and the third selection. In total, this instance will be generated with probability $2 \cdot (1/12 \cdot 1/9 \cdot 1/8) + 4 \cdot (1/12 \cdot 1/9 \cdot 1/6)$. Observe that we have $ak_A = 2$ and a 3-2-2-representation $(s_1 = 1, m_1 = 1), (s_2 = 2, m_1 = 1)$.

6   Conclusions

We designed and verified a probabilistic generation procedure for uniformly random instances of a relational database schema with just one functional dependency together with given domain sizes. The underlying combinatorial analysis of the set of all such instances reveals a subtle relationship between the explicitly required dependence requirement and an implicit diversity requirement.

Our achievements are a first step towards more ambitious future research directions. First, we plan to investigate the generation of random instances for any set of functional dependencies as well as for suitable classes of equality-generating and tuple-generating dependencies, including interrelational ones. Second, it would be worthwhile to treat database schemas obtained from a normalization process (by decomposition or synthesis), comprising keys and inclusion dependencies by foreign keys. Third, we would like or could even be forced to relax the requirement on the wanted size of the instance to be generated.

As shown in this article, the requested instance size n can only be achieved under some weakest precondition. For functional dependencies the precondition turns out to be hardly restrictive in practice, since the class of instances is closed under forming subsets. For other database dependencies, however, this property does not hold in general and, thus, instances might exist only for rather specific sizes. Moreover, even for one functional dependency the number of different instances for a given size n depends on a number-theoretic property—a specifically restricted integer partition property—of n together with the size ak_A of different values occurring under the attribute(s) of the left-hand side of the dependency and the size k_C of the domain of the additional attribute(s). At first glance this property appears to have no obvious meaning in terms of a database application. However, if we come up with a relative version of that property, expressing some range of "acceptable" quotients of ak_A and n, and further introduce a notion of "acceptable" partitions, then we might be able to characterize those relation instances that can actually occur in the anticipated database application.

Though we argued for equal probabilities of all possible outputs of an instance generator, in some well-understood situations we might prefer to obtain some specific nonuniform distribution. In particular, we might want to adapt a required probability to the degree of the acceptance of a partition. We plan to develop a parallelized prototype implementation to treat this issue and, more generally, to evaluate the practical feasibility of our approach.

Finally, our results indicate that the task to probabilistically generate relation instances is unexpectedly challenging regarding both the conceptual issues and the computational complexity. Basically, the challenge is arising from subtle interactions of requirements expressed by the database schema on the one side and requirements on the probability distribution of the outputs on the other side. Accordingly, a general answer to the question in the title is still open.

Acknowledgements. We would like to thank Sebastian Link, Bernhard Thalheim and Jan Van den Bussche for stimulating conversations about the problem.

References

1. Alattar, M., Sali, A.: Functional dependencies in incomplete databases with limited domains. In: Herzig, A., Kontinen, J. (eds.) FoIKS 2020. LNCS, vol. 12012, pp. 1–21. Springer, Cham (2020). https://doi.org/10.1007/978-3-030-39951-1_1
2. Arasu, A., Kaushik, R., Li, J.: Data generation using declarative constraints. In: Sellis, T.K., Miller, R.J., Kementsietsidis, A., Velegrakis, Y. (eds.) SIGMOD 2011, pp. 685–696. ACM (2011)
3. Beeri, C., Dowd, M., Fagin, R., Statman, R.: On the structure of armstrong relations for functional dependencies. J. ACM **31**(1), 30–46 (1984)
4. Binnig, C., Kossmann, D., Lo, E., Özsu, M.T.: Qagen: generating query-aware test databases. In: Chan, C.Y., Ooi, B.C., Zhou, A. (eds.) SIGMOD 2007, pp. 341–352. ACM (2007)
5. Bitton, D., DeWitt, D.J., Turbyfill, C.: Benchmarking database systems A systematic approach. In: Schkolnick, M., Thanos, C. (eds.) VLDB 1983, pp. 8–19. Morgan Kaufmann (1983)
6. Blum, D., Cohen, S.: Grr: generating random RDF. In: Antoniou, G., Grobelnik, M., Simperl, E., Parsia, B., Plexousakis, D., De Leenheer, P., Pan, J. (eds.) ESWC 2011. LNCS, vol. 6644, pp. 16–30. Springer, Heidelberg (2011). https://doi.org/10.1007/978-3-642-21064-8_2
7. Bruno, N., Chaudhuri, S.: Flexible database generators. In: Böhm, K., Jensen, C.S., Haas, L.M., Kersten, M.L., Larson, P., Ooi, B.C. (eds.) VLDB 2005, pp. 1097–1107. ACM (2005)
8. Chandra, B., Chawda, B., Kar, B., Reddy, K.V.M., Shah, S., Sudarshan, S.: Data generation for testing and grading SQL queries. CoRR arXiv:1411.6704v5 (2017)
9. Cohen, S.: Generating XML structure using examples and constraints. PVLDB **1**(1), 490–501 (2008). https://doi.org/10.14778/1453856.1453910
10. Demetrovics, J.: On the number of candidate keys. Inf. Process. Lett. **7**(6), 266–269 (1978)
11. Demetrovics, J., Katona, G.O.H., Miklós, D., Seleznjev, O., Thalheim, B.: Asymptotic properties of keys and functional dependencies in random databases. Theor. Comput. Sci. **190**(2), 151–166 (1998)
12. Flajolet, P., Sedgewick, R.: Analytic Combinatorics. Cambridge University Press, Cambridge (2009)
13. Flajolet, P., Zimmermann, P., Cutsem, B.V.: A calculus for the random generation of labelled combinatorial structures. Theor. Comput. Sci. **132**(2), 1–35 (1994)
14. Frank, M., Poess, M., Rabl, T.: Efficient update data generation for DBMS benchmarks. In: Kaeli, D.R., Rolia, J., John, L.K., Krishnamurthy, D. (eds.) ICPE 2012, pp. 169–180. ACM (2012)
15. Galliani, P., Väänänen, J.: Diversity, dependence and independence. In: Herzig, A., Kontinen, J. (eds.) FoIKS 2020. LNCS, vol. 12012, pp. 106–121. Springer, Cham (2020). https://doi.org/10.1007/978-3-030-39951-1_7

16. Gray, J., Sundaresan, P., Englert, S., Baclawski, K., Weinberger, P.J.: Quickly generating billion-record synthetic databases. In: Snodgrass, R.T., Winslett, M. (eds.) SIGMOD 1994, pp. 243–252. ACM (1994)
17. Houkjær, K., Torp, K., Wind, R.: Simple and realistic data generation. In: Dayal, U., et al. (eds.) VLDB 2006, pp. 1243–1246. ACM (2006)
18. Katona, G.O.H., Tichler, K.: Encoding databases satisfying a given set of dependencies. In: Lukasiewicz, T., Sali, A. (eds.) FoIKS 2012. LNCS, vol. 7153, pp. 203–223. Springer, Heidelberg (2012). https://doi.org/10.1007/978-3-642-28472-4_12
19. Kaufmann, M., Fischer, P.M., Kossmann, D., May, N.: A generic database benchmarking service. In: Jensen, C.S., Jermaine, C.M., Zhou, X. (eds.) ICDE 2013, pp. 1276–1279. IEEE Computer Society (2013)
20. Knuth, D.E.: The Art of Computer Programming, Volume I: Fundamental Algorithms, 2nd edn. Addison-Wesley, Reading (1973)
21. Knuth, D.E.: The Art of Computer Programming, Volume II: Seminumerical Algorithms, 3rd edn. Addison-Wesley, Reading (1998)
22. Lo, E., Cheng, N., Hon, W.: Generating databases for query workloads. PVLDB 3(1), 848–859 (2010)
23. Lucchesi, C.L., Osborn, S.L.: Candidate keys for relations. J. Comput. Syst. Sci. 17(2), 270–279 (1978)
24. De Marchi, F., Lopes, S., Petit, J.-M.: Samples for understanding data-semantics in relations. In: Hacid, M.-S., Raś, Z.W., Zighed, D.A., Kodratoff, Y. (eds.) ISMIS 2002. LNCS (LNAI), vol. 2366, pp. 565–573. Springer, Heidelberg (2002). https://doi.org/10.1007/3-540-48050-1_60
25. Nijenhuis, A., Wilf, H.S.: A method and two algorithms on the theory of partitions. J. Comb. Theory, Ser. A 18(2), 219–222 (1975)
26. Stojmenovic, I., Zoghbi, A.: Fast algorithms for generating integer partitions. Int. J. Comput. Math. 70(2), 319–332 (1998)
27. Tay, Y.C.: Data generation for application-specific benchmarking. PVLDB 4(12), 1470–1473 (2011)
28. Transaction Processing Performance Council, TPC: TCP Benchmarks & Benchmark Results. http://www.tpc.org

Machine Learning

Towards Proximity Graph Auto-configuration: An Approach Based on Meta-learning

Rafael Seidi Oyamada[1(✉)], Larissa C. Shimomura[2], Sylvio Barbon Junior[1], and Daniel S. Kaster[1]

[1] State University of Londrina, Londrina, PR, Brazil
{rseidi.oyamada,barbon,dskaster}@uel.br
[2] Eindhoven University of Technology, Eindhoven, The Netherlands
l.capobianco.shimomura@tue.nl

Abstract. Due to the high production of complex data, the last decades have provided a huge advance in the development of similarity search methods. Recently graph-based methods have outperformed other ones in the literature of approximate similarity search. However, a graph employed on a dataset may present different behaviors depending on its parameters. Therefore, finding a suitable graph configuration is a time-consuming task, due to the necessity to build a structure for each parameterization. Our main contribution is to save time avoiding this exhaustive process. We propose in this work an intelligent approach based on meta-learning techniques to recommend a suitable graph along with its set of parameters for a given dataset. We also present and evaluate generic and tuned instantiations of the approach using Random Forests as the meta-model. The experiments reveal that our approach is able to perform high quality recommendations based on the user preferences.

Keywords: Proximity graphs · Nearest neighbor search · Meta-learning · Auto configuration

1 Introduction

Dealing with complex data (images, long texts, audios, and etc.) is a typical task in different application areas, such as pattern recognition, image retrieval, data mining, etc. In general, complex data is represented through feature vectors composed of measures and properties extracted from the intrinsic content of the data and retrieved using dissimilarity relations between pairs of feature vectors. Those are known as *similarity queries*, as they retrieve the elements from the dataset that satisfy a given similarity-based criterion, such as the k-Nearest

This work has been supported by CAPES and CNPq funding agencies, and also has received funding from the European Union's Horizon 2020 research and innovation programme under grant agreement No 825041.

J. Darmont et al. (Eds.): ADBIS 2020, LNCS 12245, pp. 93–107, 2020.
https://doi.org/10.1007/978-3-030-54832-2_9

Neighbors query (*k-NNq*), which retrieves the k most similar elements the query element [20].

There are several access methods suitable for indexing complex data in the literature. These methods can be divided into four groups: tree-based [13], hashing-based [12], permutation-based [2], and *graph-based* [24]. In this paper, we focus on graph-based methods as recent works have shown that this method type has often outperformed other methods types in approximate similarity search [10,17,19].

Graph-based methods are very sensitive to user-defined parameters for both construction and querying. The graph structure is mainly affected by the number of neighbors an element (vertex) should be connected to. More edges in the graph generate shorter paths to be traversed. However, more edges increase the memory footprint, as well as the cost of vertex expansion during the search, since the adjacency of each vertex is larger. Additionally, depending on the graph structure, the query algorithm may not be able to find a path from the query element to every element that is part of the answer. A common approach to alleviate this problem is to execute a parameter defined number of traversals each of which is starting from a different source vertex. The number of traversals, or restarts, is also a sensible parameter as it allows improving the result accuracy at the cost of degrading the execution time. Setting suitable values for these parameters is hard as they depend on several factors, including the type of graph-based method, the dataset properties and the optimization goal (e.g., query time or memory requirements).

Recent works showed that there are no default parameters for graph-based methods (see [24] and the references therein). Considering the difficulty to reproduce experimental results for approximate nearest neighbor (ANN) algorithms in general, Aumüller et al. [3] proposed an automated benchmarking system for evaluating existing tree-based, hash-based, and graph-based methods. The authors performed experiments on different datasets so that future users can use it as a starting point for their applications. In our previous work, we performed a deep behavior analysis of graph-based methods given its settings, regarding several metrics, such as search and construction time, recall, and memory usage [24]. Our results indicated that it is not possible to assert that there is a better type of graph for all cases. Although these works identified general patterns that are useful to guide the choice of the type of graph and its parameters, it is hard to find good parametrizations for a variety of cases. Usually, a grid search procedure is employed to define a suitable graph configuration. However, this is time consuming and limited to the tested combinations.

In this paper, we propose a machine learning approach to recommend a suitable graph-based method as well as its main parameters for a given dataset and similarity query requirements. Our approach employs meta-learning techniques for providing high-performance configurations for each graph-based method by examining its dataset pattern. This work presents an instantiation of this approach for recommending parameters for dimensional datasets. The dataset characterization includes descriptions such as embedding and intrinsic dimensionality, cardinality, and statistical and information-theoretical measures. The prediction targets include query quality (in terms of query recall) and execution time, both measured using different types of graph-based methods over a collection of real and synthetic datasets. We trained a meta-model to predict the performance of the graph-based methods according to the dataset properties and query requirements to quickly evaluate characterizations to recommend the best predicted one. Our results using a Random Forest regressor have achieved a high-quality recommendation for most situations, which means that our proposal is able to generalize datasets to provide suitable configurations for graph-based methods for similarity retrieval of image databases.

This work is organized as follows. Section 2 describes the problem of parameter setting for graph-based methods for similarity searches as well as related works. Section 3 presents our approach based on meta-learning, and Sect. 4 presents the experimental evaluation and results. Lastly, on Sect. 5, we present our conclusion and future works.

2 Parameter Setting for Graph-Based Indexing Methods

The most common type of graph used for similarity searches is the proximity graph [24]. A proximity graph is a graph in which each pair of vertices $(v, u) \in V$ is connected by an edge $e = (u, v)$, $e \in E$, if and only if u and v satisfy a given property P, called neighborhood criterion, which defines the type of the graph.

Among the graph-based methods for similarity searches, the k-Nearest Neighbor Graph (k-NNG) [10,21] and the navigable small-world graph (NSW) [17] are two important types of graphs. The k-NNG has well-known properties that are useful for performing similarity searches and has been used as the base for several other graph-based methods. The brute-force construction of the k-NNG has a quadratic computational cost, other construction algorithms with lower cost have been proposed in the literature [22]. These construction algorithms generate an approximated version of the actual k-NN graph in a shorter time than the brute-force construction. One remarkable method is the NN-Descent [8] in which the main algorithm idea is "the neighbor of a neighbor is probably a neighbor". The Navigable Small World graph (NSW) is a recent proposal that is also based on connecting elements to their nearest neighbors, however, it uses short- and long-range undirected edges that grant the graph small-world properties [17]. The main advantages of the NSW are fast and highly precise approximate search execution thanks to the small-world properties, and its fast construction algorithm. Both the k-NNG and the NSW are sensible to construction parameters, particularly the number of neighbors of each vertex (NN)[1], which defines the number of edges in the graph. The parameter NN impacts both the query quality and the execution time since it affects the number and length of paths in the graph as well as the cost of evaluating the adjacency of each vertex.

There are different strategies to search for similar data in proximity graphs. The fundamental approach is to use spatial approximation, introduced by [20].

---

[1] In this paper we use NN to define the construction parameter number of neighbors of the graph-based methods, and k to define the query parameter number of neighbors in a k-NN query.

The spatial approximation property allows, starting the search from a source vertex traverse iteratively the graph using greedy steps to get spatially closer and closer to objects that are most similar to the query element. The Graph Nearest Neighbor Search (*GNNS*) is an effective algorithm that executes multiple greedy searches based on spatial approximation and aggregates the partial results into the final result [10]. In the *GNNS*, the multiple searches are called *restarts* (*R*), whose number is a user-defined parameter. The *R* parameter allows improving the quality of the result as each search starts from a different source and traverses a different path in the graph. Nevertheless, the number of restarts also impacts query execution time.

2.1   The Impact of Parameters for Graph-Based Methods

This section shows that defining suitable values for these parameters has a major impact on the effectiveness and performance of the methods and is a challenging problem. Our discussion considers typical scenarios.

The first scenario states that the user makes a careless choice and uses the same configuration across different datasets. This scenario usually happens when a configuration provides a good result for a given dataset. Then, for simplicity, the user replicates the "good" configuration for other datasets. To illustrate this scenario, we fixed the configuration, built a graph-based method for different datasets, executed *k-NN* queries using these indices, and analyzed the results. We ran this test using several configurations varying the graph type, and the construction and query parameters. Figure 1(a) shows results of a representative example, which corresponds to a *NN-Descent* graph set with $NN = 25$ running *k-NN* queries with $k = 30$ using the *GNNS* algorithm with $R = 10$ for all datasets used in this work (see details in Subsect. 3.1). The figure shows the distribution of the average recall rates throughout all datasets, being the recall rate for each dataset computed as the average recall for 100 queries with random query elements. The recall rate of a query is the fraction of the true *k*-nearest neighbors to the query element that is retrieved by the query. It is noticeable that the same set of parameters for distinct datasets leads to completely different quality rates for queries. Similar reasoning is also valid regarding query time.

The second scenario considers a single dataset. In this scenario, the user has to set the ideal parameters for the dataset subject to some constraints. Figure 1(b) presents the distribution of the average execution time for 30-*NN* queries using the *GNNS* search in the *NN-Descent*, considering different parameters, for the dataset *Color Histogram*, whose features are the 32-bin color histogram of a set of 68,040 images. The goal here is only to define the parameters *NN* and *R* for the *NN-Descent* for this dataset. The constraint is that the query should have a recall of at least 0.95. Analyzing the query time distribution, we can notice that almost two-thirds of the tested combinations of *NN* and *R* do not lie the first bucket, which means that the execution time is at least twice larger than the time demanded by the best configurations. The figure also shows the histogram of the configurations that lie in the first bucket. We can see that the variance regarding the average execution time is also large for the best configurations.

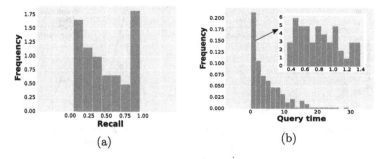

Fig. 1. Distribution of (a) recall rates given a fixed configuration over several datasets and (b) query times with recall > 0.95 varying configurations.

Additionally, regarding only the top-15 configurations, the methods present a variation of up to 50% in the execution time, which is significant.

The third scenario is the more complete one as it requires to choose the best graph type and its configuration for a given dataset. Figure 2 shows how the graph types *NSW* and *k-NNG* behave for increasing values for the *NN* parameter for the dataset Texture, which has texture features of 68,040 images. The figure shows the results for the *k-NNG* built using two construction algorithms: *NN-Descent* and brute-force (*Brute-kNNG*). Each point in the plots corresponds to the smallest number of restarts and, consequently, the smallest query time, for the corresponding type of graph and *NN* value that returned results subject to the constraint of having a recall of at least 0.95. Analyzing the plots, if the optimization goal is memory (i.e., the configuration that satisfies the constraint that consumes less memory), the best option is the *NSW* with *NN* = 5. On the other hand, if the optimization goal is query time (i.e., the fastest configuration that satisfies the constraint), we have two configurations that tie: *NSW* with *NN* = 100, and *NN-Descent* with *NN* = 130, being the latter the best cost-benefit option as it demands less memory than the former option. We can also see that choosing the graph type that is the fastest in general, which is the *NSW* in this case, but with a poor configuration (e.g., *NN* = 70), may be the worst option among the graph types. The opposite is also true since the *Brute-kNNG* is the slowest method in general, however, it is the fastest for *NN* = 150. Finally, the plots indicate that every method has an optimal configuration, which varies for different datasets and constraints. All of these reasons reinforce that the problem of recommending optimal parameters to configure graph-based methods is important and challenging.

2.2   Related Work

Works in the literature of similarity searches have defined such parameters based either on the user intuition or exhaustive evaluation. These approaches lead to suboptimal configurations and/or are excessively time consuming since the identification of adequate parameters is a challenging problem. Some works in the

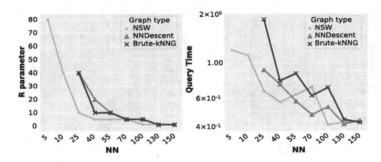

Fig. 2. a) Smallest number of restarts for each graph and *NN* value. b) Query time for the corresponding configurations of the plot on the left.

literature present extensive evaluations of access methods for similarity search. For instance, Li et al. performed a comprehensive experimental study on Approximate Nearest Neighbor (ANN) algorithms to provide a better understanding of their general behavior [16]. Similarly, the *ANN-Benchmark* was proposed to standardize the evaluation among ANN algorithms [3]. This benchmark works as a tool that enables comparing a wide range of ANN algorithms and its configuration over several real datasets. Specifically for graph-based methods, we performed an experimental evaluation in a previous work [24]. In this evaluation, we showed relevant trade-offs in the behavior of each graph according to several construction and search parameters. Although the performance patterns presented in these works can be useful, it is clear the difficulty of finding the ideal set of parameters for each algorithm considering the trade-offs among metrics, such as query time, and memory usage.

In the literature, there are works making use of machine learning concepts to advancing the state-of-the-art in database management [5,14]. However, none of them addresses parameter auto-configuration or algorithm selection. To the best of our knowledge, the only method of auto-selecting a suitable algorithm configuration for similarity searches was proposed by Muja and Lowe [18]. Their purpose is to minimize a cost function based on query time, indexing time, and memory usage. This is performed in two steps: first, a grid search strategy is used to find the parameter values that minimize the function; subsequently, a local exploration is realized to fine-tune the parameters obtained. A limitation of this work is the fact it only accepts tree-based methods.

Algorithm and parameter recommendation for machine-learning methods is an active research topic, and many successful approaches have relied on meta-learning [1,25]. Meta-learning differs from traditional learning methods (a.k.a. base-learning) in the notion of what to learn. Instead of producing a predictive function over a single problem domain, meta-learning attempts to gather knowledge from several domains to find patterns among them and provide suitable solutions for future problems. We can formally define meta-learning as follows [26]. Considering a task $t_i \in T$ (set of all tasks) along with its algorithm configuration $\theta_j \in \Theta$ (configuration space), we have a set of evaluations P, where

$P_{ij} = P(t_i, \theta_j)$ is the task t_i solved by the algorithm configuration θ_j according to a performance metric, e.g. accuracy or recall. The evaluations P refer to meta-instances, which are described through meta-features with the properties of the data enabling learning algorithms to find patterns among them, and the performances obtained by the evaluated algorithms/configurations in the different cases are the corresponding meta-targets. The meta-dataset is the set of meta-instances. A meta-model can be induced through P using the meta-dataset to predict or recommend a suitable algorithm configuration for a given new task. In this context, the novelty of our proposal is to apply meta-learning to recommend configurations of graph-based methods for similarity search.

3   A Meta-learning Approach for Proximity Graph Parameter Recommendation

This section presents a proposal of an intelligent system to recommend suitable configurations for proximity graphs, given a dataset, the optimization goal, and the search properties and constraints. Our approach employs meta-learning to induce regression meta-models able to predict the performance of query executions grounded on graph-based methods from complex data. A representative collection of datasets and diverse configurations of graph-based methods was applied to obtain a robust and general regression meta-model.

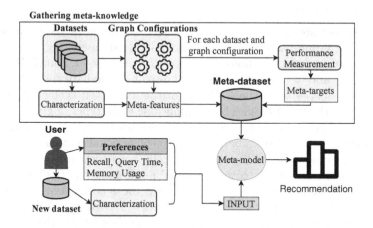

Fig. 3. Induction and usage of our proposed meta-learning recommender.

Figure 3 summarizes the process of the proposed recommender. It illustrates the steps of gathering meta-knowledge, inducting the meta-model, and generating the recommendations. The input is a set of datasets, a set of graph-based methods, and a set of parameter values. For each input dataset, we do a simple data augmentation by generating sub-datasets of smaller cardinalities and adding them to the set of datasets. The set of graph configurations are combinations of graph type and values for the considered parameters. For each dataset in the set of datasets, the recommender generates meta-instances that are composed of meta-features extracted from the dataset (Characterization) and a graph configuration. The meta-dataset is generated by meta-instances that associate the meta-features to meta-targets. A meta-target is a measure (e.g., average query time or recall) obtained by running batteries of queries using the graph-based method built for the dataset using the meta-instance's construction and query configuration values (Performance Measurement).

Then, the recommender applies a meta-learner to induce a meta-model, which is one or more regressors trained using the meta-dataset. To obtain a recommendation, a user provides a new dataset and some requirements, which include the constraints to be satisfied (e.g., minimum recall), and the optimization goal (e.g., query time or memory usage). The recommender establishes a set of meta-instances simulating different parametrizations for the input dataset and infers the corresponding performance measures (meta-targets). Finally, it ranks the meta-instances according to the performance measure and optimization goal and returns the top parametrization to the user. Notice that even though the performance measurement is hardware-dependent, an induced meta-model using meta-targets from this performance measurement should be effective for other hardware as our recommender is based on relative performances using ranking.

3.1 Overview of a Recommender Instantiation Using Random-Forests

This section details the main aspects of an instantiation of the proposed recommender for graph-based methods to index image datasets. For this work, we selected the graph-based methods *Brute-kNNG*, *NN-Descent*, and *NSW* because of their importance as base methods for approximate similarity search. We considered *k-NN* queries using the *GNNS* algorithm because it is efficient and flexible to improve the recall besides being applicable to all types of graphs selected. These types of graphs have the construction parameter *NN* in common, which refers to the number of neighbors each element is connected to in the graph. The *NN-Descent* and the *NSW* also have specific construction parameters whose impact is not as important to the methods' performance as the impact of the *NN* parameter [24]. Thus, we arbitrarily fixed these parameters values, being $\rho = 0.5$ for the *NN-Descent*, and *efConstruction* $= 100$ for the *NSW*. Therefore, given the user input, our proposal recommends the graph type, the construction parameter *NN*, and the query parameter *R*.

Input Datasets. We have employed real and synthetic datasets to analyze the behavior of each graph-based method for different configurations. The real datasets contain features from images: *Color Moments*, *Texture*, and *Color Histogram* are feature vectors extracted from 68,040 photos obtained from Corel, with dimensionalities 9, 16 and 32, respectively; *MNIST*, the pixels of a collection of 70,000 images of handwritten digits comprising 784 dimensions; and *ANN-SIFT1M*, which is a collection of 1,000,000 SIFT features (128 dimensions). The

63 synthetic datasets employed were generated following a Gaussian distribution, varying the size, the dimensionality, the number of clusters, and the distribution standard deviation, using the Python library Scikit-learn[2].

Meta-dataset. To build our meta-dataset we first performed the characterization of each dataset. Most of the meta-features employed were based on general (*cardinality, dimensionality*), statistical (*sd, skewness, t_mean, var, nr_norm, nr_outliers, median, min, range, iq_range, kurtosis, mad, max, mean*), and information-theoretical (*attr_ent, inst_to_attr*) measures[3]. We also included the Intrinsic Dimensionality (ID) of the datasets as it has often been employed in the field of similarity search to measure a dataset complexity [4]. We used the Maximum Likelihood Estimation [15] to estimate the ID, and the tool PyMFE [23] to extract the remaining measures from the datasets. Finally, the graph type and its configuration were also employed as meta-features.

The average query time and recall obtained by each configuration of each graph-based method were used as meta-targets in the meta-dataset. The performance measurement was performed using implementations in the C++ library NMSLib (Non-Metric Space Library) [6]. The queries employ the Euclidean distance (L_2). We used a superset of the results of the experiments carried on a previous work, which includes executions for combinations of the parameters $NN \in \{5, 10, 25, 40, 55, 70, 100, 130, 150\}$ and $R \in \{1, 5, 10, 20, 40, 80, 120, 160, 200, 240\}$. For additional details on the experiment settings, refer to [24].

Meta-model. We used the implementation for Random Forest on Scikit-learn (with the following parameters: $n\_estimators = 100$, $criterion = "mse"$, and $min\_samples\_split = 2$), to induce the meta-models, and a 5-fold Cross-Validation strategy to validate them. We selected the RF for its great prediction performance, reported in several recent works [9,11], simple parameterization [7], and capacity to evaluate feature importance. The recommender is composed by two Random Forests; one induced to predict the recall of a *k-NN* query using a specific graph configuration over a dataset, and the other to predict the query time. The recall is employed to filter the configurations that satisfy the user constraint about the minimum acceptable result quality while the query time is used for ranking the configurations according to the provided optimization (memory or query time).

4   Experimental Results

4.1   Analysis of Meta-feature Importance

Here we present an analysis of the importance rate of each meta-feature to predict the meta-target. These rates were measured by the meta-models performing a 5-fold cross validation over the meta-dataset. Results are presented in

---

[2] https://scikit-learn.org/.

[3] A detailed description of the general, statistical and information-theoretical meta-features is available in https://pymfe.readthedocs.io/en/latest/api.html.

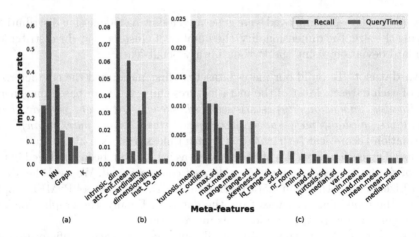

Fig. 4. The importance rate of each meta-feature per meta-target and category: (a) graph configurations, (b) general and info-theoretical, and (c) statistical.

Fig. 4. Overall, for both meta-targets evaluated, the most relevant meta-features were the construction parameter NN, the search parameters R and k and, the graph type. Nonetheless, other features also contribute to the prediction. In the meta-models, for each tree split from a set of descriptors, all the following splits depend on the graph type and its parameters, as these are the meta-features that refine and determine the final behavior of the proximity graph over a given set of dataset descriptors. Regarding recall, we can observe that the most relevant meta-feature is the construction parameter NN. This is implied by the fact that the more edges a graph has, the better its query recall rate is. Similarly, for query time, we have the query parameter R as the most important meta-feature as the higher the number of restarts R is, the longer the query execution time is, and vice-versa. Moreover, the high importance rate of the ID measure for recall analysis is an interesting result. Excluding the graph configuration meta-features, the ID had the highest rate, thus, the embedding dimensionality showed no relevance in this case.

4.2   Prediction Accuracy of the Meta-models

Subsequently, we present our results on the prediction accuracy of the meta-models regarding the real datasets used in this work. The synthetic datasets were added to the meta-database to provide a wider diversity of dataset characteristics. We evaluated our approach by using three different strategies: i) generic meta-model (GMM) – all meta-instances of our meta-dataset regarding all datasets were used for meta-training, except for the meta-instances regarding the goal dataset, which was used for meta-testing; ii) tuned meta-model using grid search (TMM-GS) – all meta-instances of our meta-dataset regarding all datasets (except for the ones regarding the goal dataset) plus meta-instances generated by the grid search performed over the goal dataset were used for

Table 1. Relative performances of the generic and tuned meta-models.

Goal Dataset	GMM				TMM-GS				TMM-S			
	Recall		Query Time		Recall		Query Time		Recall		Query Time	
	r^2	RMSE	r^2	RMSE	r^2	RMSE	r^2	RMSE	r^2	RMSE	r^2	RMSE
Histogram	0.350	0.135	0.980	0.249	0.605	0.130	0.961	0.338	0.996	0.012	0.998	0.068
MNIST	0.765	0.111	0.694	1.097	0.617	0.173	0.920	0.559	0.997	0.014	0.998	0.068
Moments	0.955	0.034	0.989	0.179	0.973	0.031	0.979	0.241	0.991	0.019	0.998	0.065
SIFT	0.807	0.132	0.932	0.524	0.568	0.247	0.803	0.932	0.983	0.049	0.984	0.260
Texture	0.978	0.024	0.962	0.344	0.990	0.022	0.951	0.378	0.996	0.012	0.998	0.058

meta-training and the goal dataset was used for testing; and iii) tuned meta-model using subsets (*TMM-S*) – meta-instances of our meta-dataset regarding all synthetic datasets (except for the ones regarding the goal dataset) plus meta-instances of subsets of the real datasets were used for meta-training, the remaining meta-instances were used for meta-testing. The first strategy simulates generating a recommendation for an unseen input dataset; the second one simulates a fine tuning of the meta-models by increasing the meta-dataset with meta-instances generated by a grid search with a limited parameter space; and lastly, the third one simulates a scenario in which the meta-model already knows datasets with similar properties to the input dataset.

Table 1 presents the relative performance achieved by each induced meta-model considering two evaluation metrics: the Coefficient of Determination (r^2) and the Root Mean Squared Error (*RMSE*). Both measure the predicted values by meta-models against true values (reached by the graph-based methods). Good fits for these metrics are, respectively, high and low values. From the results, we can observe that the strategy using the generic meta-models (GMM) reached good scores for query time and fair scores for recall for most of the datasets. This is because meta-features were more supplementary for query time than for recall. For TMM-GS, it was expected a small improvement compared to the GMM. Although in the most cases the performance was relatively similar, at final recommendation the TMM-GS outperformed GMM (further details in the next section). On the other hand, the most tuned meta-model TMM-S achieved high scores for both recall and query time. Therefore, by investing some effort to generate meta-instances of the goal dataset, the user can achieve a superior recommendation.

4.3   Effectiveness of the Recommendation

Lastly, we discuss the effectiveness of the recommendation provided by our approaches compared to a Grid Search (GS). We emulated a grid search using the subset of entries in the meta-dataset such that $NN = \{1, 25, 70, 150\}$ and $R = \{1, 10, 40, 120\}$. These were the same parameters used to evaluate the *TMM-GS*. In this analysis, we set the constraint of achieving a minimum average recall of 0.90 and evaluated two optimization criteria: (a) the shortest query time, and

(b) the lowest memory usage. Figure 5 presents the recommendations provided by the differents strategies according to each criteria. The figures (a)–(c), refer to memory optimization, and the figures (d)–(f) refer to query time optimization.

Figure 5(a) and (d) show recommendations for subsets of *Color Histogram*, and Fig. 5(b) and (e) of *Color Moments*. For memory optimization, the GMM overcame the GS in all cases, reaching the optimal most times. For query time optimization, the GMM performed worse than GS around $\frac{1}{4}$ of the times, where one of them was a wrong recommendation. We consider a wrong recommendation when the method fails to satisfy the recall constraint due to a poor prediction. In these cases, the *NN* or the query time provided by the meta-models may be smaller than the optimal values (e.g., Fig. 5(e) for $8k$ instances).

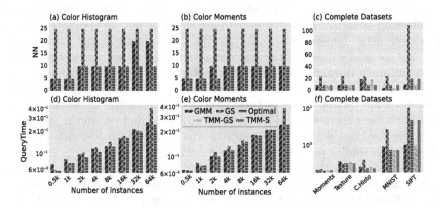

Fig. 5. Comparison of the recommendations provided by the methods.

Figure 5(c) and Fig. 5(f) show recommendations for the complete datasets provided by all the methods, including the meta-models TMM-GS and TMM-S. Overall, the TMM-GS outperformed the GMM, and the TMM-S was the best strategy, consistently reaching the optimal. For the datasets *Color Moments*, *Texture* and *Color Histogram*, our meta-models were more effective than the GS. However, for the datasets *MNIST* and *SIFT*, which are the most complex datasets used in this work due to their high dimensionality, the GMM and the TMM-GS provided wrong recommendations while the TMM-S achieved optimal results.

To better understand how much the strategies provide wrong predictions, Fig. 6 shows the true recall rates with their corresponding predictions split into intervals. In Fig. 6(a), we can observe that the GMM is able to provide predictions very close to the true values for most of the tested cases, however, it falls short for *SIFT* (Fig. 6(b)). Nevertheless, Fig. 6(c) presents the performance reached by the TMM-S where there was a huge improvement. Such a behavior not only reinforces the need of continuously enhancing the meta-dataset to improve the model generalization, but also highlights the power of our tuning proposal.

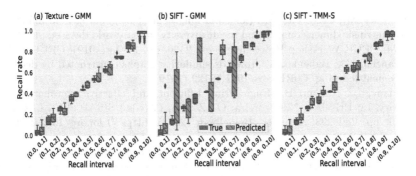

Fig. 6. Accuracy of the predictions of the meta-models per recall interval.

5   Conclusion and Further Research

In this paper, we proposed an intelligent approach capable of recommending a graph-based method and its configurations to perform similarity searches. The main idea consists in using meta-learning techniques to estimate the relative performance of different graph configurations for the given dataset to select the most suitable one. We presented an Instantiation of our approach for image databases using Random Forests. We also evaluated three variations of this instantiation, GMM, TMM-GS and TMM-S, and compared them to a standard grid search.

Our results showed that, for many situations, the generic approach GMM tied or outperformed the grid search, without requiring the user to execute performance measures on the goal dataset. However, it failed to provide valid recommendations for the most complex datasets tested. The tuned approach TMM-GS improved over GMM, nevertheless, it still provided a few invalid recommendations. On the other hand, the approach tuned with subsets, TMM-S, approached the optimal results, but it is an expensive approach though.

For future works, we intend to generate other instances of our approach with richer meta-databases, exploring more meta-features to describe the input datasets and including other meta-targets, such as construction time and real memory usage to store the structure.

References

1. Aguiar, G.J., Mantovani, R.G., Mastelini, S.M., de Carvalho, A.C.P.L.F., Campos, G.F.C., Junior, S.B.: A meta-learning approach for selecting image segmentation algorithm. Pattern Recognit. Lett. **128**, 480–487 (2019)
2. Amato, G., Gennaro, C., Savino, P.: MI-File: using inverted files for scalable approximate similarity search. Multimedia Tools Appl. **71**(3), 1333–1362 (2014)
3. Aumüller, M., Bernhardsson, E., Faithfull, A.J.: ANN-benchmarks: a benchmarking tool for approximate nearest neighbor algorithms. In: Beecks, C., Borutta, F., Kröger, P., Seidl, T. (eds.) SISAP, pp. 34–49. Springer, Cham (2017). https://doi.org/10.1007/978-3-319-68474-1_3

4. Aumüller, M., Ceccarello, M.: Benchmarking nearest neighbor search: influence of local intrinsic dimensionality and result diversity in real-world datasets. In: EDML SDM. CEUR Workshop Proceedings, vol. 2436, pp. 14–23 (2019). CEUR-WS.org
5. Baranchuk, D., Babenko, A.: Towards similarity graphs constructed by deep reinforcement learning. CoRR abs/1911.12122 (2019)
6. Boytsov, L., Naidan, B.: Engineering Efficient and effective non-metric space library. In: Brisaboa, N., Pedreira, O., Zezula, P. (eds.) SISAP 2013. LNCS, vol. 8199, pp. 280–293. Springer, Heidelberg (2013). https://doi.org/10.1007/978-3-642-41062-8_28
7. Breiman, L.: Random forests. Mach. Learn. **45**(1), 5–32 (2001)
8. Dong, W., Charikar, M., Li, K.: Efficient k-nearest neighbor graph construction for generic similarity measures. In: WWW, pp. 577–586. ACM (2011)
9. Eggensperger, K., Lindauer, M., Hoos, H.H., Hutter, F., Leyton-Brown, K.: Efficient benchmarking of algorithm configurators via model-based surrogates. Mach. Learn. **107**(1), 15–41 (2017). https://doi.org/10.1007/s10994-017-5683-z
10. Hajebi, K., Abbasi-Yadkori, Y., Shahbazi, H., Zhang, H.: Fast approximate nearest-neighbor search with k-nearest neighbor graph. In: Walsh, T. (ed.) IJCAI, pp. 1312–1317. IJCAI/AAAI (2011)
11. Hutter, F., Xu, L., Hoos, H.H., Leyton-Brown, K.: Algorithm runtime prediction: methods & evaluation. Artif. Intell. **206**, 79–111 (2014)
12. Indyk, P., Motwani, R.: Approximate nearest neighbors: towards removing the curse of dimensionality. In: Vitter, J.S. (ed.) STOC, pp. 604–613. ACM (1998)
13. Traina, C., Traina, A., Seeger, B., Faloutsos, C.: Slim-trees: high performance metric trees minimizing overlap between nodes. In: Zaniolo, C., Lockemann, P.C., Scholl, M.H., Grust, T. (eds.) EDBT 2000. LNCS, vol. 1777, pp. 51–65. Springer, Heidelberg (2000). https://doi.org/10.1007/3-540-46439-5_4
14. Kraska, T., Beutel, A., Chi, E.H., Dean, J., Polyzotis, N.: The case for learned index structures. In: Das, G., Jermaine, C.M., Bernstein, P.A. (eds.) SIGMOD, pp. 489–504. ACM (2018)
15. Levina, E., Bickel, P.J.: Maximum likelihood estimation of intrinsic dimension. In: NIPS, pp. 777–784 (2004)
16. Li, W., Zhang, Y., Sun, Y., Wang, W., Zhang, W., Lin, X.: Approximate nearest neighbor search on high dimensional data - experiments, analyses, and improvement (v1.0). CoRR abs/1610.02455 (2016)
17. Malkov, Y., Ponomarenko, A., Logvinov, A., Krylov, V.: Approximate nearest neighbor algorithm based on navigable small world graphs. Inf. Syst. **45**, 61–68 (2014)
18. Muja, M., Lowe, D.G.: Fast approximate nearest neighbors with automatic algorithm configuration. In: VISAPP, pp. 331–340. INSTICC Press (2009)
19. Naidan, B., Boytsov, L., Nyberg, E.: Permutation search methods are efficient, yet faster search is possible. PVLDB **8**(12), 1618–1629 (2015)
20. Navarro, G.: Searching in metric spaces by spatial approximation. VLDB J. **11**(1), 28–46 (2002)
21. Paredes, R., Chávez, E.: Using the k-nearest neighbor graph for proximity searching in metric spaces. In: Consens, M., Navarro, G. (eds.) SPIRE 2005. LNCS, vol. 3772, pp. 127–138. Springer, Heidelberg (2005). https://doi.org/10.1007/11575832_14
22. Paredes, R., Chávez, E., Figueroa, K., Navarro, G.: Practical construction of k-nearest neighbor graphs in metric spaces. In: Àlvarez, C., Serna, M. (eds.) WEA 2006. LNCS, vol. 4007, pp. 85–97. Springer, Heidelberg (2006). https://doi.org/10.1007/11764298_8

23. Rivolli, A., Garcia, L.P.F., Soares, C., Vanschoren, J., de Carvalho, A.C.P.L.F.: Towards reproducible empirical research in meta-learning. CoRR abs/1808.10406 (2018)
24. Shimomura, L.C., Oyamada, R.S., Vieira, M.R., Kaster, D.S.: A survey on graph-based methods for similarity searches in metric spaces. Inf. Syst. 101507 (2020)
25. Smith-Miles, K.A.: Towards insightful algorithm selection for optimisation using meta-learning concepts. In: IJCNN, pp. 4118–4124. IEEE (2008)
26. Vanschoren, J.: Meta-learning: a survey. CoRR abs/1810.03548 (2018)

Fake News Detection Based on Subjective Opinions

Danchen Zhang[✉] and Vladimir I. Zadorozhny

School of Computing and Information, University of Pittsburgh, Pittsburgh, USA
{daz45,viz}@pitt.edu

Abstract. Fake news fluctuates social media, leading to harmful consequences. Several types of information could be utilized to detect fake news, such as news content features and news propagation features. In this study, we focus on the user spreading news behaviors on social media platforms and aim to detect fake news more effectively with more accurate data reliability assessment. We introduce Subjective Opinions into reliability evaluation and proposed two new methods. Experiments on two popular real-world datasets, BuzzFeed and PolitiFact, validates that our proposed Subjective Opinions based method can detect fake news more accurately than all existing methods, and another proposed probability based method achieves state-of-art performance.

Keywords: Fake news detection · Data reliability assessment · Subjective opinions

1 Introduction

In recent years, social media, such as Facebook, Twitter, and WeChat, provides users with direct and instant communications, and people spend more and more time on these platforms. Increasingly, social media become a primary source for people to read the news. A survey from Pew Research Center, an internet research company, shows that 62% of United States adults get news from social media [1]. However, there are no rules for people to produce and spread the news in social media, and hence misinformation could spread more quickly and widely in our society. Consequently, fake news detection draws researchers' increasing attention. According to statistic data in [2], more and more works are devoted to this area.

When detecting fake news, many features and information could be considered, such as news content, news publisher profiles, and data generated in news propagation [2–6]. In this study, we focus on news user interaction in social media. More specifically, the network data constructed by the news and the users who spread the news. In such a network, some news is fake, and other news is real. Researchers could manually collect a set of news and have experts assign labels for the news veracity, and then build models to automatically predict the other unlabeled news.

© Springer Nature Switzerland AG 2020
J. Darmont et al. (Eds.): ADBIS 2020, LNCS 12245, pp. 108–121, 2020.
https://doi.org/10.1007/978-3-030-54832-2_10

Since the users may spread both real and fake news, the unlabeled news may be real or maybe fake. Reliability is a quantified measure of uncertainty about an event [8]. In this study, we define **user reliability** as the reliability of a user spreading real news, i.e., more reliable users spread more real news than fake news; less reliable users spread more fake news than real news. Besides, we define **news reliability** as the reliability of the news being real and will propose models to automatically learn the news reliability based on its related users' reliability.

It is natural to use probability to evaluate the user reliability, i.e., the reliability of a user is the probability that she/he spreads the real news. However, the effectiveness of probability depends on the observed sample size. For example, if we observe the user shares 100 real news and 0 fake news, we could say this user is 100% reliable; if we only observe the user spreads a piece of real news and the veracity of the other 99 news that the user shared remains unknown, we cannot describe this user as 100% reliable.

In reliability assessment, users spreading more unlabeled news should be more uncertain than those spreading more labeled news, and past studies [9–11] fail to consider such uncertainty in their model comprehensively. Therefore, in this study, we propose a new reliability representation and correspondingly a new fake news detection model, which could deal with uncertainty in a better way, and thus detect the fake news more accurately.

Subjective Opinions, proposed by Jøsang, describe the probability affected by the degrees of uncertainty, and Subjective Logic is a calculus for Subjective Opinions [12]. We propose the Subjective Opinions based reliability representation. A subjective opinion from a person p towards a statement s can be represented by a triple $\omega_s^p = \{t, d, u\}$, with $t, d, u \in [0,1]$, and $t + d + u = 1$. In this triple, t means trust, d means distrust, and u means uncertainty. Given the above example, when we observe the user sharing a lot of real news and no fake news, our opinion towards the statement "this user is reliable" or "this user spreads real news" can be represented as $\{0.98, 0.0, 0.02\}$. Then, when we observe the user sharing a few real news but majority news veracity stays unknown, we are highly uncertain about the user, and our opinion could be $\{0.1, 0.0, 0.9\}$. In this way, with Subjective Opinions based reliability, we could see the difference between two users.

The main contributions of this paper include:

- We are first to introduce Subjective Opinions into the fake news detection area.
- We propose a Subjective Opinion based model and a Probability based model to detect fake news automatically.
- We conduct extensive experiments on two real-world datasets, validate our proposed methods' effectiveness, and compare them in several aspects.

We introduced the background and motivation in Sect. 1 and discuss related works in Sect. 2. Next, we present our two proposed methods in Sect. 3. The experiments, results, and discussions are shown in Sect. 4 and 5. Lastly, the paper is concluded in Sect. 6.

2   Related Works

Several recent survey papers encompass the full range of research devoted to fake news [2–6]. Fake news detection mainly uses three types of information: (1) the content of news articles, including word-level, syntactic level, and semantic level information, (2) news propagation data on social networks, such as user profiles, news profiles, spreading data, and (3) network structure extracted from news articles and social media. Past works usually learn a classification model with these features to detect fake news automatically.

At the early stage of fake news detection, word level and syntactic level features were the most useful features. Several studies [14–17] show that bag-of-words features give a very effective way to reveal the linguistic cues of deception. Then, the syntactic features, such as the distribution of POS tagger and n-grams, are also able to capture the unique features of fake news [18–21]. Later, the development of neural networks in natural language processing (NLP) allows the semantic features to be extracted, further improving the detection performance, such as works in [22–24]. These studies show that both word and syntactic information are essential, and the extraction of high-quality semantic features can further increase detection effectiveness.

Meanwhile, many researchers explore news propagation features, such as the number of likes, propagation times, and related user profiles. However, many studies have found that systems cannot accurately detect fake news if they only use social network features. These features are usually used together with content mentioned above features, such as works in [17,25,26].

Besides, multiple network structures can be extracted from the news related data, such as user-follow-user networks, news-agree/conflict-news networks, publisher-publish-news network, and user-spread-news networks [9–11,27–30]. In this study, we focus on the user-spread-news network, and hence we chose the state-of-art methods Harmonic [9], HC-CB-3 [10], and TriFN [11] as baselines, which will be discussed more in Sect. 4.

To the best of our knowledge, this work is the first to apply Subjective Opinions to the area of fake news detection. Before this, it is widely used in many other areas, including trust network analysis [31], conditional inference [32], information provider reliability assessment [33], trust management in sensor networks [34]. In one of our earlier works [35], Subjective Opinions is introduced for Truth Discovery. With the data represented and recorded more comprehensively, our proposed Subjective Opinions based method is expected to have a better performance than the probability based method.

3   Proposed Methods

Consider a dataset that contains a set of news $News = \{news_1, news_2, ...,$ $news_n\}$, and a set of users $Users = \{user_1, user_2, ..., user_m\}$. Users could share the news on social media. Such data could be represented as a matrix shown in Table 1. Each row corresponds to a piece of news, each column corresponds to

Table 1. The dataset is represented by a matrix, with n news and m users.

	user$_1$	user$_2$	...	user$_m$
news$_1$	*share*	–	...	*share*
news$_2$	–	*share*	...	–
...	...	...	...	...
news$_n$	–	–	...	*share*

a user, and the cell values show whether the user shares news or not. Also, we assume that the veracity labels for a subset of news are known, and the veracity labels for the rest news need to be predicted.

In this study, we propose two semi-supervised models to evaluate the reliability for users and news, and the news reliability scores decide the news veracity. In the first model, news and user reliability is evaluated with probability and is named as **Prob_fnd**. In the second model, the reliability is evaluated with Subjective Opinions and is named as **SO_fnd**. Both two models consist of three steps: (1) update user reliability based on news labels; (2) update news reliability based on user reliability; (3) predict and update labels for news that are not in training data. These three steps iteratively run until the reliability scores converge. We find that our methods usually converge within three iterations. Table 2 compares each step of Prob_fnd and SO_fnd, and we can see that the main difference is whether probability or Subjective Opinion is used, and correspondingly whether the unknown data are ignored or recorded.

Table 2. Comparison of Prob_fnd and SO_fnd

Steps	Prob_fnd	SO_fnd
Step 1: Update *user_reliability*	Use **Probability** to describe our belief in a user sharing real news **Ignore unknown cases**	Use **Subjective Opinions** to describe our belief in a user sharing real news. **Record unknown cases with uncertainty**
Step 2: Update *news_reliability*	Use **Average** to fuse related users' reliability	Use **Consensus** to fuse related users' reliability
Step 3: Update news veracity	Predict with *news_reliability*	Predict with *news_reliability*

3.1 Method 1: Probability Based Fake News Detection (Prob_fnd)

Step-1: evaluate user reliability. For each user $user_i$, the reliability is defined as the probability that this user shares the real news, and hence we have the following formula:

$$user\_reliability(user_i) = \frac{\#(r\_n)}{\#(r\_n) + \#(f\_n)}, \tag{1}$$

where $\#(r\_n)$ is the count of real news that $user_i$ shared, and $\#(f\_n)$ is the count of fake ones. In early iterations, if the veracity of the news that the $user_i$ shared is not predicted yet, this news is not counted in this formula; if all news veracity that $user_i$ shared are unknown, reliability cannot be judged and $user_i$ is temporarily classified as unknown users.

Step-2: evaluate news reliability. For each news $news_j$, we collect all users who shared it and define the news reliability as the average $user\_reliability$ of these related users, and we have the following formula:

$$news\_reliability(news_j) = Average(user\_reliability(related\ users)). \tag{2}$$

In early iterations, if a user's reliability is unknown yet, it is temporarily ignored; if all related users' reliability is unknown, the reliability of this news will be calculated in the future iteration and temporarily classified as unknown news. Please note that we also tried to use the Median to replace Average, and experiment results show no significant difference.

Step-3: predict news veracity. Then, $\{news\_reliability\}$ is used as the feature and is put into Support Vector Machine (SVM) to learn a classification model to automatically determine the veracity label for the news. Only the news labels in training data are used as initial labels, and the model will predict veracity labels for the news in testing data.

3.2 Method 2: Subjective Opinions Based Fake News Detection (SO_fnd)

In the second method, we replace probability with Subjective Opinions. As described in Sect. 1, people's subjective opinion towards a statement can be represented as a triple $\{trust, distrust, uncertainty\}$. Information of unknown users and news is not kept in Prob_fnd, while we record such information with the $uncertainty$ in SO_fnd, and hope that reliability assessment could be more accurate with more comprehensive information considered. SO_fnd also consists of three steps, as shown below.

Step-1: evaluate user reliability. User reliability is defined as our opinion towards the statement "$user_i$ is reliable", which is defined as:

$$user\_reliability(user_i) = \{user\_trust, user\_distrust, user\_uncertainty\}, \tag{3}$$

where

$$\begin{cases} user\_trust = \frac{\#(r\_n)}{\#(r\_n)+\#(f\_n)+\#(u\_n)} * (1-\alpha), \\ user\_distrust = \frac{\#(f\_n)}{\#(r\_n)+\#(f\_n)+\#(u\_n)} * (1-\alpha), \\ user\_uncertainty = \frac{\#(u\_n)}{\#(r\_n)+\#(f\_n)+\#(u\_n)} * (1-\alpha) + \alpha. \end{cases} \tag{4}$$

α is a constant, representing people's natural uncertainty. $\#(u\_n)$ is the count of unknown news that this user shared. If all news veracity that a user shared are unknown, reliability of this user is $\{0, 0, 1\}$.

Step-2: evaluate news reliability. For each news, we collect all users who shared it and cumulatively fuse these users' reliability with Subjective Logic consensus operation (See more information about consensus operation in [13]). The fused opinion represents our belief for the statement "$news_j$ is real".

$$news\_reliability(news_j) = user_1\_reliability \oplus user_2\_reliability\oplus$$
$$... \oplus user_k\_reliability, \tag{5}$$

where $user_1$, $user_2$,..., $user_k$ are the users that shared $news_j$. The obtained $news\_reliability$ is a triple, as shown in:

$$news\_reliability(news_j) = \{news\_trust, news\_distrust,$$
$$news\_uncertainty\}. \tag{6}$$

Step-3: predict news veracity based on reliability. There are a lot of unknown users and news in the first iteration, leading to high *uncertainty* in reliability assessment, making the news veracity prediction more challenging than that in later iterations. If in such an uncertain situation, given a piece of news, the model could accumulate high enough *news_distrust*, we are confident to predict that this news is fake. Thus, we use $\{news\_distrust\}$ as the feature and put it into SVM to learn a classification model to predict the news veracity automatically (see more discussion about classifier and feature selection in Sect. 4 and 5).

Next, from the second iteration, with the number of unknown users and news decreasing, the situation is less uncertain, and the reliability assessment is hence more convincing. Then the news veracity is decided by comparing *news_trust* and *news_distrust*. I.e., the news with higher *news_trust* are predicted to be real, and ones with higher *news_distrust* are predicted to be fake.

4 Experiments

4.1 Data

FakeNewsNet [36] is selected as the validation dataset in this study. It consists of two real-world datasets, BuzzFeed and PolitiFact. BuzzFeed contains 90 real news and 90 fake news, with 15,257 users interacting with (re-tweet or like) the news. PolitiFact contains 120 real news, 120 fake news, and 23,865 users interacting with the news.

In the preprocessing procedure, if a user ($user_i$) shares only one piece of news ($news_j$), this user is removed. The reason is that (1) if the $news_j$ veracity is unknown, we cannot infer $user_i$ reliability, and hence $user_i$ cannot provide information; (2) if the $news_j$ veracity is known, as $user_i$ does not share other news, model needs no information from it. Please note that, after preprocessing, if the news no longer has related users, we directly label it as fake news and do not update its label in iterations. We do know such a straightforward strategy may lead to failure, but such loss on unpopular news is acceptable in real-world scenarios.

After preprocessing, 3,002 users are left in BuzzFeed, and 4,139 users are left in PolitiFact. Also, we find the PolitiFact data is denser than BuzzFeed data, i.e., people share more news in PolitiFact.

4.2 Experiment Settings

Following procedures in [9–11], we learn and evaluate our models with 5-fold cross-validation, i.e., 20% of data is used as testing, while 80% of data is used to train the model. Each cross-validation is repeated 50 times, and the average performance with standard deviation is reported. Accuracy, Precision, Recall, and F1 of detecting fake news are selected as the evaluation metrics.

Prob_fnd has no parameters, while SO_fnd has one parameter α, which describes people's natural uncertainty. Following [9–11], we select $\alpha = 0.9$, because it achieves the highest performance with both datasets in cross-validation.

Please note that, in Step-3 of both Prob_fnd and SO_fnd, SVM is used to predict news veracity. We tried different classification models, including SVM, Naive Bayes, Decision Tree, Random Forest, and Logistic Regression. We found that SVM could provide the best performance for two models on two datasets. Besides, with different α in SO_fnd, SVM provides more robust performance than other models. Therefore, in this study, SVM is selected.

4.3 Baselines

Harmonic from [9]. This method is very similar to our proposed Prob_fnd, iteratively evaluating the reliability scores of both users and news, and both methods ignore the unknown news and users in the calculation. The major difference is that Harmonic explicitly differentiate reliable users from unreliable users, and real news is those that accumulate more scores from reliable users, while fake news is those that accumulate more scores from unreliable users. On the other hand, in Prob_fnd, news reliability is defined as the average reliability of the users that shared it without explicitly different reliable and unreliable users.

HC-CB-3 from [10]. This method is developed based on Harmonic. It utilizes the word-level features of news content with a logistic regression model. If the news is shared by more than λ people, social-network based Harmonic is used; otherwise, content based classification is used.

TriFN from [11]. This method designed a Tri-Relationship embedding framework, which utilizes the information from news content, news-user interaction, and news-publisher relationship. TriFN shows much better performance than several other baselines, which use content based or social-network based features, and they are not included in this paper due to page limit.

4.4 Results

Experiment results are shown in Table 3, and their comparison is better illustrated in Fig. 1. Best and second-best performed runs are labeled with '**' and '*'. In this study, the Wilcoxon Signed Ranks test is only conducted among the results of Prob_fnd and SO_fnd. As baseline papers only report the averaged results with standard deviation, the significance test cannot be conducted. Since all standard deviation values are relatively small (<0.1), when comparing the model performance in this section, we are comparing the reported average values.

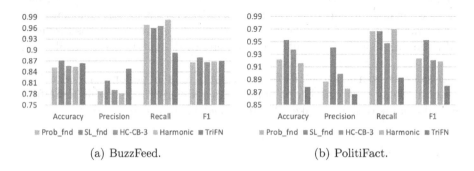

(a) BuzzFeed.   (b) PolitiFact.

Fig. 1. Repeated 5-fold cross-validation results on two real-world datasets.

Table 3. Repeated 5-fold cross-validation results on two real-world datasets.

		Prob_fnd	SO_fnd	HC-CB-3	Harmonic	TriFN
BuzzFeed	Accuracy	.852 ± .055	**.871 ± .051****	.856 ± .052	.854 ± .052	.864 ± .026*
	Precision	.788 ± .086	.816 ± .079*	.791 ± .076	.782 ± .075	**.849 ± .040****
	Recall	.969 ± .043*	.960 ± .004	.966 ± .045	**.983 ± .041****	.893 ± .013
	F1	.866 ± .052	**.880 ± .050****	.867 ± .050	.869 ± .050	.870 ± .019*
PolitiFact	Accuracy	.922 ± .036	**.953 ± .029****	.938 ± .029*	.916 ± .042	.878 ± .020
	Precision	.887 ± .056	**.941 ± .048****	.899 ± .057*	.876 ± .074	.867 ± .034
	Recall	.967 ± .034*	.967 ± .034*	.948 ± .046	**.970 ± .030****	.893 ± .023
	F1	.924 ± .035*	**.953 ± .030****	.921 ± .041	.919 ± .044	.880 ± .017

x^{**}: the run with the best performance.
x^*: the run with the second best performance.

Our proposed SO_fnd has the best performance on reported Accuracy and F1 in both datasets. To be more specific, on the BuzzFeed dataset, SO_fnd got the best Accuracy 87.1% and F1 score 88.0%, and second-best precision

81.6%; on the PolitiFact dataset, SO_fnd has the best Accuracy 95.3%, F1 score 95.3%, precision 94.1%, and second-best recall 96.7%. It shows that SO_fnd can differentiate fake news from real news much more accurately than other methods. Besides, on both datasets, we find that SO_fnd significantly outperforms Prob_fnd on Accuracy, Precision, and F1 $(p-value < 0.01)$. It indicates that keeping a record of unknown cases as an uncertainty value is essential, which can highly improve the fake news detection accuracy.

We can also see that on two datasets, both the baselines and our proposed methods have lower precision and higher recall. It indicates that most fake news could be correctly detected, but many pieces of real news are wrongly classified as fake news. Such a model is better than one with higher precision and lower recall. The reasons are: (1) the broad propagation of fake news may lead to inestimable damages, and hence we could sacrifice some real news to get a high recall on fake news detection; (2) we can hire experts to check these identified fake news manually, and since the data size decreases a lot, the manual effort cost is lowered down; (3) if a piece of real news is falsely recognized as fake news and removed, people could still search online or ask experts if they really need it.

Besides, we can find that Prob_fnd has very similar performance with Harmonic, implying that whether or not explicitly differentiate reliable users from unreliable users does not make a big difference in these two datasets.

5   Discussion

5.1   Is SO_fnd Performance Sensitive to Natural Uncertainty Parameter?

SO_fnd has one parameter α, which describes people's natural/basic uncertainty. Above reported results are obtained when $\alpha = 0.9$, which is the highest performance with both datasets in cross-validation. We report the Accuracy and F1 of SO_fnd when α changes in range $[0.1, 0.9]$. We repeat the cross-validation procedure 50 times, and the average performance is reported in Fig. 2.

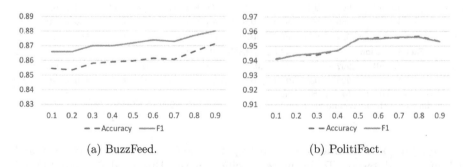

(a) BuzzFeed.   (b) PolitiFact.

Fig. 2. Accuracy and F1 of SO_fnd varying with different α on BuzzFeed and PolitiFact.

From Fig. 2, we can observe that though SO_fnd prefers larger α in both datasets when α varies across $[0.1, 0.9]$, the accuracy and F1 do not change a lot, with the increments less than 2%. It shows SO_fnd is relatively robust to the parameter α in range $[0.1, 0.9]$.

5.2 How Does the Training Data Size Affect the Performance of the Methods?

In this subsection, we explored the performance of Prob_fnd and SO_fnd when they are trained by different sizes of data. As shown in Fig. 3, the size of training data increases from 10% to 90%, and the accuracy is evaluated for each model on both BuzzFeed and PolitiFact. We repeat the training and testing procedure 50 times for each run, and the average performance is reported.

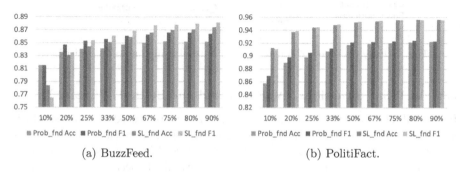

(a) BuzzFeed.   (b) PolitiFact.

Fig. 3. Accuracy and F1 of Prob_fnd and SO_fnd varying with different training data size on BuzzFeed and PolitiFact.

From Fig. 3, we can observe that, Accuracy and F1 score of Prob_fnd and SO_fnd all increase in both datasets when training data size rises. Also, SO_fnd's performance outperforms Prob_fnd in most cases, except when they are trained with 20% or less data on BuzzFeed.

Shu et al. reported TriFN's performance with the different training set sizes in [11]. On BuzzFeed, when training data is 40% and less, TriFN's Accuracy and F1 is less than 80%; however, Prob_fnd's Accuracy and F1 are above 80% even with 10% training data, and SO_fnd's Accuracy and F1 are above 80% with 20% or more training data. On PolitiFact, TriFN's Accuracy and F1 are above 80% with 40% or more training data; however, SO_fnd's Accuracy and F1 are above 90% even with 10% training data, and Prob_fnd's Accuracy and F1 are above 90% with 33% or more training data. It shows that, compared to TriFN, our proposed two models are able to achieve a similar or even better performance with much less labeled training data.

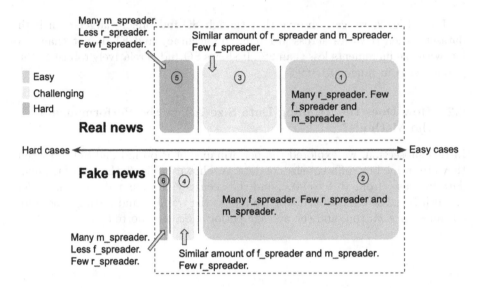

Fig. 4. Easy classified, challenging, and hard classified news in PolitiFact.

5.3 In What Situations, Will Prob_fnd and SO_fnd Win and Fail?

In this subsection, we explore in what situations two proposed methods shall win and shall fail. This experiment is conducted on PolitiFact because two methods' performance difference is larger on it than BuzzFeed. First, we use all news labels in PolitiFact to calculate *user_reliability* in Formula 1. Second, we mark users whose *user_reliability* > 0.8 as **real news spreader (r_spreader)**, mark users whose *user_reliability* < 0.2 as **fake news spreader (f_spreader)**, and mark other users as the **mixed news spreader (m_spreader)**. Among 4,132 users, there are 994 r_spreader, 2,619 f_spreader and 569 m_spreader. Surprisingly, 2,594 users are spreading only fake news, and 979 users are spreading only real news. Third, as shown in Fig. 4, based on the distribution of three types of users, we identify three levels of difficulty for news classification:

- **Easily classified news.** News that is shared mainly by r_spreader, as shown in area 1 in Fig. 4, are very likely to be real news; news that is spread mainly by f_spreader, as shown in area 2, are very likely to be fake news. Usually, r_spreader and f_spreader could be easily identified with training data, and hence models can easily classify them.
- **Challenging news.** If the news is shared by a similar amount of m_spreader and r_/f_spreader, as shown in areas 3 and 4 in Fig. 4, the classification performance is affected by the reliability assessment of m_spreader. The reliability assessment accuracy for m_spreader vary in different models, and the classification of such news is challenging. We found that our proposed two models were able to identify them successfully.
- **Hard classified news.** If the news is shared mainly by m_spreader, as shown in area 5 and 6 in Fig. 4, it is hard to classify them. The classification

performance is directly decided by (1) the reliability assessment accuracy for the m_spreader, and (2) how the news reliability assessment is designed. We checked the failure cases for both methods in repetitive experiments and found that there were 15 out of 17 frequently appearing failure cases in Prob_fnd, and 7 out of 9 frequent failure cases in SO_fnd, can be attributed to the large number of m_spreader.

Two other failure cases for Prob_fnd and SO_fnd are: (1) a piece of real news (news id 84) is spread by more f_spreader and hence is wrongly classified. (2) a piece of real news (news 22) is wrongly classified because its related user information (reliability) cannot be assessed from the data, and it is directly classified as fake news.

From Fig. 4, we can also observe that fake news is mainly spread by f_spreader (area 2 is very large), but only half real news is mainly spread by r_spreader (area 1), with the other half real news spread by a lot of m_spreaders (area 3 and 5). It indicates that most fake news in PolitiFact is easily classified news, and only a few are challenging or hard classified fake news, while nearly half of real news is challenging or hard to classify. With assessed news reliability of SO_fnd, when *news_distrust* is high, the news is likely to be fake; when *news_distrust* is low, the news is likely to be real (because challenging and hard classified fake news are few). However, when *news_trust* is high, the news is likely to be real; when *news_trust* is low, the news may be hard classified real news, or maybe fake news. It explains why *news_distrust* has a better performance than *news_trust* when used as the SVM classification feature in the first iteration of the SO_fnd. Hence, *news_distrust* is selected instead of *news_trust*.

6   Conclusion and Future Works

In this study, to detect the fake news that spreads on the social network, we propose two new methods. Validated on two real-world datasets, our proposed probability based method, Prob_fnd, can achieve state-of-art performance. Furthermore, our proposed Subjective Opinions based method, SO_fnd, can record the model's uncertainty more accurately in reliability evaluation, and hence has a much better performance than all existing models. Also, we explored our model's sensitivity to the parameters, training data size's effect on model performance, and also our models' winning and losing cases.

In this process, we do notice that there is a set of news lacking related user information, and we plan to work on the news content mining to predict the veracity of the news. As a next step, we will also consider introducing the user profile features, such as age, account verification, registration time, and follower count.

References

1. Sihombing, S.O.: Predicting intention to share news through social media: an empirical analysis in Indonesian youth context. Bus. Econ. Horiz. **13**(4), 468–477 (2017)

2. Bondielli, A., Marcelloni, F.: A survey on fake news and rumour detection techniques. Inf. Sci. **497**, 38–55 (2019)
3. Kumar, S., Shah, N.: False information on web and social media: a survey. arXiv preprint arXiv:1804.08559 (2018)
4. Shu, K., et al.: Fake news detection on social media: a data mining perspective. ACM SIGKDD Explor. Newsletter **19**(1), 22–36 (2017)
5. Conroy, N.J., Rubin, V.L., Chen, Y.: Automatic deception detection: methods for finding fake news. Proc. Assoc. Inf. Sci. Technol. **52**(1), 1–4 (2015)
6. Chen, Y., Conroy, N.J., Rubin, V.L.: Misleading online content: recognizing clickbait as "false news". In: Proceedings of the 2015 ACM on Workshop on Multimodal Deception Detection (2015)
7. Walker, W.E., et al.: Defining uncertainty: a conceptual basis for uncertainty management in model-based decision support. Integr. Assess. **4**(1), 5–17 (2003)
8. Wang, Y., et al.: A survey of queries over uncertain data. Knowl. Inf. Syst. **37**(3), 485–530 (2013)
9. Acchini, E., Ballarin, G., Della Vedova, M. L., Moret, S., de Alfaro, L.: Some like it hoax: automated fake news detection in social networks. arXiv preprint arXiv:1704.07506 (2017)
10. Della Vedova, M. L., Tacchini, E., Moret, S., Ballarin, G., DiPierro, M., de Alfaro, L.: Automatic online fake news detection combining content and social signals. In 2018 22nd Conference of Open Innovations Association (FRUCT), pp. 272–279. IEEE, May 2018
11. Shu, K., Wang, S., Liu, H.: Exploiting tri-relationship for fake news detection. arXiv preprint arXiv:1712.07709 (2017)
12. Jøsang, A.: Subjective Logic. Springer, Heidelberg (2016). https://doi.org/10.1007/978-3-319-42337-1
13. Jøsang, A.: The consensus operator for combining beliefs. Artif. Intell. **141**(1–2), 157–170 (2002)
14. Rubin, V.L., Lukoianova, T.: Truth and deception at the rhetorical structure level. J. Assoc. Inf. Sci. Technol. **66**(5), 905–917 (2015)
15. Wang, W.Y.: "Liar, liar pants on fire": a new benchmark dataset for fake news detection. arXiv preprint arXiv:1705.00648 (2017)
16. Potthast, M., Kiesel, J., Reinartz, K., Bevendorff, J., Stein, B.: A stylometric inquiry into hyperpartisan and fake news. arXiv preprint arXiv:1702.05638 (2017)
17. Kumar, S., West, R., Leskovec, J.: Disinformation on the web: Impact, characteristics, and detection of wikipedia hoaxes. In: Proceedings of the 25th international conference on World Wide Web, pp. 591–602. International World Wide Web Conferences Steering Committee, April 2016
18. Hassan, N., Li, C., Tremayne, M.: Detecting check-worthy factual claims in presidential debates. In: Proceedings of the 24th ACM International on Conference on Information and Knowledge Management, pp. 1835–1838. ACM, October 2015
19. Ott, M., Choi, Y., Cardie, C., Hancock, J.T.: Finding deceptive opinion spam by any stretch of the imagination. In: Proceedings of the 49th Annual Meeting of the Association for Computational Linguistics: Human Language Technologies, vol. 1, pp. 309–319. Association for Computational Linguistics, June 2011
20. Feng, S., Banerjee, R., Choi, Y.: Syntactic stylometry for deception detection. In: Proceedings of the 50th Annual Meeting of the Association for Computational Linguistics: Short Papers, vol. 2, pp. 171–175. Association for Computational Linguistics, July 2012

21. Afroz, S., Brennan, M., Greenstadt, R.:. Detecting hoaxes, frauds, and deception in writing style online. In: 2012 IEEE Symposium on Security and Privacy, pp. 461–475. IEEE, May 2012

22. Ajao, O., Bhowmik, D., Zargari, S.: Fake news identification on twitter with hybrid CNN and RNN models. In: Proceedings of the 9th International Conference on Social Media and Society, pp. 226–230. ACM, July 2018

23. Song, C., Tu, C., Yang, C., Liu, Z., Sun, M.: CED: credible early detection of social media rumors. arXiv preprint arXiv:1811.04175 (2018)

24. Zubiaga, A., et al.: Discourse-aware rumour stance classification in social media using sequential classifiers. Inf. Process. Manage. **54**(2), 273–290 (2018)

25. Liu, Y., Jin, X., Shen, H.: Towards early identification of online rumors based on long short-term memory networks. Inf. Process. Manage. **56**(4), 1457–1467 (2019)

26. Li, Q., Zhang, Q., Si, L.: Rumor detection by exploiting user credibility information, attention and multi-task learning. In: Proceedings of the 57th Annual Meeting of the Association for Computational Linguistics, pp. 1173–1179, July 2019

27. Gupta, M., Zhao, P., Han, J.: Evaluating event credibility on twitter. In: Proceedings of the 2012 SIAM International Conference on Data Mining, pp. 153–164. Society for Industrial and Applied Mathematics, April 2012

28. Jin, Z., Cao, J., Zhang, Y., Luo, J.: News verification by exploiting conflicting social viewpoints in microblogs. In: Thirtieth AAAI Conference on Artificial Intelligence, March 2016

29. Ruchansky, N., Seo, S., Liu, Y.: CSI: a hybrid deep model for fake news detection. In: Proceedings of the 2017 ACM on Conference on Information and Knowledge Management, pp. 797–806. ACM, November 2017

30. Guacho, G.B., Abdali, S., Shah, N., Papalexakis, E.E.: Semi-supervised content-based detection of misinformation via tensor embeddings. In: 2018 IEEE/ACM International Conference on Advances in Social Networks Analysis and Mining (ASONAM), pp. 322–325. IEEE, August 2018

31. Jøsang, A., Hayward, R., Pope, S.: Trust network analysis with subjective logic. In: Proceedings of the 29th Australasian Computer Science Conference, vol. 48. Australian Computer Society Inc. (2006)

32. Josang, A.: Conditional reasoning with subjective logic. J. Multiple-Valued Logic Soft Comput. **15**(1), 5–38 (2008)

33. Pelechrinis, K., Zadorozhny, V., Kounev, V., Oleshchuk, V., Anwar, M., Lin, Y.: Automatic evaluation of information provider reliability and expertise. World Wide Web **18**(1), 33–72 (2013). https://doi.org/10.1007/s11280-013-0249-x

34. Oleshchuk, V., Zadorozhny, V.: Trust-aware query processing in data intensive sensor networks. In: SENSORCOMM. IEEE (2007)

35. Zhang, D., Zadorozhny, V.I., Oleshchuk, V.A.: SLFTD: a subjective logic based framework for truth discovery. In: Welzer, T., et al. (eds.) ADBIS 2019. CCIS, vol. 1064, pp. 102–110. Springer, Cham (2019). https://doi.org/10.1007/978-3-030-30278-8_13

36. Shu, K., et al.: FakeNewsNet: a data repository with news content, social context and dynamic information for studying fake news on social media. arXiv preprint arXiv:1809.01286 (2018)

Improving on Coalitional Prediction Explanation

Gabriel Ferrettini$^{(\boxtimes)}$, Julien Aligon, and Chantal Soulé-Dupuy

Université de Toulouse, UT1, IRIT, CNRS/UMR 5505, Toulouse, France
{gabriel.ferrettini,julien.aligon,chantal.soule-dupuy}@irit.fr

Abstract. Machine learning has proven increasingly essential in many fields but a lot obstacles still hinder its use by non-experts. The lack of trust in the results obtained is foremost among them, and has inspired several explanatory approaches in the literature. These approaches provide a great insight on the predictions of a model, but at a cost of a long computation time. In this paper, we aim to further improve the detection of relevant attributes influencing a prediction, on the strength of feature selection methods.

Keywords: Data analysis · Machine learning · Prediction explanation

1 Introduction

One of the main limits to the use of machine learning solutions is the "black box" problem inherent to an opaque model, producing results without insight of how they were produced. As an answer to this problem, several methods exist to explain a predictive model, in a global way [1]. A problem arise when a domain expert user (for instance a biologist) has to study the behavior of particular dataset instances over a predictive model (for instance in the context of cohort study). In this case, a global explanation is not enough to give the information needed by the study. In this direction, previous studies offer the possibility of explaining single instance prediction, over a model, as in [14] and [3]. One major problem of these contributions is the high complexity of the proposed algorithms $(O(n^2))$. Because of this computational weight, explaining each instance over a predictive model can be very time consuming, especially if the dataset has a large number of attributes.

Our work fits the general ambition to help a domain expert user to get involved in data analysis operations, especially in learning tasks. On this way, obtaining explanations for predictive models, in a reasonable time, is essential. In a previous work [5], we proved the feasibility of lowering the computation time of existing solutions, with a very limited loss of explanation accuracy while saving a high computation time. In this paper, we continue this work to find better approximations of these solution, through the exploration of new ways to find groups of attributes.

J. Darmont et al. (Eds.): ADBIS 2020, LNCS 12245, pp. 122–135, 2020.
https://doi.org/10.1007/978-3-030-54832-2_11

The paper is organized as follows. Section 2 explores previous works already done in the domain of prediction explanation. In particular, the identification of attributes having a significant influence on a model is fundamental. To that end, the automated discovery of groups of linked attributes is an important challenge to overcome. Notably, we rely on attribute grouping methods from the literature, notably inspired by the feature selection methods. Then, Sect. 3 describes the base methods used to generate predictions explanation. The extension of our work [5] is proposed in Sect. 4 to find faster methods of explanation. This is achieved through new way to find groups of attributes for the coalitional method described in Sect. 3. Experiments are presented in Sect. 5, showing the interest of our methods in terms of computation time and their limited impacts in terms of loss of accuracy, significantly improving the results of [5]. Finally, Sect. 6 concludes the paper by giving new perspective of works, including the new possibilities opened by our results.

2 Related Works

Explaining the influence of each attribute (of a dataset) on the output of a predictive model has been explored largely. An example of the works pertaining to global attribute importance on a model is available in [1]. The most recent methods are based on swapping the values of attributes in a dataset and analysing which swap affects the most the predictions trained by a model. The more modifying the attributes values affects the predictions, the most this attribute is considered important for the model, as a whole. Many ways of explaining single predictions have been explored but these methods often struggle between being too simplistic, or too complex to be interpreted by a human, notwithstanding the problem of computation time, which can become problematic for more advanced user assistance systems. The possible applications of prediction explanations are investigated by [11]. According to their paper, the interest for explaining a predictive model is threefold. It can help to (1) understand, (2) judge the quality and (3) choose a model. A great number of works pertaining to prediction explanation led to [8], which theorized a category of explanation methods, named *additive* methods, and produced a review of the different methods developed in this category, such as [4] and [13]. These methods provides, for a given prediction, a weight to each attribute of the dataset, representing its influence on a model, locally. Different *additive* methods exist to calculate relevant weights but the end result is always this vector of weights. This vector is easy to interpret, even for someone without expertise on machine learning. Yet, these methods have a major deterrent: their computation time makes them difficult to use for the average user. That is why [8] explores methods to generate explanations faster, but at the cost of very restricting hypotheses, as the independence of each attribute of the dataset, or the linearity of the model, which is not always the case. Thus, we are aiming for a simplification to reduce computational time of methods like [14], but applicable in a more generic way than [8]. In this work, we want to facilitate the generation of prediction explanation, without having to restrict ourselves to a given set of models. This paper is the continuity of [5] in which we already established possible methods of simplification. One of these methods relies on the automatic detection of groups of attributes. In this paper, we aim to identify and compare additional methods detecting groups, in order to compare their influence on the efficiency of the simplification method.

The selection of relevant attributes to be grouped can take inspiration from the works in the field of feature selection [2,16]. In particular, the methods proposed in a dimensional reduction goal seem to reach our scope. Indeed, these methods have to automatically detect interactions between attributes for reducing a potential high dimensionality in a dataset. Thus, two main approaches, feature extraction (mainly the principal component analysis) and filter methods (which measure the relevance of features by their correlations) can be considered. The fact that the principal component analysis (PCA) and the filter methods rely only on information provided by a dataset (independent of the model used in an analysis) is a great advantage for our work, in contrast with techniques such as SVM-RFE [10] or FS-P [9], based on a specific model. Indeed, different predictive models can classify differently a same instance. Thus, an explanation on this instance can be different, from one model to another, and cannot depend of a selection of influence attributes made by a unique predictive model, such as SVM. The PCA is a largely recognised method to provide new features from sets of correlated attributes. The Correlation-based feature selection (CFS) methods [6] are promising candidates. In particular, the use of a multicollinearity measure by a variance inflation factor (VIF), can provide sets of attributes having linear correlations between them. This avoids calculating collinearity between pairs of attributes, using the Pearson's measure, for example. However, the VIF measure is unable to compute non linear correlations, on the contrary of the Spearman correlation factor. Even if this factor only works between pairs of attributes, the capacity to detect non linear correlations makes it a good candidate.

3   Prediction Explanation

In this section, we present the basis of our current work: the methods used to generate prediction explanations. First, we introduce our baseline, the *complete explanation*, and then we present our simplification of this baseline, the *coalitional explanation*.

3.1   Complete Explanation

The baseline of our work takes inspiration from the work of [14]. This influence calculation method is based on the computation of attribute influences for all possible subgroups. This framework is close to the situation of a game called "coalitions", where each group of attributes can have an influence on the model prediction. The influence of an attribute is measured according to its importance in each coalition. We can then refer to the coalition games as defined by Shapley in [12]: A coalitional game of N players is defined as a function mapping subsets of players to gains $g : 2^N \mapsto \mathbb{R}$. The parallel can easily be drawn with our situation, where we wish to assess the influence of a given attribute *in every possible coalition of attributes*. We then look at not only the influence of the attribute, but also its use in all subsets of attributes. We thus define the *complete influence* of an attribute $a_i \in A$ on the classification of an instance x for the class C:

$$\mathcal{I}_{a_i}^C(x) = \sum_{A' \subseteq A \setminus a_i} p(A', A) * (inf_{f,(A' \cup a_i)}^C(x) - inf_{f,A'}^C(x)) \tag{1}$$

With $p(A', A)$ a penalty function accounting for the size of the subset A'. Indeed, if an attribute changes a lot the result of a classifier, in a large group of attributes, it can be considered as very important for the prediction compared to the other ones. On the opposite, an attribute changing the result of a classifier, when this classifier is based on a small set of attributes, cannot be considered to have an influence as decisive as the first one. The Shapley value [12] is a promising candidate, and defines this penalty as:

$$p(A', A) = \frac{|A'|! * (|A| - |A'| - 1)!}{|A|!} \tag{2}$$

The base influence $inf_{f,A}^C(x)$, defined in [14], is the difference between the prediction without prior information, and the prediction with every attribute in the group of attributes A:

$$inf_{f,A}^C(x) = f(x_A) - f(\varnothing) \tag{3}$$

This *complete influence* of an attribute now takes into consideration its importance among all the possible attribute configurations, which is closer to the original intuition behind attribute influence. However, because we ambition to explain a single instance on a model, the *complete influence* can be extremely computationally expensive: $\bigcirc(2^n * l(n, x))$, with n the number of attributes, x the number of instances in the dataset and $l(n, x)$ the complexity of training the model to be explained It is then not practical to use the *complete influence* and it becomes necessary to seek a more efficient way. However, the *complete influence* can be considered as an excellent baseline [14]. Thus, our new explanation approaches can be evaluated by measuring how they deviate from the *complete influence*.

3.2   Coalitional Explanation

A more efficient strategy is to only identify the groups of correlated attributes, as proposed in our previous work [5]. This strategy avoids having to calculate all possible subgroups of influence. We then obtain a *coalitionnal influence* of an attribute $a_i \in g, g \in G$:

$$simple\mathcal{I}_{a_i}^C(x) = \sum_{g' \subseteq g \setminus a_i} p(g', g) * (inf_{f,(g' \cup a_i)}^C(x) - inf_{f,g'}^C(x)) \tag{4}$$

Given the fact we can set a maximum cardinal c for our subgroups, the complexity is, in the worst case, $O(2^c * \frac{n}{c} * l(n, x)) \approx O(n * l(n, x))$. This method calculates less groups than the *complete influence*, but tries to make up for it by only grouping the attributes actually related to each other. In order to determine which attribute groups are relevant to consider, we need to use an automatic attribute groups construction method.

4   Coalition Computing Methods

We propose, in this section, different ways to compute attribute coalitions and study their effects on the efficiency of the *coalitionnal* influence. We base our first algorithm on the work of [7]. The other algorithms are based on the variance inflation factor (VIF) and the principal component analysis (PCA) of a dataset. For each algorithm, we implement a parameter which control the size of the subgroups that are generated. A higher value of this parameter generates larger groups whereas a smaller value produces smaller groups.

4.1   Model-Based Coalition

In this method, the attribute groups are created by using the model itself to detect interacting attributes. In this approach, no correlation is detected, but only an interaction in the sense of the model usage of the attributes. This is done by randomizing the values of the dataset, and studying the evolution of the model predictions. It consists in measuring the differences of predictions on the whole dataset before and after the randomization. When attributes are considered to be part of the same group, their values are swapped together with the values of another instance, classified by the model as the same class as the starting instance. Each attribute outside of the group has its value swapped completely randomly. Once this have been done, the new instances are classified by the model. The ratio of differences between the old and the new classification is called the fidelity. A higher fidelity meaning a lower variation of the predictions. At each iteration, the attribute which removal lowers the less the fidelity is removed, until it is not possible to keep the fidelity above a fixed threshold. Then the group is considered as fixed. This attribute grouping algorithm has been developed in [7] and is detailed in Algorithm 1.

4.2   Principal Component Analysis Based Coalition

The objective of a principal component analysis is to transform correlated attributes into new attributes linearly uncorrelated between them. Our reasoning, for this approach, is to consider the set of correlated attributes (summarized by the new attribute of the PCA) as a group of influence.

Given a dataset $D = (A, X)$ composed of a set of n attributes $A = \{a_1, ..., a_n\}$, and a set of instances X where $x \in X, x = \{x_1, ..., x_n\} \forall i \in [1..n], x_i \in a_i$.

Algorithm 1. Model-based coalition extraction

Input: Sensitivity parameter $\delta > 0$, the number of attributes m, and a fidelity function
$fid()$. Two auxiliary functions $L(X) = \bigcup_{i \in X}\{\{i\}\}$ and $F(X) = L(\bigcup_{Y \in X} Y)$, which
produces sets of singletons (e.g. $L(\{1,2,3\}) = F(\{\{1,2\},\{3\}\}) = \{\{1\},\{2\},\{3\}\}$)

Output: σ a coalition of attributes

$\sigma \leftarrow \{\}$
$R \leftarrow \{m\}$ ▷ R contains a group to test for
$A \leftarrow \{\}$ ▷ A contains the removed attributes
$\Delta \leftarrow fid(L([m])) + \delta$
while $R \neq \{\}\ or\ A \neq \{\}$ **do**
  if $A = \{\}$ and $fid(\{R\} \bigcup F(\sigma)) < \Delta$ **then**
                ▷ if we are already below Δ before removing any attribute assign the
remaining attributes to singleton groups
      $\sigma \leftarrow \sigma \bigcup L(R)$
      $R \leftarrow \{\}$
      $A \leftarrow \{\}$
  else
                ▷ Find an attribute j whose removal from R decreases the fidelity least
      $j \leftarrow argmax_{j \in R} fid(\{\{R \backslash \{j\}\} \bigcup \{\{j\}\} \bigcup \{A\} \bigcup F(\sigma))$
      if $|R| = 1$ or $fid(\{\{R \backslash \{j\}\} \bigcup \{\{j\}\} \bigcup \{A\} \bigcup F(\sigma))$ **then**
                ▷ If the fidelity drops below Δ add the group of attributes to the results
and look for the next group of attributes
        $\sigma \leftarrow \sigma \bigcup \{R\}$
        $R \leftarrow A$
        $A \leftarrow \{\}$
      else
                   ▷ If the fidelity stays above Δ continue removing the grouping R
        $R \leftarrow R \backslash \{j\}$
        $A \leftarrow A \bigcup \{j\}$
      end if
  end if
end while
return σ

We can apply a principal component analysis which produces a new dataset
$D' = (A', X')$ such as $A' = \{a'_1, ..., a'_m\}$ with each new attribute being a linear
composition of the previous attributes : $\forall i, a'_i \in A', \exists \{\alpha_1, ..., \alpha_n\} \in R^n, a'_i =
\alpha_1 * a_1 + ... + \alpha_n + a_n$.

Each new instance is associated with an instance of the previous dataset.
$\forall x' = \{x'_1, ..., x'_m\} \in X', \exists! x \in X, \forall i \in [1, .., m] \exists \alpha_1, ..., \alpha_n \in R^n, x'_i = \alpha_1 * x_1 +
... + \alpha_n + x_n$.

Given this set of factors $\alpha_1, ..., \alpha_n$, for each attribute, we consider each factor
as an evaluation of the importance of the attributes in the group. We can then
constitute a coalition of attributes by exploiting the groups formed by the most
important factors. This gives us the Algorithm 2. For the sake of simplicity, we
consider each $a' \in A'$ as a vector of its α_i factors.

Algorithm 2. PCA-based coalition extraction

Input: a threshold t and the set of attributes A' of the PCA
Output: σ a coalition of attributes

    $\sigma \leftarrow \{\}$
    for all $a' \in A'$ **do**   ▷ for each attribute generated by the PCA
        $g \leftarrow \{\}$ ▷ g, a new possible group
        $\alpha max \leftarrow max(a' = \alpha_1, ..., \alpha_n)$ ▷ find the most important factor
        for all $\alpha_i \in a'$ **do**
            if $\alpha_i \geq \alpha\ max * (1 - t)$ **then**
                add a_i to g ▷ the attribute is included in the group if close to the max
            end if
        end for
        add g to σ
    end for
    return σ

4.3 Variance Inflation Factor Based Coalition

The variance inflation factor (VIF) is an estimation of the multicollinearity of the attributes of the dataset in regard to a given target attribute.

Given a dataset $D = (A, X)$, the VIF value of $a \in A$ is calculated by running a standard linear regression with a as the target for the prediction. Then, given R the coefficient of determination of the linear regression, we have:

$$VIF(a) = \frac{1}{1 - R^2} \tag{5}$$

It is commonly accepted that a variance inflation factor superior to 10 indicates a strong multicollinearity of the attribute with other attributes of the dataset. Moreover, when an attribute is removed from the dataset, the VIF of the attributes multicollinear with it decrease. Then, we can automatically detect groups of attributes by calculating the VIF of each attribute (considered as a target) of the dataset, and then comparing them with a new VIF calculation with an attribute removed. For this purpose, we consider two possible approaches:

– Considering as a priority the calculation of strongly multicollinear groups of attributes: Those are groups of attributes with a dependency to one another. In the context of this approach, attributes whose VIF varies strongly when an attribute is removed from the dataset will be considered as part of the group.
– Considering as a priority the calculation of weakly or non multicollinear groups of attributes: Given the fact that correlated attributes tend to bring the same information to the model, it may be preferable to prioritize groups for which the addition or removal of an attribute will change greatly the information brought by the group.

These two approaches are named *VIF coalition* and *reverse VIF coalition*, respectively. This gives us the Algorithm 3, for the *VIF coalition*. The *reverse VIF coalition* can be obtained simply by replacing the condition for adding

Algorithm 3. VIF-based coalition extraction

Input: a threshold t, the set of attributes of the dataset A and a function $VIF(A)$
   calculating the array of all the VIF of all the subsets of a set of attributes
Output: σ a coalition of attributes
   $\sigma \leftarrow \{\}$
   $oldvifs \leftarrow VIF(A)$ $\triangleright$ calculating the initial VIFs of the attributes
   for all $a \in A$ **do**
      $g \leftarrow \{\}$
      add a to g
      $newvifs \leftarrow VIF(A/a)$
      for all $a' \in A$ **do**
         if $newvifs(a') < oldvifs(a') * (0.4 + t)$ **then**
            add a' to g
         end if
      end for
      add g to σ
   end for
   return σ

---

an attribute to a group by *if* $newvifs(a') > oldvifs(a') * (1 - t * 0.05)$. This supplementary ratio of 0.05 have been obtained by preliminary experiments, which showed that just keeping the $1 - t$ factor led to a generation of all the possible subgroups, which defeat the principle of an approximation.

4.4   Spearman Correlation Based Coalition

A limit of the variance inflation factor is the sole consideration of multicolinearity, while a correlation between attributes might not be linear. This problem is addressed through the Spearman correlation coefficient, which takes into account non linear correlations. Spearman being not multicollinear, the calculation of the correlation between attributes has to be done by pairs. Thus, the method consists in generating the matrix of all the correlations of each pair, and then deciding which attributes are part of a group. For this method, we have the same two possibilities as for the *VIF* method: we can either prioritize the calculation of strongly correlated attributes, or on the contrary, prioritize groups of non correlated attributes. These two approaches are named respectively *Spearman coalition* and *reverse Spearman coalition*.

Given a dataset $D = (A, X)$, with $A = \{a_1, ..., a_n\}$ the correlation matrix C is obtained by computing the spearman correlation coefficient of each attribute couple : $C(1, 2) = corr(a_1, a_2)$. Thus C is symmetrical and have 1 as the value of its whole diagonal. For each line i of the matrix C, we consider as grouped with a_i the attributes strongly (or weakly) correlated with a_i, for the *Spearman coalition* (or the *reverse Spearman coalition*).

The Algorithm 4 details the *Spearman coalition* method. In order to perform the *reverse Spearman coalition* method can be obtained by replacing the condition for adding an attribute to a group by $corrmat(a, a') < min(corrmat(a)) + max(corrmat(a)) * t$ and $min(corrmat(a)) < 0.5$. This allows to add the least

---

Algorithm 4. Spearman-based coalition extraction

Input: a threshold t, the set of attributes of the dataset A and a function $spearman(A)$ calculating the matrix of all the absolute spearman correlation coefficient of all the subsets of a set of attributes. a max and min functions which returns the maximum and minimum of a matrix line.

Output: σ a coalition of attributes

$\quad \sigma \leftarrow \{\}$

$\quad corrmat \leftarrow spearman(A)$ ▷ calculating the correlation matrix

$\quad$ **for all** $a \in A$ **do**

$\quad\quad g \leftarrow \{\}$

$\quad\quad$ **for all** $a' \in A$ **do**

$\quad\quad\quad$ **if** $corrmat(a,a') > max(corrmat(a)) * (1 - t)$ and $max(corrmat(a)) > 0.1$ **then**

$\quad\quad\quad\quad$ ▷ If the most correlated attribute have a coefficient less than 0.1, we consider a as a singleton

$\quad\quad\quad\quad$ add a' to g

$\quad\quad\quad$ **end if**

$\quad\quad$ **end for**

$\quad\quad$ add g to σ

$\quad$ **end for**

$\quad$ **return** σ

---

correlated attributes up to a threshold : if the minimum is superior to 0.5, we consider the attribute as too correlated to the others and consider it as a singleton.

5 Evaluating the Coalition Computation Methods

In this section we aim to evaluate the performances of each coalition calculation method, considering their precision when compared to the *complete* influence, and their computational time. We also give an overview of the group characterisation for each coalition method.

5.1 Experimental Protocol

Our experiments are run on the OSIRIM[1] cluster. This cluster is equipped with 4 AMD Opteron 6262HE processors with $16 \times 1{,}6$ GHz cores, for a total of 64 cores, and 10×512 GB of RAM. Our tests are realized from the data available on the Openml platform [15]. We select the biggest collection of datasets[2] on which classification tasks have been run. We also consider six classification tasks: naïve Bayes, nearest neighbors, J34 decision tree, J34 random forest, bagging naïve Bayes and support vector machine. Due to the heavy computational cost of the complete influence (considered as the reference of our experiments), we select

---

[1] http://osirim.irit.fr/site/en.
[2] Available in https://www.openml.org/s/107/tasks.

the datasets having at most nine attributes. Thus, a collection of 324 datasets is obtained. Considering the six types of workflows, we have a total of 1944 runs. For each of those runs, we generate each type of influence proposed in this paper, for each instance of the 324 datasets: the *complete* influence for the baseline, along with the *coalitional* influence. The *coalitional* influences are generated using the different group generation methods described in Sect. 4, which are based on an $\alpha \in]0, 0.5[$ parameter (small values of α resulting in smaller subgroups, and high values in bigger ones). We generate the possible subgroups with 5 different values of α to study the influence of subgroup size. To compare the different explanation methods, we consider the explanation results as a vector of attribute influences noted $\mathcal{I}(x) = [i_1, ..., i_n]$ with n the number of attributes in the dataset. Thus, each of the attributes a_k is given an influence $i_k \in [0, 1]$ by the method $\mathcal{I}$: $\forall k \in [1..n], i_k = \mathcal{I}_{a_i}(x)$, with x an instance of the dataset. We then define a difference between two vectors of influences i, j as the normalised euclidean distance:

$$d(i, j) = \frac{1}{2\sqrt{n}} \sum_{k=1}^{n} \sqrt{(i_k - j_k)^2} \tag{6}$$

Considering this formula, we define an error score based on the difference between an explanation method and the *complete* influence method. Given an instance x, an explanation method $\mathcal{I}(x)$, and the *complete influence* method $\mathcal{I}^C(x)$:

$$err(\mathcal{I}, x) = d(\mathcal{I}(x), \mathcal{I}^C(x)) \tag{7}$$

For each instance of each dataset, we generate the error score of every method, allowing us to compare their performances across the different collected datasets . Each error score is the distance of one of the coalitional methods from the *complete* method. Thus, lesser error is indicative of a more precise estimation of the *complete* method.

5.2   Calculation Time and Error Scores

Table 1. Mean number of instances for datasets with a given number of attributes

Number of attributes	1	2	3	4	5	6	7	8	9
Mean number of instances	1020	1529	3728	1171	2370	1748	983	2414	409

Figures 1 and 2 give the performance and computational time in milliseconds of each coalitional method, respectively (for different values of their threshold parameter).

For readability, Table 1 details the mean number of instances for each number of attributes. This can have an impact on computation time, and explains the variations of Fig. 1. This figure includes the computation time for generating the

groups of attributes and for explaining each instance of the dataset. The decrease
of the computation time for the case of 9 attributes is explained by the important
decrease in the mean number of instances. This makes each retraining faster to
do, even if there are potentially twice more subgroups to take into account.

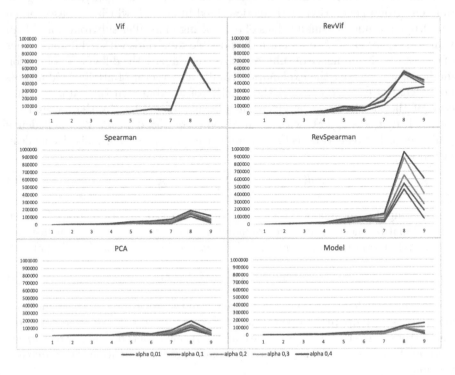

Fig. 1. Calculation time of each coalitional method versus the number of attributes in
the dataset

Figure 2 depicts the mean error score, aggregating the error score (Eq. 7) of
each explanation method for each of our 324 datasets. In this figure, the closer
the curve is to 0, the closer it is to the *complete* influence method.

As we can see, in an overall analysis, the *VIF* method seems to be the
worst, with a poor performance and a long computational time. This can be
explained by the fact that the attributes of the generated group are correlated
to one another, which mean that the information brought by these groups and
subgroups is very redundant. We can suppose a lot of groups are calculated (see
Sect. 5.3 for more details), but they often bring nearly the same information
each. *Spearman* has a far better computation time than *VIF*, but still has a
poor performance overall, probably for the same reasons. As an example, *PCA*
has a better performance but a computation time very similar to *Spearman*.
RevSpearman has an overall better performance than part of other methods,
but this performance is paid by the longest computation time, without reaching

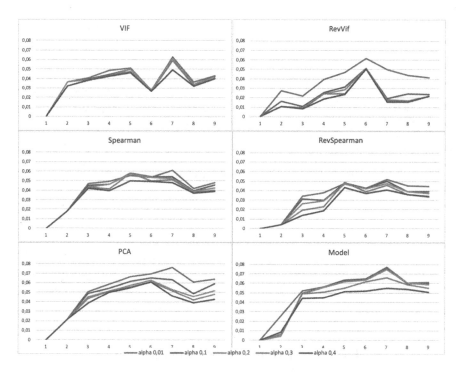

Fig. 2. Error score between each coalitional method and the complete influence, versus the number of attributes in the dataset

the best performance. This can be explained by the group calculation method, which does not take into account the possible correlation of two attributes which are both not correlated with the original attribute of the group (no transitivity). This lead, as for *VIF* and *Spearman*, to the calculation of redundant information, which increases the computation time without improving much the performance. The *PCA*, *RevVIF*, and *Model* methods each seem to have their strong and weak points. The *RevVIF* is clearly more precise than the other two, but at a cost of greatly increased computation time. Instead of focusing on the correlated groups, the *RevVIF* method relies on the least correlated, thus a greater diversity of information is taken into account. While the *Model* and *PCA* methods are less exhaustive in their approaches, they seem to have a far lower computational time, the evolution of computation time against the number of attributes being far less steep than for *RevVIF*.

5.3 Group Characterisation

Figures 3 and 4 compare the average number and average size of the groups of attributes generated by each coalitional method, respectively (for the two ends alpha = 0.01 and 0.4).

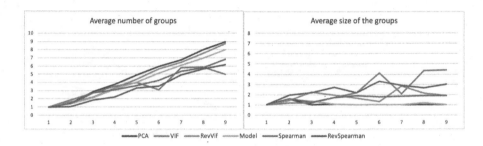

Fig. 3. Group characterisation with alpha = 0.01

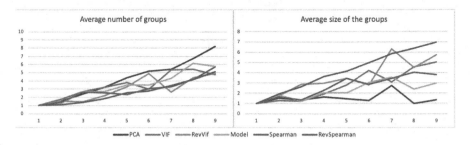

Fig. 4. Group characterisation with alpha = 0.4

We can note that *RevVIF*, *RevSpearman* and *VIF* are the three methods generating the highest average group sizes, compared to the other methods. This phenomenon can explain why these methods minimize best the error scores as discussed in Sect. 5.2. Indeed, the larger the groups are, the more exhaustive they are in terms of coalition influence that can correctly explain an instance with respect to a predictive model. More surprisingly, the high average number of groups seem not to induce a good error score. For example, the *RevSpearman* method generate, for the two alpha thresholds, the lowest number of groups, for most of the cases, whereas its error rate is one of the best. This can be explained by the generation of a lot of small groups (singletons or couples), rather than a few large ones. After all, the *complete influence* is the equivalent of the *coalitional influence* using a single group containing all the attributes.

6   Conclusion and Perspectives

In this paper, we proposed a comparative study between several attribute grouping methods (inspired by the feature selection field) in an objective of individual prediction explanation. Our tests, conducted with 324 real datasets, show that *RevVIF*, *PCA* and *Model* methods are all of interest. *RevVIF* is preferable for datasets with few attributes, while *PCA* and *Model* should fare better for a large set of attributes. Then, a new interesting perspective would be to study the evolution of computation times with larger datasets. The main problem here is it becomes impossible to compute the *Complete influence* for large datasets. Thus, it is impossible to monitor the performance of our different methods with this baseline. To address this problem, a possible way could be to run a general attribute importance study for large datasets, first, and use this information to calculate the influence of the most important attributes during the individual explanation generation.

References

1. Altmann, A., Toloşi, L., Sander, O., Lengauer, T.: Permutation importance: a corrected feature importance measure. Bioinformatics **26**(10), 1340–1347 (2010)
2. Bolón-Canedo, V., Sánchez-Maroño, N., Alonso-Betanzos, A.: A review of feature selection methods on synthetic data. Knowl. Inf. Syst. **34**(3), 483–519 (2013). https://doi.org/10.1007/s10115-012-0487-8
3. Casalicchio, G., Molnar, C., Bischl, B.: Visualizing the feature importance for black box models. arXiv e-prints, April 2018
4. Datta, A., Sen, S., Zick, Y.: Algorithmic transparency via quantitative input influence: theory and experiments with learning systems. In: 2016 IEEE Symposium on Security and Privacy (SP). pp. 598–617, May 2016
5. Ferrettini, G., Aligon, J., Soulé-Dupuy, C.: Explaining single predictions: a faster method. In: Chatzigeorgiou, A., et al. (eds.) SOFSEM 2020. LNCS, vol. 12011, pp. 313–324. Springer, Cham (2020). https://doi.org/10.1007/978-3-030-38919-2_26
6. Hall, M.A.: Correlation-based feature selection for machine learning. Ph.D. thesis (1999)
7. Henelius, A., Puolamaki, K., Boström, H., Asker, L., Papapetrou, P.: A peek into the black box: exploring classifiers by randomization. Data Min. Knowl. Disc. **28**(5–6), 1503–1529 (2014). qC 20180119
8. Lundberg, S., Lee, S.I.: A unified approach to interpreting model predictions. In: NIPS (2017)
9. Mejía-Lavalle, M., Sucar, E., Arroyo, G.: Variable selection using SVM based criteria. In: International Workshop on Feature Selection for Data Mining, p. 131–1350 (2006)
10. Rakotomamonjy, A.: Variable selection using SVM based criteria. J. Mach. Learn. Res. **3**, 1357–1370 (2003)
11. Ribeiro, M.T., Singh, S., Guestrin, C.: "Why should i trust you?": explaining the predictions of any classifier. In: Proceedings of the 22Nd ACM SIGKDD International Conference on Knowledge Discovery and Data Mining, KDD 2016, pp. 1135–1144. ACM, New York (2016)
12. Shapley, L.S.: A value for n-person games. Contrib. Theory Games **28**, 307–317 (1953)
13. Shrikumar, A., Greenside, P., Kundaje, A.: Learning important features through propagating activation differences. In: Proceedings of the 34th International Conference on Machine Learning, ICML 2017, vol. 70. pp. 3145–3153 (2017)
14. Strumbelj, E., Kononenko, I.: An efficient explanation of individual classifications using game theory. J. Mach. Learn. Res. **11**, 1–18 (2010)
15. Vanschoren, J., van Rijn, J.N., Bischl, B., Torgo, L.: OpenML: networked science in machine learning. SIGKDD Explor. **15**(2), 49–60 (2013)
16. Yu, L., Liu, H.: Efficient feature selection via analysis of relevance and redundancy. J. Mach. Learn. Res. **5**, 1205–1224 (2004)

Data Processing

JSON Functionally

Jaroslav Pokorný[(✉)] [iD]

Faculty of Mathematics and Physics, Charles University, Prague, Czech Republic
pokorny@ksi.mff.cuni.cz

Abstract. Document databases use JSON (JavaScript Object Notation) for data representation. In the category of NoSQL databases they support an ability to handle large volumes of data at the absence of an explicit data schema. On the other hand, schema information is sometimes essential for applications during data retrieval. Consequently, there are approaches to schema construction in the JSON community. We will suppose JSON collections equipped by a schema compatible in its expressivity to the JSON Schema recommendation. We use a formal approach based on typed functional data objects. We accommodate a classical approach to functional databases based on a typed λ-calculus to obtain a powerful non-procedural query language over JSON data with sound semantics.

Keywords: Document databases · JSON · Typed lambda calculus · Functional data objects · Querying JSON data · Database integration · MongoDB

1 Introduction

Document databases (DBs), also known as document stores or document-oriented DBs, are one of the main categories of NoSQL DBs. For example, DB-Engines Ranking[1] considers more than 40 document DBs. Document DBs handle collections of objects (called *documents*) represented in hierarchical formats such as XML or JSON. Originally, JSON[2] (JavaScript Object Notation) is a popular data format based on the data types of JavaScript programming language. Similarly to XML it belongs to a category of mark-up languages. Each document is composed of a (nested) set of fields and is associated with a unique identifier for indexing and retrieving purposes. Generally, these systems offer richer query languages than those in other NoSQL categories, being able to exploit the structuredness of the objects they store.

JSON occurs in a number of NoSQL DBs. For example, documents are represented as JSON objects in ArangoDB[3]. OrientDB[4] is a NoSQL solution with a hybrid document-graph engine that adds several compelling features to the document DB model. Also Couchbase[5] uses a JSON-based document store, similarly Apache CouchDB[6] stores

---

[1] http://db-engines.com/en/ranking (retrieved on 22. 5. 2020).

[2] http://www.json.org/ (retrieved on 22. 5. 2020).

[3] https://www.arangodb.com/ (retrieved on 22. 5. 2020).

[4] https://orientdb.com/ (retrieved on 22. 5. 2020).

[5] https://docs.couchbase.com/home/index.html (retrieved on 22. 5. 2020).

[6] https://couchdb.apache.org/ (retrieved on 22. 5. 2020).

© Springer Nature Switzerland AG 2020
J. Darmont et al. (Eds.): ADBIS 2020, LNCS 12245, pp. 139–153, 2020.
https://doi.org/10.1007/978-3-030-54832-2_12

JSON documents with the option of attaching non-JSON files to those documents. Here, among document stores, we refer to MongoDB[7], one of the most adopted. Considering such data stores as semistructured DBs, it is relevant to take into account querying such DBs and associated JSON-like query languages. We could cite some special JSON query languages, e.g., JSONiq[8]—a simplified version of XQuery language adapted for JSON.

As it is typical for NoSQL DBs, they are mostly schemaless. On the other hand, a schema-oriented approach is being based on application query patterns. This is departure from RDBMS where schemas are designed for optimizing storage, in case of NoSQL they are designed for access. Hence, NoSQL follows 'Query Driven Design'. Some document DBs offer a possibility to express JSON schema, e.g., in the language JSON Schema [3, 13]. This language is an attempt to provide a general purpose schema language for JSON, so we can optionally enforce rules governing document structures. Authors of [1] identify a JSON type language and design a schema inference algorithm enabling reasonable schema inference for massive JSON data collections.

We will consider just the document DBs with a schema in this paper. The goal is to propose new possibilities for querying JSON data. In our approach, we accommodate some classical approaches to functional DBs, e.g. [4, 8], based on a typed λ-calculus, to obtain a powerful non-procedural query language called JSON-λ with sound semantics. The associated model of JSON data deals with data as with functions. Our goal will be to capture most of the features offered by the functional approach used for modelling XML data and its querying described in [9, 10].

Section 2 presents a short overview of JSON data modelling including the JSON schema format. Section 3 offers a document querying in MongoDB. In Sect. 4, we describe a functional type system appropriate for typing JSON data and constructing JSON schema. Section 5 introduces a version of a typed λ-calculus for manipulating JSON data and a number of examples of its use. Section 6 concludes the paper.

2   Modelling JSON Data

JSON data model describes the basic data structures and semantics of the underlying JSON data [5]. It covers key aspects for JSON data format. JSON defines three major object types for document fields: *object*, *array*, and *value*. An object is an unordered set of name/value pairs, where values can be of type string, number, or other objects. Objects are in { } braces, each name wrapped in "double quotes" is followed by ":", name/values pairs are separated by ",". Arrays are ordered collections of elements (with no constraint on their structure). That is, arrays can mix both basic and complex types. Arrays are bounded by "["and"]", their elements are separated by ",". A JSON value may be either an object, array, number, string, true, false, or null. A *JSON instance* contains a single JSON value.

Clearly, JSON is simpler than XML. For example, it does not consider attributes. Obviously, XML attributes could be also considered as JSON objects, e.g., encoded by

---

[7] https://docs.mongodb.com/manual/ (retrieved on 22. 5. 2020).

[8] http://www.jsoniq.org/docs/JSONiqExtensionToXQuery/html-single/index.html (retrieved on 22. 5. 2020).

prefixing the attribute name with the @ symbol. Similarly to XML, JSON objects could be modelled by trees [2]. To present differences and similarities of XML and JSON data, we use the documents in Fig. 1 and Fig. 2, respectively.

```
<Book>
  <Title> Fundamentals of Database Systems </Title>
  <Authors>
    <Author> Elmasri,R.</Author>
    <Author> Navathe,S.B.</Author>
  </Authors>
  <Date>2015</Date>
  <Publisher>Pearson</Publisher>
</Book>
```

Fig. 1. Data XML-formatted

```
{
  "Book":
    {
      "Title": "Fundamentals of Database Systems",
      "Authors":["Elmasri,R.", "Navathe,S.B."],
      "Date":"2015",
      "Publisher":"Pearson"
    }
}
```

Fig. 2. The same data as in Fig. 1 JSON-formatted

The ability to store nested or hierarchical data within a text file structure makes JSON a powerful format to use as we are working with larger text datasets.

2.1 JSON Schema

JSON schema is a format that may be used to formalize constraints and requirements to JSON files. The language JSON Schema[9], similarly to XML Schema, SQL-like relational schemas, etc., is a powerful tool for validating the structure of DB data. However, it is different from a similar notion used in XML data model. i.e., XSD. A *JSON schema* is a JSON document, and that document must be an object. Object members (or *properties*) defined by JSON are called *keywords*, or *schema keywords*. With JSON Schema we can specify what properties exist, which type(s) can be used, if properties are required and how the JSON document is composed. The JSON schema in Fig. 3 describes a more complex name type and an associated object.

---

[9] https://json-schema.org/ (retrieved on 22. 5. 2020).

```
{                                          {
  "name":{                                   "name":{
   "type":"object",                            "firstname":"Ramez",
   "properties":{                              "surname":"Elmasri"
    "firstname":{"type":"string"},                     }
    "surname":{"type":"string"}        }
 }}}
```

Fig. 3. JSON schema fragment and related JSON data

It is also best practice to include an $id property as a unique identifier for each schema. We can set it to a URL at a domain, e.g.,

```
{"$id": "http://mydomain.com/schemas/myschema.json"}
```

Also some basic integrity constraints (ICs) are allowed to formulate as it is shown in Fig. 4 (without firstname and surname).

```
{
    "$schema":"http://json-schema.org/draft-04/schema",
    "type":"object",
    "properties":{
        "book":{
            "type":"object",
            "properties":{
                "title":{"type":"string"},
                "authors":{"type":"array",
                            "minItems":1,
                            "maxItems":3,
                            "items":{"type":"string"}},
                "issued":{"type":"number"},
                "required":["title","authors"],
                "additionalProperties":false
                            }
                 }  },
        "required":["book"],
        "additionalProperties":false
    }
```

Fig. 4. JSON schema fragment with ICs

Semantics of objects and elements of arrays of a JSON schema instance is straightforward. For example, an object instance is valid against minItems and maxItems if its number of authors is from interval <1,3>, etc. The type of authors' items in this array is string. The first restriction additionalProperties specifies if the array cannot contain items which are not specified in the schema.

3 Querying JSON Data in MongoDB

MongoDB instance is composed of a set of named *collections* of BSON documents, nested up to an unbounded depth. BSON (Binary Serialized dOcument Notation) is a binary serialization of JSON, with which such documents share the schemaless, arbitrarily nested structure. A collection may have zero or more documents. Documents are addressed in the DB via a unique key _id. Documents within a collection can have different fields. MongoDB also supports data types that are not part of original JSON specification, such as Date, Timestamp, Binary, ObjectID, RegExp, Long, Undefined, DBRef, Code, and MinKey. This is known as Extended JSON.

From Version 3.6, MongoDB supports JSON Schema and provides a JSON Schema Validator from within the application that runs like a trigger to check any changes to the data via inserts or alterations. In the next example, a document key is not included. Notation is simplified a little, e.g. " " braces are omitted for object names.

```
{name:{firstname:"John", lastname:"White"},
address:"Mostecka 25, 118 00 Prague 1",
grandchildren:["Klara","Magda","Richard"],
age:23
}
```

Default DB of MongoDB is 'db'. A query is specified using the find command, e.g.

```
db.<collection>.find({<age>:{$in:[<value>,
                                  <value>]}})
```

specifies that the age of persons documents should be one of 2 values, e.g.,

```
db.persons.find({age:{$in:[23,25]}})
```

Comparison operators like $lt, $lte, $gt, $gte, $ne are allowed. They correspond to $<$, $<=$, $>$, $>=$, and $\neq$, respectively. More conditions separated by ";" represent a conjunction. For example,

```
db.persons.find({age: 23, grandchildren:["Magda"]})
```

Another option is to use $exists.

```
db.<collection>.find({<name>:{$exists: true}})
```

The query searches for documents with an existing field.

We can observe that the above examples enable to express some forms of AND queries. Explicit $or enables to express OR queries. More advanced retrieval uses querying on embedded documents (in MongoDB terminology) using paths in JSON graph.

In Sects. 4–5 we will propose a calculus-oriented approach to querying JSON data, which requires a JSON schema expressed by a set of typed functions. This language JSON- λ will be more powerful than querying allowed by MongoDB.

4 Typing JSON Data

In our approach, JSON uses typed objects. To include typed objects into a DB processing, we introduce a set **O** of *abstract objects*. The set **O** serves as a reservoir for construction of JSON objects. An empty abstract object ε is also the member of **O**. The *content* of an abstract object will be either a string from STRING, in the easiest example, or a group of (sub)objects, or empty. There is difference between the empty object ε and empty content of an empty object.

Consider now, e.g., the object {"Date":"2015"}. It is a JSON instance of the Date object, which will be conceived as a (partial) function from **O** into STRING. For an o ∈ **O**, Date(o) returns the date 2015. The Date function is changing in time similarly as relations during the life of a relation DB. Similarly, the name type from Fig. 3 can be conceived as a set of two functions from **O** into **O** (including abstract first names and surnames). The current name object, i.e. the one stored in a given JSON DB, is a function assigning to each o ∈ **O** at most a couple of abstract objects from **O**.

4.1 Typing JSON Objects

Summarizing the notions given above, we will distinguish among object types and objects. *Objects* are of object types. Because object types are functions, objects are their values. Obviously, the values need mark-up given by the name of the object. Actually, a presentation of objects is done by real JSON objects.

First, we introduce a general functional type system supporting a structure of JSON data.

Definition 4.1. The existence of some *(primitive) types* $S_1,..., S_k$ ($k \geq 1$) is assumed. They constitute a *base* **B**. More complex types are obtained in the following way:

(a) Every member of the base **B** is a *(primitive) type* over **B**.
(b) If T_1, T_2 are types over **B**, then ($T_1 \rightarrow T_2$) is a *(functional) type* over **B**.
(c) If $T_1,..., T_n$ ($n \geq 1$) are types over **B**, then $\{T_1,..., T_n\}$ is a *set type* over **B**.
(d) If $T_1,..., T_n$ ($n \geq 1$) are types over **B**, then $[T_1,..., T_n]$ is an *array type* over **B**.

The *type system* **T** *over* **B** (or **T** if **B** is assumed) is the least set containing types given by (a)–(d).

If members of **B** are interpreted as mutually disjoint non-empty sets, then ($T_1 \rightarrow T_2$) denotes the set of all (total or partial) functions from T_1 into T_2. An object *o* of the type T is called a *T-object* and can be denoted o/T. $\{T_1,..., T_n\}$-objects contain an unordered set of respective $T_1,..., T_n$ objects. $[T_1,..., T_n]$-objects are arrays of respective $T_1,..., T_n$ objects.

For example, NUMBER, STRING, BOOL ∈ B. The type BOOL is defined as the set {TRUE, FALSE}. It allows typing some objects as sets and relations. They will not considered here as separate units. Both can be modelled as unary and n-ary characteristic functions, respectively. Thus, both notions are redundant in **T**.

For example, mathematical functions may be easily typed. Arithmetic operations +, −, *, / are examples of ((NUMBER, NUMBER) → NUMBER)-objects. Logical connectives, quantifiers and predicates are also typed functions: e.g., **and**/((BOOL, BOOL) → BOOL), R-identity $=_R$ is ((R,R) → BOOL)-object, universal R-quantifier Π_R, and existential R-quantifiers Σ_R are ((R → BOOL) → BOOL) - objects. As for our notational convention, we use an infix notation for logical functions. Similarly, we write '$\forall x...$' and '$\exists x...$' for application of the universal and existential quantifier, respectively. With **T**, it is possible to type functions of functions, nested tables, ISA-hierarchies, etc.

4.2 Typing JSON Regular Expressions

First, in the type system $\mathbf{T}_{reg}$ we will describe regular expressions over character data and named character data. We start with the base **B** containing primitive types BOOL, NUMBER and STRING. Moreover, outside **B** we use a set NAME of strings. Obviously, one type of strings would be enough, but we want to distinguish between names of objects and the most important part of objects content - character data.

Our regular expressions will be restricted comparing to regular expressions in XML [9]. The reason is that in a set type keys of $T_1,..., T_n$ must be unique. When the names within a set object are not unique, the behaviour of software that receives such an object would be unpredictable.

Definition 4.2. Let **B** = {STRING, NUMBER, BOOL}, a set NAME of names and **T** the type system over **B**. Then we define the *type system* $\mathbf{T}_{reg}$ over **B** as follows.

1. Every member of the base **B** is an *(primitive) type* over **B**.
2. Let name ∈ NAME. Then
    name: STRING is an *(elementary) type* over **B**,   */named character data/*
    name: is an *(empty elementary) type* over **B**.
3. Let T be a set type or named character data. Then
    T* is a *type* over **B**.   */zero or more/*
    T+ is a *type* over **B**.   */one or more/*
    T? is a *type* over **B**.   */zero or one/*
4. Let T be a type given by a step 3. Let name ∈ NAME. Then name: T is a *type* over **B**.   */named type/*

Restrictions:

- Let $[T_1,..., T_n]$ be an array type. Then any T_i can be T*, T+, or T?.
- Let $\{T_1,..., T_n\}$ be a set type. Then any T_i can be T?.

The *type system* $\mathbf{T}_{reg}$ *over* **B** (or $\mathbf{T}_{reg}$ if **B** is understood) is the least set containing types given by (1)–(4).

Then name:STRING denotes the set of character data named name, and name: denotes the empty character object. T? denotes the set of objects of type T ∪ NIL.

Now we will define JSON object types. We suppose for each name used in name:STRING or in name: the existence of the NAME name denoting an associate object type. The same holds for each name ∈ NAME.

Definition 4.3. Let T_{reg} over **B** be the type system from Definition 4.2 and **O** be the set of abstract objects. Then the *object type system* T_O *induced by* T_{reg} (or T_O if T_{reg} is understood) is the least set containing the object types given by the following rule:

- Let name:T be from T_{reg}. Replace all names in name:T by their upper-case version. Then NAME:T is a member of T_O.

The functional semantics of object types from T_O associates with NAME:STRING the set of all functions from **O** into name:STRING. For a non-elementary type T from T_O, the semantics of NAME:T is also functional, but the functions are more complex. Let B, C, and D be elementary object types, i.e. they denote the function space **O** $\rightarrow$ STRING. Then e.g. A:{C, D?} denotes a function space

$$\mathbf{O} \rightarrow (\mathbf{O} \rightarrow \text{STRING}) \times (\mathbf{O} \rightarrow \text{STRING} \rightarrow \text{BOOL}).$$

Note that ($\mathbf{O} \rightarrow$ STRING $\rightarrow$ BOOL) abbreviates (($\mathbf{O} \rightarrow$ STRING)$\rightarrow$ BOOL). Due to the properties of Cartesian product we can easily work with its components. For example, if A:{B, C, D} is an object type with A, B, C, and D as above, then A.B denotes functions of type ($\mathbf{O} \rightarrow \mathbf{O} \rightarrow$ STRING). Note, that it is the same space as for A:{B}. Let there is an object of this type. Then for each A abstract object we obtain an B abstract object and then B's character data. We observe that with names it is not necessary to use any positional notation.

4.3 Toward a JSON Functional Schema

We use a part of the JSON schema in Fig. 4 and one valid book object in Fig. 5, i.e., a simple BIBLIO DB is at disposal. The FIRSTNAME:STRING denotes the set of all functions associating with each abstract object from **O** at most one object of type firstname:STRING. The object of this type stored in the BIBLIO DB in Fig. 5 is defined for two abstract objects with values 'Anthony' and 'Joe', respectively. Obviously, in other BIBLIO DB the object of type FIRSTNAME could be defined also for abstract objects associated with no book object. There are people (authors) who are not book authors. Object types from T_O related to the book object in Fig. 5 include

```
TITLE:STRING
FIRSTNAME:STRING
SURNAME:STRING
LOCALITY:STRING
ZIP:STRING
ISSUED:NUMBER
ADDRESS:{LOCALITY, ZIP}
BOOK:{TITLE, AUTHORS, ISSUED?}
AUTHORS: [AUTHOR, AUTHOR]
NAME:{FIRSTNAME, SURNAME}
AUTHOR: {NAME, ADDRESS?}
```
(1)

In T_O we could specify, e.g., the BOOK object type by one complex expression as

```
{
  "book":{
    "title":"Business objects",
    "authors":["author":{
                "name":{
                  "firstname":"Anthony",
                  "surname":"Newman"
                         }
                "address":{
                  "locality":"Malostranske 25, Praha",
                  "ZIP":"118 00"
                            }
                          },
              "author":{
                "name":{
                  "firstname":"Joe",
                  "surname":"Batman"
                          }}]
        }}
```

Fig. 5. JSON document containing a book object

BOOK:{TITLE:STRING,
  AUTHORS:[AUTHOR:{NAME:{FIRSTNAME:STRING, SURNAME:STRING},
             ADDRESS?{LOCALITY:STRING, ZIP:STRING}},
         AUTHOR: {NAME:{FIRSTNAME:STRING, SURNAME:STRING},
             ADDRESS?{LOCALITY:STRING, ZIP:STRING}
         }],
ISSUED?:NUMBER}   (2)

JSON DB contains only one BOOK object in this example. In the case of NAME object type, the associated function is defined on two abstract objects. Obviously, NAME in this case means something else than NAME in Definition 4.3.

To consider books with exactly two authors is rather restrictive. We could take into account the variant AUTHORS:[AUTHOR+], i.e. books with one or more authors. Then the expression (2) would be much simpler.

Obviously, abstract objects are not visible. Intuitively, we can imagine objects stored in a JSON DB, which is described by appropriate typed object variables. A valuation of these variables provides a *DB state*. In practice, we could consider JSON DBs containing one JSON object of type BOOKS[BOOK+] containing books of type BOOK.

Thus, we will conceive a *JSON-database schema*, S_{JSON}, as a set of variables of types from T_O. Given a database schema S_{JSON}, a *JSON-database* is any valuation of variables in S_{JSON}. For convenience, we denote the variables from S_{JSON} by the same names as names from T_O, e.g. BOOK, AUTHOR, etc. Then object types in (1) represent a JSON-database schema. Explicit ICs on the JSON-database are not considered in this paper.

5 Querying JSON Data with λ-Terms

Recent query languages over JSON data have roots in languages for querying semistructured data. There the most important query languages deal with XML data. They enable easily to apply the notion of path in the query expressions as well as regular path expressions. We use this strategy here, too.

Due to the functional features of T_O, our approach will be based on the typed λ-calculus extended with arrays. The λ-calculus serves as a manipulation tool which directly supports manipulating objects typed by T_O.

First, we introduce a general definition of λ-terms (shortly terms).

Definition 5.1. Starting with a collection **Func** of constants, each of a fixed type, and denumerably many variables for each type from **T**, the *language of terms* (LT) is inductively defined as follows. Let types T, T_1,…, T_n ($n \geq 1$) are members of **T**.

1. Every variable of type T is a *term* of type T.
2. Every constant (a member of **Func**) of type T is a *term* of type T.
3. If M is a term of type $((T_1,...,T_n) \rightarrow T)$ and N_1,…,N_n are terms of type T_1,…,T_n, respectively, then
   $M(N_1,...,N_n)$ is a *term* of type T.   /*application*/
4. If x_1,…,x_n are distinct variables of types T_1,…,T_n, respectively, and M is a term of type T, then
   $\lambda x_1,...,x_a(M)$ is a *term* of type $((T_1,...,T_n) \rightarrow T)$.   /*λ-abstraction*/
5. If M is a term of type $\{T_1,...,T_n\}$ and N is of type $T \in \{T_1,...,T_n\}$. Then
   $N(M)$ is a *term* of type T.   /*set element*/
6. If N_1,…,N_n are terms of types T_1,…,T_n, respectively, then
   $[N_1,...,N_n]$ is a *term* of type $[T_1,...,T_n]$.   /*array*/
7. If M is a term of type $[T_1,...,T_n]$, then
   $M[1]$,…,$M[n]$ are *terms* of types T_1,…,T_n, respectively.   /*elements of array*/

Terms can be interpreted in a standard way by means of an interpretation assigning to each constant symbol from **Func** an object of the same type, and by a semantic mapping from LT into all functions and Cartesian products given by the type system **T**. In short, we assume a standard 'fixed' interpretation in which an application is evaluated as the application of the associated function to given arguments, a λ-abstraction 'constructs' a new function of the respective type, etc.

5.1 λ-Calculus and JSON Data

We restrict our λ-calculus to JSON data, i.e. we will suppose the type systems T_{reg} and T_O induced by T_{reg}. To add some expressiveness to LT, we permit some useful Boolean functions such as comparing predicates =, <, ≤, …, quantifiers, and logical connectives in **Func**. We will extend slightly the notion of variable. To achieve querying tags, it is necessary to consider not only variables typed by T_O. We need also variables like x:y, where x/NAME and y/T with T from T_{reg} or T_O. Obviously, the resulted type system and the language remain still very general, i.e. they are not *restricted* in the sense of permitting only JSON-data as the query output. For example, we will show that also relational data can be extracted from JSON data.

It is easily verified that terms of LT are usable to expressing queries. Each term defines a function after its evaluation over a given DB. For queries we use applications of functions and λ-abstractions. A typical *query term* is of form

$$\lambda \,..\, (\lambda \,..\, ...(\text{expression})...),$$

where **expression** is of type BOOL. A query term consists of two parts: the query part (here **expression**) and a constructor part (here the lambda part of the query term). A significant role is assigned to the lambda part. Similarly to XML query languages, we can construct the answer to a query, e.g., a new JSON document with a rich nested structure.

Another possibility of querying, as we shall see, is based on application terms. We examine now some terms and queries. We will use variables, e.g., *e*/**O**, other letters will denote abstract objects. Functional semantics of objects allows specifying paths via compositions of functions. For example, for a book abstract object *b* we can get the first author's surname for the book associated with *b*.

SURNAME(NAME(AUTHORS(b)[1]))

The variables AUTHORS, NAME and SURNAME from S_{JSON} are valuated by actual objects of respective types. Then this application returns character data, i.e. the value of a SURNAME object. To simplify the notation, we can use a more convenient "path-like" notation

b.AUTHORS[1].NAME.SURNAME

Then we can easily use comparisons like

b.AUTHORS[1].NAME.SURNAME = 'Newman'

5.2 Querying JSON Data—Examples

The first feature of most JSON-like query languages is the matching data using patterns. Consider again book's documents with one entry in Fig. 5 and the query D1: Find the addresses of the book author Anthony Newman. In JSON-λ language the query is expressed as follows:

λx (.BOOK.AUTHOR.NAME.SURNAME = 'Newman' **and**
    .BOOK.AUTHOR.FIRSTNAME = 'Anthony' **and**
    .BOOK.AUTHOR.ADDRESS = x)

Similarly to the JSON style, it is possible to omit parts of paths. We are using "." for specification root objects. The dot starting all three paths expresses that the path begins in an abstract book object. The object is common for all three paths. There is an equivalent expression that uses an existential quantifier and *e* variable for this purpose.

Obviously, $x/\mathbf{O}$. We can derive this fact from the context of x in the body of λ-abstraction. Each evaluation is running over all values of x, because x is free variable in the λ-abstraction body. Thus, as a result, we obtain a set of $\mathbf{O}$-objects in this case, which is not very user friendly. The set will be a singleton in the case when there is only one author Anthony Newman in the BIBLIO DB. Of course, for real addresses, the LOCALITY and ZIP would be necessary. Two authors Anthony Newman (even with the same address) could be assigned to two different abstract objects. To obtain the content of an abstract object we introduce notation of underlining. Then $\underline{x}$ returns the content of the abstract object valuating x. Replacing x by $\underline{x}$ in query term of D1(JSON-λ), we could obtain a presentation of the result like

```
{ "locality":"Malostranske 25, Praha",
  "ZIP":"118 00"
}
```

i.e. the result is a JSON object it this case. To obtain better semantics we should write

$$\lambda \text{ address:x}(\dots$$

in the lambda part of D1(JSON-λ). In this case, the choice of JSON names in the result can be user-controlled explicitly. This reminds introducing new XML tags (opening and closing) into a result of an XQuery query given by its RETURN clause.

We can also require fair STRING objects. For example, the query D2: Find all addresses, we formulate in JSON-λ as
D2(JSON-λ):

$$\lambda x, y \text{ (.ADDRESS.LOCALITY} = x \textbf{ and } \text{.ADDRESS.ZIP} = y)$$

After the query evaluation, we obtain a set of couples like ("Malostranske 25, Praha", "11800"), etc. That is, the result is a binary relation it this case.

In more convenient notation, we can group logical conditions belonging to the same path in D1(JSON-λ). Then, we can write

$$\lambda x \text{ (.BOOK.AUTHOR.NAME.(SURNAME} = \text{'Newman'}$$
$$\textbf{and } \text{FIRSTNAME} = \text{'Anthony')} \textbf{ and } \text{.BOOK..ADDRESS} = x)$$

The descendant operator ".." indicates any number of intervening levels. Of course, it's just an abbreviation for a more complex expression. Then the lambda part of D1(JSON-λ) can be even shortened to

$$\lambda x \text{ (.BOOK..NAME.(SURNAME} = \text{'Newman'}$$
$$\textbf{and } \text{FIRSTNAME} = \text{'Anthony')} \textbf{ and } \text{.BOOK..ADDRESS} = x)$$

According to the DB notions, till now discussed JSON-λ features represent a *selection* of data based on simple logical conditions. The term

$$\lambda x \text{ (.BOOK..NAME.(SURNAME} = \text{'Newman'} \textbf{ and } \text{FIRSTNAME} = \text{'Anthony')}$$
$$\textbf{and } \text{.BOOK..ADDRESS} = x \textbf{ and } \text{.BOOK.ISSUED} > 2015)$$

ensures to select the addresses of authors whose books were published after 2015.

The following powerful feature of JSON-λ simulates the *object join operation* over a common value. Moreover, we will show how this operation combines data from different JSON DBs. The second JSON DB of our example, ADDRESSBOOK, contains records from an address book. Its entry in Fig. 6 contains only data about one person.

```
{
   "addressbook":{
          "person":{
              "ID":"111-22-3333",
              "surname":"Newman",
              "name":"Anthony"
              "titled":"Dr. A. Newman",
              "address":"Malostranské 25, Praha 1",
              "links":["tel":"2191 4268",
                       "tel":"2191 4323",
                       "email":"newman@ksi.mff.cuni.cz"]
                 } }
}
```

Fig. 6. JSON document containing an addressbook object

We try to join objects from both DBs in the query D3.
D3: Who from our contacts are authors of books? Give also their e-mail addresses.
We need to distinguish between two data sources, e.g. using a prefix notation.
D3(JSON-λ):

λ x, y, m (BIBLIO:.BOOK..NAME.(SURNAME = x **and**
   FIRSTNAME = y) **and** ADDRESSBOOK:.PERSON.(SURNAME = x **and**
   NAME = y **and** LINKS[3] = m))

The result is a ternary relation of STRING data. To obtain the answer in more JSON-like style, we can replace the lambda part of the query term, e.g., by

λ e-contact:[surname:x, name:y, email:m]

i.e. the result will be a set of E-CONTACT objects composed from triples of other objects. Because this is a part of a query expression, it is not necessary to solve the problem of assigning new abstract objects to parts of the result.

In general, a constructing JSON data in the answer is ensured by the lambda part of a query term (see, D3(JSON-λ)). A "flattening" of a hierarchy is also possible to do. It reminds a denormalization of relations. For example, we can easily formulate a query in JSON-λ, which produces a list of triples (title, firstname, surname). An author can occur in the result many times, dependent on the number of his/her books.

We can write more structured queries in JSON-λ.
D4. For each author find the book titles, where the author is the first author.

D4(JSON-λ):

> λ firstname x.NAME.FIRSTNAME, surname:x.NAME.SURNAME
> (λtitle:y(BOOK.(AUTHORS[1](x) **and** TITLE = y)))

D5. Find the names of authors for each book.
D5(JSON-λ):

> λ title:y (λname:<u>x.NAME</u> (∃i .BOOK..(AUTHORS[i](x) **and** TITLE = y)))

We have used here the NAME component of the variable x. Names will contain properties firstname and surname.

Another category of queries could use the universal quantifier and implication similarly to, e.g., the domain relational calculus. We conclude the description of JSON-λ with usage of aggregate functions in queries. Suppose now the query
D6. For each book, find the number of its authors.
D6(JSON-λ):

> λ x, n (.BOOK..(TITLE = x **and** COUNT(AUTHORS) = n))

The query returns a relation whose each row is composed from a book title and associated number of its authors. Suppose here AUTHORS:[AUTHOR+] in JSON-database schema (1). The type of n variable is derived from COUNT type. Remind that COUNT assigns to each set or array its cardinality.

6   Conclusions

In this paper, we have shown a DB-oriented view on JSON data based on a functional approach to typing. JSON schema is a set of typed functions. Then, a version of typed λ-calculus (LT language) was used as a formal background for querying JSON data. Comparing to MongoDB querying, LT is more expressive due to logical connectives, quantifiers, arithmetic operations, and aggregation functions included in **Func**. Query answers can be relations, tree structures of STRING values, and even new JSON data. Queries in MongoDB return only subsets of a collection. Because the proposed LT language is very general, it would be necessary to use only its appropriate subset in practice.

With the LT language we can do even an integration of NoSQL and relational DBs [11, 12]. Integration of relational and JSON data can be done without problems.

There is also a standardized approach to integration of SQL and JSON in the SQL:2016 [6]. There the SQL/JSON path language and the SQL/JSON operators are defined. More about JSON integration with relational DBs can be found in [7].

Acknowledgments. This work was supported by the Charles University project Q48.

References

1. Baazizi, M.A., Lahmar, H.B., Colazzo, D., Ghelli, G., Sartiani, C.: Schema inference for massive JSON datasets. In: Proceedings of EDBT 2017, pp. 222–233 (2017)
2. Bourhis, P., Reutter, J.L., Vrgoč, D., Suárez, F.: JSON: data model and query languages. Inf. Syst. **89**, 123–135 (2020)
3. Droettboom, M., et al.: Understanding JSON Schema Release 7.0. Space Telescope Science Institute (2019)
4. Duzi, M., Pokorny, J.: Semantics of general data structures. In: Charrel, P.-J., Jaakkola, H., Kangassalo, H. (eds.) Information Modelling and Knowledge Bases IX, pp. 115–130. IOS Press, Amsterdam (1998)
5. Lv, T., Yan, P., He, W.: Survey on JSON data modelling. J. Phys. Conf. Ser. **1069**, 683–687 (2018)
6. Michels, J., et al.: The new and improved SQL: 2016 standard. SIGMOD Rec. **47**(2), 52–60 (2018)
7. Petković, D.: JSON integration in relational database systems. Int. J. Comput. Appl. (0975–8887) **168**(5), 14–19 (2017)
8. Pokorný, J.: Database semantics in heterogeneous environment. In: Jeffery, K.G., Král, J., Bartošek, M. (eds.) SOFSEM 1996. LNCS, vol. 1175, pp. 125–142. Springer, Heidelberg (1996). https://doi.org/10.1007/BFb0037401
9. Pokorný, J.: XML functionally. In: Desai, B.C., Kioki, Y., Toyama, M. (eds.) Proceedings of IDEAS2000, pp. 266–274. IEEE Computer Society (2000)
10. Pokorný, J.: XML-λ: an extendible framework for manipulating XML data. In: Abramowicz, W. (ed.) BIS 2002, Poznan, pp. 160–168 (2002)
11. Pokorný, J.: Integration of relational and NoSQL databases. In: Nguyen, N.T., Hoang, D.H., Hong, T.-P., Pham, H., Trawiński, B. (eds.) ACIIDS 2018. LNCS (LNAI), vol. 10752, pp. 35–45. Springer, Cham (2018). https://doi.org/10.1007/978-3-319-75420-8_4
12. Pokorný, J.: Integration of relational and graph databases functionally. Found. Comput. Decis. Sci. **44**(4), 427–441 (2019)
13. Pezoa, F., Reutter, J.R., Suarez, F., Ugarte, M., Vrgoč, D.: Foundations of JSON schema. In: Proceedings of WWW 2016, pp. 263–273 (2016)

Semantic Web

Template-Based Multi-solution Approach for Data-to-Text Generation

Abelardo Vieira Mota$^{(\boxtimes)}$, Ticiana Linhares Coelho da Silva$^{(\boxtimes)}$, and José Antônio Fernandes De Macêdo$^{(\boxtimes)}$

Insight Data Science Lab, Fortaleza, Brazil
abevieiramota@gmail.com, {ticianalc,jose.macedo}@insightlab.ufc.br

Abstract. Data-to-text generation is usually defined into two parts: planning how to order and structure the information, and generating a text grammatically correct and fluent, that is faithful to the facts described in the input knowledge base source. A typically knowledge base consists of Resource Description Framework (RDF) triples which describe the entities and their relations. There are plenty of end-to-end solutions proposed to generate natural language descriptions from RDF, however, they require large and noise-free training datasets, lack control over how the text will be generated and there is no guarantee that the generated text verbalizes all and only the input. We address these problems by proposing a modular solution that uses templates and generates multiple texts over the data-to-text generation phases, returning the best one. Our experiments on a real-world dataset demonstrate that our approach generates higher quality texts and outperforms some baseline models regarding BLEU, METEOR, and TER.

Keywords: Natural Language Generation · Knowledge bases · Data to text generation · Semantic web

1 Introduction

Data-to-text generators produce natural language texts from a source data representation. Some of these source representations were designed to be used by computers, and humans can not easily understand them. For instance, Resource Description Framework (RDF), which represents information as triples $\langle subject, predicate, object \rangle$, can be extremely difficult for non-experts users to understand. RDF has been widely used in knowledge bases, as DBpedia [20], that contains data extracted from Wikipedia. One way to make these knowledge bases more accessible to humans is to convert their data to natural language texts.

However, it would be expensive and slow to perform this task manually, moreover it would require familiarity with the knowledge base, which in general, no user should be expected to have. These are reasons that motivate the development of automatic methods for generating texts from RDF data. Natural

J. Darmont et al. (Eds.): ADBIS 2020, LNCS 12245, pp. 157–170, 2020.
https://doi.org/10.1007/978-3-030-54832-2_13

Language Generation (NLG) is a field of study concerned with the development of computer systems for automatically generate natural language texts from non-linguistic data [26].

Consider a user that searches for information about Barack Obama over the DBpedia knowledge base. For sake of brevity, suppose that the following set of triples are returned:

$$\langle BarackObama, birthDate, 1961\text{-}8\text{-}4 \rangle$$
$$\langle BarackObama, birthPlace, Hawaii \rangle$$
$$\langle Hawaii, capital, Honolulu \rangle$$

There is more than one way to verbalize this data. One of them is *"Barack Obama was born in Honolulu, Hawaii, on August 4, 1961."*. Another one is *"Honolulu, capital of Hawaii, is the city where Obama was born in 1961/08/04."*. These generated texts are different regarding the fact ordering, the entity ordering, and how the information is represented. All these choices should be made by the NLG system to verbalize the data.

The paper [26] highlights a consensus on the basic decisions an NLG system should care: (i) Content Determination, to decide which subset of data to verbalize; (ii) Discourse Planning, to decide the order in which the data will be verbalized, and the discourse itself. For instance, it should decide to present first more general information and then detailing it; (iii) Sentence Aggregation, to decide how to partition the data, so each part becomes a single sentence; (iv) Lexicalization, to decide which words to use to verbalize relations between entities; (v) Referring Expression Generation, to decide which words to use to refer to entities; and finally, (vi) Linguistic Realization, to decide about grammar aspects of the text, as words agreement and punctuation.

In this paper, we tackle the problem of generating a text grammatically sound and that correctly represents all the information contained in the input set of triples. Various recently published works on generating texts from RDF triples use deep learning with an end-to-end architecture [6,16,21,29], following a trend on other Natural Language Processing tasks [12]. End-to-end deep learning architectures have the advantage of not requiring specialist knowledge on the domain or on linguistics, but to do so these models require large and noise-free training datasets [8], lack control over how the text will be generated, and there is no guarantee that the generated text verbalizes all and only the input. An alternative solution, called modular architecture, to these problems has been investigated. In such case, a deep learning model is used in all modules [9], or only in the realization module [23]. Another alternative is the modular template-based system, defined by [5] as a system that maps a non-linguistic input directly to a linguistic surface structure. The modular template-based approach is an alternative to deep learning, because it offers simplicity and allows more control of the generation process, which is a requirement for some NLG systems in production [14].

However, modular template-based systems provide, in general, poor results when there are global constraints on the texts to be generated that can not be satisfied by local constraints on the modules [25]. This problem is called generation gap [12]. In this paper, we address the generation gap using a multi-solution modular architecture, in which each module generates multiple outputs, generating at the end multiple texts that are fed to a model responsible for selecting the text that should be finally returned. We show that the quality of a multi-solution approach is higher than a single-solution. We also compare it with other proposed approaches from the state-of-the-art.

This paper is organized as follows. In Sect. 2 we give a formal definition of the problem. Then, in Sect. 3 we detail our proposed architecture and its modules. In Sect. 4 we explain how we designed the experiments and their results. In Sect. 5 we discuss the related work. Finally, in Sect. 6 we present the conclusions and future work.

2 Preliminaries

In this section, we first introduce the template concept and the N-gram models used in our approach, and finally we formulate our problem statement.

2.1 Templates

In our solution, the generated text comes from templates of sentences, that are texts with slots to be filled with references to entities or values. We define a template as a tuple $\langle s, Z \rangle$, where $s = [t'_1, t'_2, ..., t'_n]$ is a sequence of triples t'_i in which both the *subject* and *object* are variables, and Z is the template text. For example, consider the following template for the sentence *"Barack Obama was born in Honolulu, Hawaii, on August 4, 1961"*.

$$\langle s = [\langle \boldsymbol{slot_1}, birthDate, \boldsymbol{slot_2} \rangle,$$
$$\langle \boldsymbol{slot_1}, birthPlace, \boldsymbol{slot_3} \rangle,$$
$$\langle \boldsymbol{slot_3}, capital, \boldsymbol{slot_4} \rangle],$$
$$Z = \text{``}\boldsymbol{slot_1} \text{ was born in } \boldsymbol{slot_4}, \boldsymbol{slot_3}, \text{ on } \boldsymbol{slot_2}.\text{''} \rangle$$

The generated text from the template is obtained by replacing the slots $slot_1$, $slot_2$, $slot_3$, and $slot_4$, respectively, with references to the entities *BarackObama*, *Honolulu, Hawaii*, and the value *1961-8-4*.

Before using a template, it is necessary to verify if the template is appropriate to verbalize the input data and which entities should replace each slot. A template is appropriate to a sequence of RDF triples $T = [t_1, t_2, ..., t_n]$ if filling the template with the data in T, the generated text verbalizes all and only the triples in T, respecting the order in which they appear in T. The template used as an example is appropriate to the triples shown in page 2, if they were put in a sequence in the same order as they are shown. Different from the input of the problem, that is a set of triples, the input of a template is a sequence of triples.

2.2   N-gram Model

An N-gram model estimates the probability of a word w_{m+1} coming after a sequence of words $w = [w_1, w_2, ..., w_m]$ looking only to its last $N - 1$ words, i.e., $[w_{m-N+1}, ..., w_m]$. Let $w_i^j = [w_i, w_{i+1}, ..., w_j]$, where $i \leq j$, denote the subsequence of w, from the i-th element to the j-th element and $w_i^j w_k$ the concatenation of the subsequence w_i^j and the word w_k. In order to account for the context before the first word and after the last word, we add the sequence $[\langle s \rangle, ..., \langle s \rangle]$, with $N - 1$ elements, before and after the sequence of words w, with the special symbol $\langle s \rangle$, resulting in the sequence W. Using the chain rule and a context of $N - 1$ words, we can estimate the probability of a sequence of words:

$$P(w) = P(W) \approx \prod_{k=N}^{|W|} P(W_k | W_{k-N+1}^{k-1}) \tag{1}$$

Given $C(W_i^j)$ the number of occurrences of the sequence W_i^j in a corpus, we estimate $P(W_k | W_{k-N+1}^{k-1})$ using Maximum Likelihood Estimation as:

$$P(W_k | W_{k-N+1}^{k-1}) = \frac{C(W_{k-N+1}^{k-1} W_k)}{C(W_{k-N+1}^{k-1})} \tag{2}$$

Smoothing techniques can be used to move some probability of more frequent words to words that were not present in the corpus and that would receive probability 0 otherwise. We refer the reader to the book [17] for further details.

2.3   Problem Definition

A knowledge base is defined as a set of RDF triples, where each RDF triple is represented as $t = \langle subject, predicate, object \rangle$, representing the information that the entity identified as *subject* is related to the entity or value identified as *object* through the predicate identified as *predicate*. Given $\mathcal{K} = \{t_1, t_2, ..., t_n\}$, a subset of the knowledge base, our goal is to generate a natural language text $\mathcal{S}$ which consists of a sequence of words $[w_1, w_2, ..., w_l]$, where w_l denotes the l-th word in the sentence $\mathcal{S}$. The generated sequence $\mathcal{S}$ is required to be grammatically correct, fluent, and should verbalize all and only the facts described in $\mathcal{K}$.

3   Our Approach

In this section we describe our modular template-based multi-solution approach.

Figure 1 shows the pipeline of our proposal. The pipeline follows the tasks described in [26]. The only difference is that our solution receives the knowledge base $\mathcal{K}$ that must be verbalized, so there is no need to deal with the task Content Determination, and the tasks Lexicalization and Linguistic Realisation are solved by the Template Selection module, that chooses templates from a template database. The reference database associates *subjects/objects* of triples to natural language expressions that can be used to refer to them.

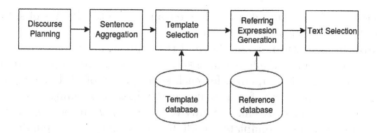

Fig. 1. Our proposed architecture

The paper [9] also follows the tasks described in [26]. Basically, [9] returns only one output in each phase, besides using deep learning techniques to implement each module. Our hypothesis, in this work, is that by returning multiple outputs in each phase, we have more chances to generate a text more fluent and customized to the type of user. We prove this assumption in the experimental section.

Rather than using all possible outputs for each module, which would generate a combinatorial explosion, we limit them to the top possible outputs, according to some ranking model. We use N-gram models as ranking models, using the probability that they give to a sequence as a score. We clarify how each module performs using the running example below. Given a knowledge base:

$$\mathcal{K} = \{\langle Bakso, ingredient, Noodle\rangle,$$
$$\langle Bakso, country, Chinese\_cuisine\rangle\}$$

1. **Discourse Planning**: given $\mathcal{K}$, this module is responsible for returning the triples ordered in a sequence, defining the order in which these triples should be verbalized. Every possible order is scored by this module according to an N-gram model of predicates. One possible ordering is
   $[\langle Bakso, country, Chinese\_cuisine\rangle, \langle Bakso, ingredient, Noodle\rangle]$, and the N-gram model should score the sequence of its predicates
   $["country", "ingredient"]$. The output is the top k sequence of triples according to the score given by the N-gram model.
2. **Sentence Aggregation**: given T one of the sequences of triples from the previous module, this module is responsible for splitting T into subsequences, each of them to be verbalized as a sentence. For every way of splitting T, this module generates a sequence of triple predicates interleaved with a | symbol, representing a splitting boundary or a _ symbol, meaning that the predicates of both sides were placed in the same subsequence. This module then scores that sequence using an N-gram model of predicates and | and _ symbols. Given the sequence of triples ordered by the previous phase, $[\langle Bakso, country, Chinese\_cuisine\rangle, \langle Bakso, ingredient, Noodle\rangle]$, one of the possible way of splitting it is to put all triples in the same subsequence
   $[\,[\langle Bakso, country, Chinese\_cuisine\rangle, \langle Bakso, ingredient, Noodle\rangle]\,]$, and the N-gram model will score the corresponding sequence

["*country*", "*_*", "*ingredient*"]. The output is the top b ways of splitting T according to the score given by the N-gram model.

3. **Template Selection**: given P one of the splittings of triples, from the previous module, this module is responsible for selecting appropriate templates, from a database of templates, for each subsequence of P. Remember that a template is appropriate for a sequence of triples T if filling it with T, the generated text verbalizes all and only the triples in T, respecting their order. In order to evaluate a template, we fill its slots with the corresponding triples' *subject/object*, and evaluate the resulting text with an N-gram model. We emphasize that the resulting text is not already ready to be returned by the solution, as the triples' *subject/object* are referred using their values themselves, and not with appropriate textual references. Given the partition $[[\langle Bakso, country, Chinese\_cuisine \rangle, \langle Bakso, ingredient, Noodle \rangle]]$, one appropriate template is:

$$TEM = \langle [\langle \boldsymbol{slot_1}, country, \boldsymbol{slot_2} \rangle,$$
$$\langle \boldsymbol{slot_1}, ingredient, \boldsymbol{slot_3} \rangle],$$
$$\text{"}\boldsymbol{slot_1} \text{ is from } \boldsymbol{slot_2} \text{ and contains } \boldsymbol{slot_3}.\text{"} \rangle$$

and the N-gram model should evaluate the sequence:
["*Bakso*", "*is*", "*from*", "*Chinese_cuisine*", "*and*", "*contains*", "*Noodle*", "*.*"]
The output is $TEMS$ the combinations of the top p templates, from a database of templates, for each of the subsequences of the splitting of triples P. Because of that, its computational cost is exponentially proportional to p.

4. **Referring Expression Generation**: given $TEMS$ one of the combinations of templates for the partitioning P, from the previous module, this module is responsible for selecting textual references, from a database of textual references, of the triples' *subject/object* to fill the $TEMS$ templates' slots. In order to evaluate a textual reference to fill one slot of one of the templates in $TEMS$, we fill that slot with that reference, and its remaining slots with the corresponding triples' *subject/object*, and evaluate the resulting text with the an N-gram model. In the example, given the template TEM, imagine we want to fill $slot_1$ with a reference for the entity $Bakso$. A possible reference for $Bakso$ is "The dish Bakso". So the N-gram model will evaluate the sequence ["*The dish Bakso*", "*is*", "*from*", "*Chinese_cuisine*", "*and*", "*contains*", "*Noodle*", "*.*"]. The output is the combination of templates $TEMS$ for the partition P, and for each of its templates' slots, the top q textual references, from a database of textual references, that can be used to fill their slots, according to the corresponding *subject/object* in triples in P. Because of that, its computational cost is exponentially proportional to q.

5. **Text Selection**: given the combination of templates $TEMS$ and the corresponding q textual references, for each of their slots, from the previous phase, this module is responsible for selecting the top text generated by filling the templates with one textual reference for each of their slots. Consider a possible output from the previous phase the template TEM and the textual references

for its slots:

slot1 $\in$ { "Bakso", "Chinese dish Bakso", "The dish Bakso"}

slot2 $\in$ { "China", "chinese cuisine", "the chinese cuisine"}

slot3 $\in$ { "noodle", "noodles"}

One combination of references is **slot1** = "The dish Bakso", **slot2** = "China", **slot3** = "noodle", and the N-gram model will evaluate the text *"The dish Bakso is from China and contains noodle"*. We note that the Text Selection module can become a limiting factor if it selects low-quality texts.

In the next section, we present the experimental evaluation conducted to assess the validity of our approach in terms of quality and run-time performance.

4 Experiments

4.1 Dataset

We evaluated our solution using the WebNLG [11] dataset[1], released as part of the WebNLG 2017 shared task [4]. It was generated through a semi-automatic process using DBpedia [20], and contains 9674 entries of the form $\langle category, tripleset, references \rangle$, where *category* is one of 15 categories like "Astronaut" and "University"; *tripleset* is a set of triples $\langle subject, predicate, object \rangle$, ranging from 1 to 7 triples, containing information about one entity and possible related entities; and *references* is a set of English texts verbalizing the information represented by *tripleset*, ranging from 1 to 8 texts. We used the same dataset partitioning used in the shared task, where there are a *training* set (6940 entries), a *development* set (872 entries) and a *test* set (1862 entries), and the *test* set is divided into two subsets: *test-seen* (971 entries), containing entries from categories seen in the *training* or *development* sets, and *test-unseen* (891 entries), that contains the remaining.

4.2 Experimental Setup

To generate the template database and the reference database, we used the enhanced version of the WebNLG dataset [10], that contains the templates for the *references*, the order in which the *tripleset* was verbalized, and how its triples were grouped into sentences. The template database associates each template to one of 15 categories from WebNLG benchmark, according to the category of the entry from which the template was extracted. The Template Selection module first tries to retrieve templates of its input category; if there is none, it then retrieves templates from other categories.

We extracted datasets of sequences to train the N-gram model of each module described in the previous section. Given *tripleset*, a set of triples; *txt*, a text that verbalizes *tripleset*, we use the following sequences to train the N-gram models:

---

[1] Currently there are more than one release of this dataset. We used the first release, the same release used in the 2017 shared task.

1. **Discourse Planning**: the sequence of predicates of triples in *tripleset*, ordered according to the order in which the triples are verbalized in *txt*;
2. **Sentence Aggregation**: the same sequence as for the previous module, but adding a symbol between the predicates indicating if two adjacent predicates occurred in the same sentence in *txt*, or the |, otherwise;
3. **Template Selection**: the sequence obtained by replacing the references to entities in *txt* by the entities identifiers (the *subject/object* of the triples in *tripleset*). For example, from the *txt* "The teacher Francisca works in Universidade Federal do Ceará." we generate the sequence "**id768** works in **id835**", assuming "The teacher Francisca" is a reference to the entity identified by **id768**, and "Universidade Federal do Ceará" to **id835**.
4. **Referring Expression Generation**: similar to the previous module, but rather than to replace a textual reference by its entity identifier, we replace it by an identifier to the textual reference itself. Using the previous example, rather than replacing "The teacher Francisca" by its entity identifier **id768**, we replace it with an identifier to the textual reference itself, that we generate simply replacing the spaces by an underline, resulting in the text "*The_teacher_Francisca works in Universidade_Federal_do_Ceará.*".
5. **Text Selection**: the *txt* itself.

As a tool to train, store and use N-gram models, we used KenLM [15], which uses Kneser-Ney smoothing [19].

The parameters involved in this work are the order of each N-gram model (from each module described in the previous section), and k, b, p, q which are the numbers of outputs from the Discourse Planning, Sentence Aggregation, Template Selection, and Referring Expression Generation modules, respectively. We perform a widely used method, called grid search [3], to choose appropriate values for those parameters. Basically, we pre-defined a set of values for each parameter, the values are described in Table 1. In grid search, the set of trials is formed by assembling every possible combination of values. Next, we rank the trials according to the achieved BLEU. Then, we start the fine search by looking at the range where the best-ranked values for all parameters fall within. This means the trial of the parameter values which provides the highest BLEU is the best configuration. We use lower values for the parameters p and q, than the k and b, because they contribute exponentially to the experiment cost. The order of the N-gram models and the number of outputs from the modules were discovered by training using the *training* set, and evaluated using the *development* set. After the discovery of the best values for those parameters, we use the *training* and *development* sets to build the models, and evaluate them.

4.3 Evaluation Metrics

We evaluated our solution using the *test-seen* set, and we used the same automatic metrics used in WebNLG shared task: BLEU [24], METEOR [2], and TER

Table 1. Grid Search hyperparameters

Discourse planning		Sentence aggregation		Template selection		Referring expression generation		Text selection
k	order	b	order	p	order	q	order	order
5, 10	3, 4	5, 10	3, 4	1, 2	3, 4	1, 2	3, 4	3, 4

[27][2]. These metrics were originally proposed for evaluation of machine translation as an alternative for human evaluation, and they work comparing the text to be evaluated with a set of reference texts. We report the metric values for our approach and six competitors: (i) *adaptcentre* an end-to-end deep learning solution, which is the best solution of the WebNLG shared task, regarding to BLEU metric for *test-seen* set, and (ii) *upf-forge*, a modular rule-based solution, which is the best, regarding the human evaluation they conducted [1], (iii) *deepnlg-e2ernn* we refer the reader to [9], (iv) *seq2seq-wc-word* we refer the reader to [16], (v) *gcn* we refer the reader to [18], (vi) *BIU-Chimera-v1* we refer the reader to [23].

We also provide and discuss some generated texts from our approach and the competitors.

4.4 Experimental Results

Table 2 shows the values for BLEU, METEOR, and TER on the *test-seen* set, and it is ranked by BLEU. We call *template-pipe-multi* our approach trained with the best hyperparameters according to the grid-search. It achieves competitive results with the current best approaches evaluated with the WebNLG benchmark. It is in the third place according to BLEU and METEOR scores, and in the first place, according to TER. We also report the scores obtained by a variant of our approach using a single-solution at each module, and using the same order of the N-gram models. We call it *template-pipe-single*. As we expected, there was a tradeoff between text quality and run-time performance. While on the *test-seen* set the model *template-pipe-multi* spent 40 s and received a BLEU of 57.87, the model *template-pipe-single* received a BLEU of 55.27, and spent 1.5 s, more than 20 times faster. This proves our hypothesis that by returning more outputs in each module, we can generate a text more fluent and more customized to the type of user (with higher BLEU).

We also analyzed the texts generated by *template-pipe-multi*, *adaptcentre* and *upf-forge* for 70 randomly selected entries from the *test* set, uniformly distributed in relation to the entries' number of triples. We found some types of errors:

---

[2] We used the same preprocessing and the same tools. All scores reported here are calculated in the same way. METEOR and TER scores were rounded to 2 decimal places; BLEU score was not rounded.

Table 2. Scores on *test-seen* set.

Approach	BLEU	METEOR	TER
adaptcentre	60.59	0.45	0.38
deepnlg-e2ernn	58.36	0.42	0.40
template-pipe-multi	57.87	0.43	0.37
seq2seq-wc-word	55.82	0.41	0.40
gcn	55.35	0.39	0.40
template-pipe-single	55.27	0.42	0.40
BIU-Chimera-v1	53.20	0.44	0.47
upf-forge	40.88	0.41	0.56

- there are texts that contains words not existent in English, like "capition" in this text from *adaptcentre*: *"the english language is spoken in the united states where akron, ohio is the **capition**."*; for some of them it looks like a typo, as in this text from *upf-forge*: *"the main ingredient in batagor are fried fish dumpling with tofu and vegetables **inpeanut** sauce."*;
- some texts contains repeated information, as this one from *adaptcentre*: *"(...) the language spoken in texas is english and one of the languages is english. (...)"*;
- our solution, *template-pipe-multi*, generate a text that is not a well formed English sentence: *"california gemstone benitoite."*;
- the text *"**johns hopkins university** is the parent company of johns hopkins university (...)"*, from our solution, *template-pipe-multi*, fails to refer to the entity *Johns_Hopkins_University_Press* as its subject;
- some texts lack cohesion between its sentence, as this text from *adaptcentre* *"amsterdam airport schiphol serves the city of amsterdam. The runway name is 18l/36r aalsmeerbaan and is 2014."*;

Those problems could be attributed to the systems that generated the texts, but the data also has some problems. Some predicates are verbalized in ways that implies different meanings. It is the case of the predicate *leader*, that sometimes means that the object is **the** leader of the subject, sometimes means that it is **one of the** leaders. For a tripleset containing two triples with the predicate *leader*, *upf-forge* generated a text containing *"(...) manuel valls is the leader of france, the leader of which is gerard larcher. (...)"*. Some predicates are verbalized with various verb tenses. It is the case for *club*, that is verbalized, in the *test* set, as *"Michele Marcolini played for Vicenza Calcio."*, but also as "Michele Marcolini plays for Vicenza Calcio."

5   Related Works

There is not still a consensus on what precisely Natural Language Generation comprises [12]. As the name implies, it is related to processes that generate natural language texts, but it does not say anything about from which type of input. It can be a table, an image, or a graph, but it can also be a text, as it is the case of Text Summarization. The papers [26] and [12] narrow this definition and say that NLG refers to systems that generate texts from non-linguistic data. We adopt that definition, as there are specific decisions that an NLG system must do that other text generation systems do not have to do. For example, an automatic translation system already receives, in its input, the order in which information has to be verbalized, or which discourse structure to use.

Reference [26] says that at that time, it was becoming a consensus that a set of basic activities should be carried out by an NLG system. It was, in short, to decide how the information will be structured, the discourse relations, the organization in sentences, the words to be used to refer to concepts and entities, and finally more surface aspects of a text, like punctuation and the case of letters. How these activities are organized in modules defines how modular or integrated is an NLG system's architecture, being called end-to-end a system that has just one module that has all these responsibilities. Before the growth of the use of data-driven methods, rule-based modular systems were prevalent [12]. As more computational resources became available, and more research was conducted on data-driven methods, more end-to-end systems were proposed, using deep learning methods.

Different types of NLG systems have been proposed to generate texts from RDF data. Reference [7] proposes *LOD-DEF*, a system that automatically generates short descriptions of entities, using templates. It extracts a database of templates through a semi-automatic process; then, it collects statistics of RDF predicates usage in order to define class models, that specify which predicates entities of that class are relevant, how they should be ordered, and their set of templates. To describe a given entity, it first decides which class model to use, and using the templates of the chosen class model it selects templates in a way that they express all the values in the input. Our approach differs from their approach in that all of our modules are multi-solution and are data-driven.

One advantage of template-based solutions is to be cheap to adapt to other languages, as it was shown by [13]. They adapted to English a template-based solution for generating football match reports in Dutch, translating the templates from Dutch to English through a semi-automatic process, using a machine translation tool, and then manually correcting its results. They report the problem of automatically translating idiomatic expressions, as some may occur in one language but not in the other.

Another approach to generate text is to model it as a process of translation between the input and the resulting text. The paper [16] compares word-based and character-based sequence-to-sequence models. They conclude that sequence-to-sequence models can be used to verbalize structured data, even surpassing human performance, when evaluated with automatic metrics, but they credit this to their capacity to learn patterns in the training data. They have not found evidence that one of the word-based or character-based approach was superior to the other. They also made experiments assessing the capacity of sequence-to-sequence models to generalize beyond the texts they were trained on, and generate novel texts. Reference [29] explores the idea that they could improve the quality of a sequence-to-sequence model changing its training objective. Rather than simply transforming the RDF graph into a sequence of tokens, and then feeding the model, [6] and [21] propose new ways to encode RDF, better preserving its graph structure. They both conclude that graph-based encoders improve the model's result. To use deep learning with a low amount of labeled data, [28] proposed to use Reinforcement Learning to improve a model with unlabeled data.

Recent works have proposed to use deep learning with more modular architectures. The paper [9] compares the use of deep learning techniques in a pipeline architecture, inspired by the tasks defined in [26], and in an end-to-end architecture. They used the deep learning techniques Gated-Recurrent Unit (GRU) and Transformer, and the WebNLG dataset [4]. They concluded that the pipeline architecture generates more fluent texts than the end-to-end architecture.

Reference [23] also proposes a pipeline architecture, but with only two modules, one responsible for planning the text, defining the order of the information and how it should be grouped in sentences, and other responsible for transforming that plan into a text. The first module was implemented as a ranking model, selecting the best text plan according to a score calculated as a product of probabilities of some text plan features, like the frequency of splitting the triples in sentences as the text plan. Different from [9], only the last module was implemented using deep learning techniques. They also got results that suggest that more modular architectures outperform end-to-end architectures, pointing that it occurs because, in this way, the neural module has fewer responsibilities. They point, as another advantage, the fact that more modular architectures allow more control over the output.

6   Conclusion

In this paper, we address the problem of automatically generating texts that are grammatically correct and sound from a set of input RDF triples. We propose a template-based multi-solution approach following the pipeline proposed in [26]. The experiments show that our approach outperforms some baselines from the state-of-the-art, regarding BLEU, METEOR, and TER quality measures. We also show that the multi-solution approach performs better than the single-solution. Although our approach did not outperform the best reported systems, and it has not the ability to generalize beyond the templates in the database of templates, our solution allows more control, comparing to end-to-end systems, over the generation process and the texts that are generated, as it is modular and uses templates. Also the automatic metrics to evaluate NLG solutions are only a surrogate to evaluate the quality of the generated texts, as they rely on a set of texts to be used as reference, and that set may not be representative of the set of all texts that could be considered a good text. The fact that the texts generated by the competitor *upf-forge* was considered the best, according to the human evaluation, but was not in the first ranks, regarding the automatic metrics, supports that idea. As a future direction, we aim at applying this solution with other ranking models and exploring techniques, like sentence fusion [22], to automatically derive new templates given a template database.

Acknowledgments. This work is partially supported by the FUNCAP SPU 8789771/2017, and the UFC-FASTEF 31/2019.

References

1. WebNLG challenge: human evaluation results. Technical report (2018)
2. Banerjee, S., Lavie, A.: METEOR: an automatic metric for MT evaluation with improved correlation with human judgments. In: Proceedings of the ACL Workshop on Intrinsic and Extrinsic Evaluation Measures for Machine Translation and/or Summarization, pp. 65–72 (2005)
3. Bergstra, J., Bengio, Y.: Random search for hyper-parameter optimization. J. Mach. Learn. Res. **13**(1), 281–305 (2012)
4. Colin, E., Gardent, C., Mrabet, Y., Narayan, S., Perez-Beltrachini, L.: The WebNLG challenge: generating text from DBPedia data. In: Proceedings of the 9th International Natural Language Generation Conference, pp. 163–167 (2016)
5. Deemter, K.V., Theune, M., Krahmer, E.: Real versus template-based natural language generation: a false opposition? Comput. Linguist. **31**(1), 15–24 (2005)
6. Distiawan, B., Qi, J., Zhang, R., Wang, W.: GTR-LSTM: a triple encoder for sentence generation from RDF data. In: Proceedings of the 56th Annual Meeting of the Association for Computational Linguistics (Volume 1: Long Papers), pp. 1627–1637 (2018)
7. Duma, D., Klein, E.: Generating natural language from linked data: unsupervised template extraction. In: Proceedings of the 10th International Conference on Computational Semantics (IWCS 2013)-Long Papers, pp. 83–94 (2013)
8. Dušek, O., Howcroft, D.M., Rieser, V.: Semantic noise matters for neural natural language generation. arXiv preprint arXiv:1911.03905 (2019)
9. Ferreira, T.C., van der Lee, C., van Miltenburg, E., Krahmer, E.: Neural data-to-text generation: a comparison between pipeline and end-to-end architectures. arXiv preprint arXiv:1908.09022 (2019)
10. Ferreira, T.C., Moussallem, D., Krahmer, E., Wubben, S.: Enriching the WebNLG corpus. In: Proceedings of the 11th International Conference on Natural Language Generation, pp. 171–176 (2018)
11. Gardent, C., Shimorina, A., Narayan, S., Perez-Beltrachini, L.: Creating training corpora for NLG micro-planning. In: 55th Annual Meeting of the Association for Computational Linguistics (ACL) (2017)
12. Gatt, A., Krahmer, E.: Survey of the state of the art in natural language generation: core tasks, applications and evaluation. J. Artif. Intell. Res. **61**, 65–170 (2018)
13. Gatti, L., van der Lee, C., Theune, M.: Template-based multilingual football reports generation using Wikidata as a knowledge base. In: Proceedings of the 11th International Conference on Natural Language Generation, pp. 183–188 (2018)
14. Harris, M.D.: Building a large-scale commercial NLG system for an EMR. In: Proceedings of the Fifth International Natural Language Generation Conference, pp. 157–160 (2008)

15. Heafield, K., Pouzyrevsky, I., Clark, J.H., Koehn, P.: Scalable modified Kneser-Ney language model estimation. In: Proceedings of the 51st Annual Meeting of the Association for Computational Linguistics, Sofia, Bulgaria, pp. 690–696, August 2013. https://kheafield.com/papers/edinburgh/estimate_paper.pdf
16. Jagfeld, G., Jenne, S., Vu, N.T.: Sequence-to-sequence models for data-to-text natural language generation: word- vs. character-based processing and output diversity. arXiv preprint arXiv:1810.04864 (2018)
17. Jurafsky, D., Martin, J.H.: Speech and Language Processing: An Introduction to Speech Recognition, Computational Linguistics and Natural Language Processing. Prentice Hall, Upper Saddle River (2008)
18. Kipf, T.N., Welling, M.: Semi-supervised classification with graph convolutional networks. arXiv preprint arXiv:1609.02907 (2016)
19. Kneser, R., Ney, H.: Improved backing-off for M-gram language modeling. In: 1995 International Conference on Acoustics, Speech, and Signal Processing, vol. 1, pp. 181–184. IEEE (1995)
20. Lehmann, J., et al.: DBpedia-a large-scale, multilingual knowledge base extracted from Wikipedia. Seman. Web 6(2), 167–195 (2015)
21. Marcheggiani, D., Perez-Beltrachini, L.: Deep graph convolutional encoders for structured data to text generation. arXiv preprint arXiv:1810.09995 (2018)
22. Marsi, E., Krahmer, E.: Explorations in sentence fusion. In: Proceedings of the Tenth European Workshop on Natural Language Generation (ENLG 2005) (2005)
23. Moryossef, A., Goldberg, Y., Dagan, I.: Step-by-step: separating planning from realization in neural data-to-text generation. arXiv preprint arXiv:1904.03396 (2019)
24. Papineni, K., Roukos, S., Ward, T., Zhu, W.J.: BLEU: a method for automatic evaluation of machine translation. In: Proceedings of the 40th Annual Meeting on Association for Computational Linguistics, pp. 311–318. Association for Computational Linguistics (2002)
25. Reiter, E.: Pipelines and size constraints. Comput. Linguist. 26(2), 251–259 (2000)
26. Reiter, E., Dale, R.: Building applied natural language generation systems. Nat. Lang. Eng. 3(1), 57–87 (1997)
27. Snover, M., Dorr, B., Schwartz, R., Micciulla, L., Makhoul, J.: A study of translation edit rate with targeted human annotation. In: Proceedings of Association for Machine Translation in the Americas, vol. 200 (2006)
28. Zang, H., Wan, X.: A semi-supervised approach for low-resourced text generation. arXiv preprint arXiv:1906.00584 (2019)
29. Zhu, Y., et al.: Triple-to-text: converting RDF triples into high-quality natural languages via optimizing an inverse KL divergence. In: Proceedings of the 42nd International ACM SIGIR Conference on Research and Development in Information Retrieval, pp. 455–464 (2019)

Distributed Tree-Pattern Matching in Big Data Analytics Systems

Ralf Diestelkämper[1(✉)] and Melanie Herschel[1,2]

[1] University of Stuttgart, Stuttgart, Germany
{ralf.diestelkaemper,melanie.herschel}@ipvs.uni-stuttgart.de
[2] National University of Singapore, Singapore, Singapore

Abstract. Big data analytics systems such as Apache Spark offer built-in support for nested data, which abounds, for instance, as JSON data available online. However, these systems typically have to transform the data to gain access to (deeply) nested data for further processing. This adds complexity to big data analytics pipelines and may result in an unnecessary runtime overhead. Therefore, this paper introduces tree-pattern matching as a first-class operator in big data analytics systems. It reduces the complexity of big data analytics pipelines and accelerates the pipeline processing by up to four times, compared to state-of-the-art pipelines for nested data. The novelty of our operator lies in the distributed and data-parallel processing supported by its underlying tree-pattern matching algorithm. Experiments validate that our operator, implemented in Spark, can improve pipeline complexity and runtime.

Keywords: Tree-pattern matching · Nested data · Big data analytics

1 Motivation

Online, vast amounts of data are distributed, shared, and published. A noticeable portion of the data is in nested data formats. For instance, Twitter provides tweets in JSON format [12], DBLP offers their database in XML format [13], and public sensor data are frequently downloadable as JSON files. Further examples are provided in [20]. Big data analytics systems such as Apache Spark, Flink, and Hive natively support reading these nested formats but use their own hierarchical data formats for internal processing, e.g., Apache Parquet.

Example 1.1. To illustrate nested data (which we will use as a running example), consider the sample Twitter data in Table 1, highly simplified from real Twitter data for conciseness. Each tuple includes a tweeted *text*, an authoring *user* tuple with attributes *id_str* and *name*, and a nested collection of *user_mentions*, which holds tuples featuring *id_str* and *name* for each user mentioned in the tweeted *text*. Each tweet has a *retweet_cnt* that indicates the number of retweets.

© Springer Nature Switzerland AG 2020
J. Darmont et al. (Eds.): ADBIS 2020, LNCS 12245, pp. 171–186, 2020.
https://doi.org/10.1007/978-3-030-54832-2_14

Table 1. Twitter-like example input data

Table 2. Example output data

	text	user		user_mentions		retweet_cnt
			id_str	name		
1	Hello @ls @jm @ls	id_str / name — lp / Lisa Paul	ls	Lauren Smith		0
			jm	John Miller		
			ls	Lauren Smith		
2	Hello World	id_str / name — ts / Tom Sims				0
3	Hello @lp	id_str / name — jm / John Miller	id_str / name — jt / Jane Tik			1

	name
101	Lisa Paul
102	Lauren Smith
103	John Miller

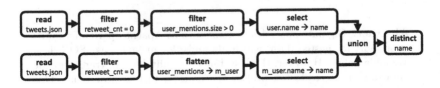

Fig. 1. Example processing pipeline without tree-pattern matching

A key feature of big data analytics systems is the ability to scale out on increasing computing resources. The systems process data in pipelines of individual operators (e.g., filters, joins, maps) that distribute computations in a data-parallel fashion. The most common operators to restructure nested data are flatten and nesting. These operators are necessary to give subsequent operators direct access to deeply nested tuples since directly addressing arbitrary combinations of nested data is not supported in big data analytics systems. As a consequence, pipelines processing nested data become unnecessarily complex and, thus, difficult to understand, maintain, and inefficient.

Example 1.2. Assume that our goal is to retrieve all names of persons who either have authored a user-mentioning tweet or are themselves mentioned in at least one original (i.e., non-retweeted) tweet. The example pipeline, shown in Fig. 1, computes these names, returning Table 2. The pipeline determines the names of the authoring users in its upper branch and the names of the mentioned users in its lower branch before uniting and deduplicating them. While this pipeline answers our initial question, we observe that the filter on the *retweet_cnt* occurs in both branches of the pipeline unlike the filter on the *user_mentions*. The upper branch explicitly filters tweets without *user_mentions*, whereas the lower branch implicitly prunes these tweets by flattening the *user_mentions*. The flatten operator is necessary to elevate the mentioned users to the top-level of the hierarchical data.

Our sample pipeline illustrates how a simple "access and return" query for names appearing at different locations in the hierarchy results in a pipeline with duplicated operators and different operators to implement similar constraints. For XML data, tree-pattern matching has been extensively studied to query complex structures in nested data. The next example gives a basic understanding of tree-pattern matching (defined later).

Example 1.3. Using a tree-pattern matching operator, as shown in Fig. 2, the pipeline (black) that answers the same question as in Example 1.2 has three operators, as opposed to the ten operators in Fig. 1. The tree-pattern matching operator requires a tree-pattern as parameter, which we show in blue in Fig. 2. In the visualization, node labels correspond to attribute labels to be matched by the input data. The interest in returning only *names* is indicated by the double frame of the node labeled *name*. Edges between nodes express structural constraints, requiring either a parent-child relationship (single-lined) or an ancestor-descendent relationship (double-lined). Thus, the *name* node will match both *name* attributes in the *user* attribute and in the *user_mentions* attribute of our input data. The tree-pattern further supports cardinality constraints (e.g., at least one tuple in a collection nested under *user_mentions*) and value constraints (e.g., *retweet_cnt* = 0). Using Table 1 as input, the tree-pattern matching operator matches only the first tuple. However, it matches that tuple twice: with the *name* of *user* and with the *name* of *user_mentions*.

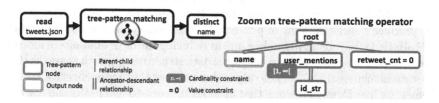

Fig. 2. Example processing pipeline with tree-pattern matching (Color figure online)

Contributions. As illustrated above, tree-pattern matching may simplify big data analytics pipelines that process nested data. Given that pipelines with fewer operators also potentially incur less time-consuming data shuffling, we present the definition and implementation of a tree-pattern matching operator for big data analytics systems. In addition to reducing pipeline complexity, it shall maintain the key features of distributed processing, including data-parallel computation. This prevents us from using existing tree-pattern matching algorithms that heavily rely on global state. They use stacks or state-machines, requiring massive synchronization in a distributed setting, which counters the advantage of using a big data analytics system.

Our tree-pattern matching algorithm leverages the property of big data systems to strictly separate the schema from its homogeneously structured data. This allows us to define a two-phase algorithm: In the first phase, it matches a given tree-pattern against the schema of the dataset, narrowing down the data to consider in the second phase, where it validates constraints that the tree-pattern imposes on the instance data. We seamlessly integrate the tree-pattern matching algorithm as an operator into Spark's Dataframe API. Experimental validation shows that our tree-pattern matching operator not only reduces the complexity of big data analytics pipelines but also improves the overall runtime of some big data analytics pipelines.

Structure. Section 2 covers related work. In Sect. 3, we provide the formal foundation for our two-phase tree-pattern matching algorithm, which we present in Sect. 4. Section 5 describes our implementation in Apache Spark and reports experimental results. We conclude in Sect. 6.

2   Related Work

Multiple surveys have been published on state-of-the-art research for tree-pattern matching [10,16,18,19]. Due to space constraints, we only briefly review the algorithm families for tree-pattern matching most relevant to our work.

Structural join approaches split tree-patterns into smaller parts, match these smaller parts against the data, and merge these parts to a complete tree-pattern match [2,23]. These approaches typically employ region encoding to identify and index elements in the data. However, they have the caveat that they produce a large amount of potentially unnecessary intermediate results.

Holistic twig join approaches aim at reducing the large amounts of intermediate results. Thus, they make use of global data structures [8], such as stacks [4,15] and state machines [14,17]. These algorithms also exploit more effective labeling schemes, such as Dewey labeling, that encodes the root-to-leaf paths and the nesting depth to identify and index the data more efficiently than region encoding. The TwigVersion [21] algorithm further identifies repetitive structures in the nested data to improve the tree-pattern matching. The S^3 [11] approach extends this idea by creating a QueryGuide structure that extracts all paths from the nested data. Then it applies a matching on these paths before accessing the actual data. While TwigVersion and S^3 use a similar idea to consider constraints on the structure and the data separately, they still operate on the complete input XML document, labeling and indexing each element in the data.

The mentioned algorithms are all optimized for matching tree-patterns on a single XML document on a stand-alone computer. They either produce a large amount of potentially unnecessary intermediate results or make use of global data structures. Both properties are unacceptable for distributed execution. Distributing large amounts of intermediate results across distributed computing resources leads to network contention and, thus, to low overall performance. Maintaining global data structures inhibits the algorithms to scale horizontally across the computing resources because of lock contention on the global data structures. In contrast, our approach is designed to scale on a distributed cluster.

3   Preliminaries on Nested Data Model and Tree-Patterns

This section briefly introduces the nested data model relying on [1,9] and the tree-patterns we target in this paper. They are in accordance with the data formats processed in big data analytics systems.

3.1   Data Model

Nested collections contain tuples whose labeled attributes have one of three types: primitive types (e.g., integers), nested tuples, or nested collections. Tuples in nested collections form a *nested collection instance*, and all comply to the same *schema*.

Definition 3.1. (Nested collection schema). *Given an infinite set of names* $\mathbb{L}$, *root* $\notin \mathbb{L}$, *and* $A_i \in \mathbb{L}$, *a nested type* $\mathcal{R}$, *called nested collection schema, is recursively defined by the following grammar:*

$$\mathcal{P} := \text{INT} \mid \text{STR} \mid \text{BOOL} \mid \ldots \qquad \mathcal{R} := \{\{\mathcal{T}\}\}$$
$$\mathcal{T} := \langle A_1 : \mathcal{A}, \ldots, A_n : \mathcal{A} \rangle \qquad \mathcal{A} := \mathcal{P} \mid \mathcal{T} \mid \mathcal{R}$$

Definition 3.2. (Nested collection instance). *A collection whose type* τ *complies to a valid nested collection schema* $\mathcal{R}$ *is a nested collection instance* I *of type* $\mathcal{R}$, *denoted as* $\tau(I) = \mathcal{R}$.

Next, we define *paths*, which allow us to uniquely identify and access nested attributes, tuples, and collections.

Definition 3.3. (Path). *In the context of tuple* $t \in I$, *a path* p *is recursively defined by* $p = t.p'$, $p' = x \mid x.p'$, $x = A \mid A[i]$. *The* x *is an attribute* A *of a nested tuple, a value, or the* i-*th element of a nested collection* A, *denoted as* $A[i]$. *The context of* p' *is recursively updated to the context* x.

For simplification, we denote a path p with context tuple t by p^t when the context is not clear. We refer to the enumeration of all paths that exist in a context t as the path set PS^t. While the definition of paths defines them on tuple instances, we will slightly abuse the notation to also write paths on (nested) schema elements. In both cases, by convention, we will name the unnamed outermost collection (type) of I ($\mathcal{R}$) as *root*.

Example 3.1. The value ls appearing in the first tuple of Table 1 has full path $root[1].user\_mentions[1].id\_str$. To designate attribute $retweet\_cnt$ at schema level, we use the path $root[pos].retweet\_count$, where pos is a placeholder for any possible position.

Next, we formally introduce tree-patterns and tree-pattern matches. The matches are defined in two parts: (i) on the schema and (ii) on the instance.

3.2   Tree-Patterns

In our introductory example in Sect. 1, we have illustrated different aspects of a tree-pattern, which include tree-pattern nodes and edges, value constraints, and cardinality constraints. Here, we formally define these.

Definition 3.4. (Value constraint). *A value constraint* $vc = \langle comp, const \rangle$ *with respect to an attribute A of primitive type $\mathcal{P}_A$ is a tuple holding a comparison operator* $comp \in \{=, \neq, >, \geq, <, \leq, contains\}$ *and a constant value const in the domain of $\mathcal{P}_A$, denoted as* $\tau(const) = \mathcal{P}_A$.

Definition 3.5. (Cardinality constraint). *A cardinality constraint with respect to an attribute A of type $\mathcal{R}$ is a tuple $cc = \langle min, max \rangle$ with $min, max \in \mathbb{N} \cup \infty$ defining the minimum and the maximum number of occurrences of tuples in the instance of A.*

Definition 3.6. (Tree-pattern node). *A tree-pattern node n is a 4-tuple $n = \langle A, vc, cc, on \rangle$, where $A \in \mathbb{L} \cup \{\{root\}\}$ denotes an attribute name, vc either $\perp$ or a value constraint, cc either $\perp$ or a cardinality constraint, and on a boolean indicating if n is an output node when true, or not when false.*

Example 3.2. The value constraint on attribute $retweet\_cnt$ is $vc_{rtc} = \langle =, 0 \rangle$. Cardinality constraint $cc_{um} = \langle 1, \infty \rangle$ applies on $user\_mentions$. Examples of tree-pattern nodes are $n_{rtc} = \langle retweet\_cnt, vc_{rtc}, \perp, false \rangle$ or $n_{name} = \langle name, \perp, \perp, true \rangle$.

Definition 3.7. (Structural constraint). *A structural constraint with respect to two tree-pattern nodes n_1 and n_2 is a boolean value $sc = \{true|false\}$ that encodes a parent-child relationship (PC) between n_1 and n_2 when true or an ancestor-descendant relationship (AD) when false.*

Definition 3.8. (Tree-pattern edge). *A tree-pattern edge is a triple $e = \langle n_1, n_2, sc \rangle$, where $n_1 \neq n_2$ are tree-pattern nodes and sc is a structural constraint with respect to nodes n_1 and n_2.*

Example 3.3. The edge connecting the root node n_{root} with n_{name} describes an AD relationship, defined by $e_{root\_name} = \langle n_{root}, n_{name}, false \rangle$.

Definition 3.9. (Tree-pattern). *A tree-pattern is a triple $T = \langle r, N, E \rangle$. Here, r is a tree-pattern node, N is a set of tree-pattern nodes (including r), and E is a set of tree-pattern edges. N and E form a single tree rooted at r.*

3.3   Tree-Pattern Matching

Tree-patterns are used to identify data within an instance I whose structure is defined by a tree-pattern T. Essentially, tree-patterns only match the data if all nodes N and all edges E have a counterpart in the actual data. Further, the data must fulfill all value, cardinality, and structural constraints that the pattern defines. In the literature, this matching is formalized by embeddings [10,18].

According to our data model, all tuples of a nested instance comply to the same schema. Hence, we can divide the classical definition of embeddings into a data-independent schema-matching and a data-dependent data-matching. During schema-matching, we check for matches in (i) the node names in the tree-pattern and (ii) compliance to all structural constraints. During data-matching, we check for fulfilling all constraints, including cardinality and value constraints.

Definition 3.10. (Schema-matching). *Given $T = \langle r, N, E \rangle$ and a nested collection schema $\mathcal{R}$, a schema match M fulfills the following constraints over $\mathcal{R}$:*

1. *All nodes $n \in N$ match an attribute label $A_R \in \mathcal{R}$, denoted $M(n) = A_R$:*
   $\forall n = \langle A, vc, cc, on \rangle \in N, \exists A_R \in \mathcal{R} \models A = A_R$
2. *All PC relationships $e_{PC} \in E$ match in $\mathcal{R}$, denoted $M(e_{PC}) = \langle A_P, A_C \rangle$:*
   $\forall \langle n_P, n_C, true, on \rangle \in E, \exists A_P, A_C \in \mathcal{R} \models M(n_P) = A_P \wedge M(n_C) = A_C \wedge$
   $(path(A_C) = path(A_P).A_C \vee path(A_C) = path(A_P)[pos].A_C)$
3. *All AD relationships $e_{AD} \in E$ match in $\mathcal{R}$, denoted $M(e_{AD}) = \langle A_A, A_D \rangle$:*
   $\forall \langle n_A, n_D, false, on \rangle \in E, \exists A_A, A_D \in \mathcal{R} \models M(n_A) = A_A \wedge M(n_D) = A_D \wedge$
   $path(A_A)$ *is a prefix of* $path(A_D)$

Overall, each match M maps T to a tree with nodes M_N and edges M_E, i.e., $M(T) = \langle M_N, M_E \rangle$ where $M_N = \bigcup_{n \in N} M(n)$ and $M_E = \bigcup_{e \in E} M(e)$. In this tree, nodes (edges) are uniquely identified by their path (pair of paths). All value constraints vc, cardinality constraints cc, and output flags on are transferred from the nodes in T to their matching nodes in M. There can be more than one schema match of T in $\mathcal{R}$, and we define the schema-matching $\mathcal{M}$ as the set of all possible schema-matches of T in $\mathcal{R}$.

Example 3.4. In our example, schema-matching produces two matches M_1 and M_2, as illustrated in Fig. 3. The matches differ in only one path. M_1 results from $M(name) = root[pos].user.name$, while for M_2, we have $M(name) = root[pos].user\_mentions[pos].name$.

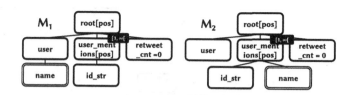

Fig. 3. Schema matches M_1 (left) and M_2 (right) obtained in our running example

Essentially, the above schema-matches serve as a blueprint for the full tree-pattern match over the input data. They guarantee that all required attribute labels are present and all structural constraints are satisfied. Therefore, in the data-matching step, we only need to check, for each match $M \in \mathcal{M}$, the cardinality constraints and value constraints on each tuple t of an instance I.

Definition 3.11. (Data-matching). *Given a schema match M and a tuple $t \in I$, we say that t is a data match of M iff the following conditions hold:*

1. *All value constraints hold:*
   $\forall n \in M_N, vc_n \neq \bot \models$ *the value of $path(n)^t$ satisfies vc*
2. *All cardinality constraints hold:*
   $\forall n \in M_N : cc_n \neq \bot \models$ *subtree of M rooted at n matches tuples in the nested relation at $path(n)^t$ at least min_{cc} times and at most max_{cc} times*

Example 3.5. Considering M_2, shown in Fig. 3, and the second tuple t_2 of Table 1, we see that the cardinality constraint for node $root[pos].user\_mentions$ is not satisfied, because the nested collection instance rooted at $root[2].user\_mentions$ does not contain at least one tuple with attributes id_str and $name$.

Algorithm 1: $tpm(T, I)$

Input: Tree-pattern T, dataset I of type $\mathcal{R}$
Output: Dataset I' of type $\mathcal{R}'$
1   $\mathcal{M} \leftarrow matchSchema(T, \mathcal{R})$
2   $I' \leftarrow matchData(\mathcal{M}, I)$
3   **return** I'

Algorithm 2: $matchSchema(T, \mathcal{R})$

Input: Tree-pattern T, schema $\mathcal{R}$
Output: SchemaMatches $\mathcal{M}$
1   $\mathcal{M} \leftarrow \emptyset$
2   $\mathcal{R}_D \leftarrow deweyID(\mathcal{R})$
3   $I_{\mathcal{R}} \leftarrow deweyIdx(\mathcal{R}_D)$
4   $RC \leftarrow I_{\mathcal{R}}(T.r.name)$
5   **for** $rc \in RC$ **do**
6     $C \leftarrow \emptyset$
7   **for** $l \in leaves(T)$ **do**
8       $C \leftarrow C \cup \langle node : l, candidates : \{\{lc | lc \in I_{\mathcal{R}}(l.name) \wedge prefix(rc, lc) = true\}\}\rangle$
9   **for** $c \in \{\{\langle cc_1.node : lc_1, ..., cc_{|C|}.node : lc_{|C|}\rangle | lc_i \in cc_i.candidates \wedge cc_i \in enum(C)\}\}$ **do**
10       $M_c \leftarrow merge(rc, c)$
11   **if** $validate(M_c) = true$ **then**
12         $\mathcal{M} \leftarrow \mathcal{M} \cup \{\{transferConstraints(M_c)\}\}$

13   **return** $\mathcal{M}$

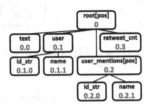

Fig. 4. Schema with assigned DeweyIDs (grey)

4 Tree-Pattern Matching

Given a tree-pattern T and a dataset instance I of schema $\mathcal{R}$, we propose a two-phase algorithm to match T onto I as summarized in Algorithm 1. The two phases correspond to the definitions of the schema-matching and the data-matching provided in Sect. 3. The $matchSchema$ function computes the schema matches $\mathcal{M}$ as defined by Definition 3.10. The algorithm only accesses the data of I in its second phase, when calling the $matchData$ function. This function yields the output collection that contains just those tuples that match the tree-pattern, following Definition 3.10. The separation of the schema-matching and data-matching phases allows for distributed processing of tree-pattern matching, which is imperative when processing data in big data analytics systems. In the following, we describe the two phases of the algorithm in detail.

4.1 Schema Matching

Algorithm 2 computes the set of schema matches $\mathcal{M}$. During the initialization phase (ll. 1–4), the algorithm assigns each attribute in $\mathcal{R}$ a DeweyID to obtain the annotated schema $\mathcal{R}_D$. Intuitively, the DeweyID [14] encodes the nesting of attributes. The algorithm creates an index $I_\mathcal{R}$ that maps each unique node label to a set of these DeweyIDs. Using this index, it retrieves the list of all root candidates RC, i.e., nodes in $\mathcal{R}_D$ that match the root node r of T (l. 4).

Example 4.1. In our example, the algorithm assigns the DeweyIDs shown in Fig. 4. For instance, $name$ is mapped to the list $\{\{0.1.1, 0.2.1\}\}$. Reusing our sample tree-pattern of Fig. 2, we obtain $RC = \{\{0\}\}$.

While iterating over the root candidates (ll. 5–12), the algorithm computes the schema matches $\mathcal{M}$ for each root candidate $rc \in RC$. To this end, it first associates each leaf node l of the tree-pattern T to a set of candidate attributes of $\mathcal{R}_D$, identified by DeweyID, in a map C (ll. 6–8). Candidate matches to l are nodes that match l's label, retrieved from index $I_\mathcal{R}$ ($lc \in I_\mathcal{R}(l.name)$) and that are descendants of the root candidate ($prefix(rc, lc) = true$).

Example 4.2. Our sample tree-pattern has the leaves $name, id\_str, retweet\_cnt$, for which the algorithm computes the following mapping C:

$$C = \left\{\left\{ \begin{array}{c} \langle name : \{\{0.1.1, 0.2.1\}\}\rangle \\ \langle id\_str : \{\{0.2.0\}\}\rangle \\ \langle retweet\_cnt : \{\{0.3\}\}\rangle \end{array} \right\}\right\}$$

In lines 9–12, the algorithm computes the schema matches from C. Conceptually, it creates the cross product of the DeweyIDs stored in each label's list in C (l. 9). Then, for each combination c comprising $|C|$ DeweyIDs, the algorithm merges the root to leaf paths into a schema match candidate M_c using the DeweyIDs (l. 10). Next, it validates that M_c fulfills all structural constraints defined by tree-pattern T. If the validation succeeds, it transfers value and cardinality constraints from T to matching nodes of M_c and adds M_c to $\mathcal{M}$.

Example 4.3. Continuing Ex. 4.2, C results in enumerating:

$$c_1 = \langle name{:}0.1.1, id\_str{:}0.2.0, retweet\_cnt{:}0.3 \rangle$$

$$c_2 = \langle name{:}0.2.1, id\_str{:}0.2.0, retweet\_cnt{:}0.3 \rangle$$

Considering c_1, the three paths, which are compactly represented by DeweyIDs, result in a candidate schema match

$$M_1 = \langle \{0, 0.1, 0.1.1, 0.2., 0.2.0, 0.3\},$$
$$\{(0, 0.1), (0.1, 0.1.1), (0, 0.2), (0.2, 0.2.0), (0, 0.3)\} \rangle$$

This match corresponds to M_1 of Fig. 3. It can be easily verified that c_2 results in the schema match M_2 shown in Fig. 3.

When the algorithm has computed the matches, it advances to next phase.

4.2 Data Matching

In the second phase, the algorithm computes the tuples that comply to any of the schema matches $M \in \mathcal{M}$. For that purpose, function *matchData* (not shown due to space constraints) relies on the recursive function *checkTuple* (see Algorithm 3) to check the value and cardinality constraints of each M against every tuple $t \in I$, individually. For each tuple t, the function is initialized with M's root node n and an empty path $p =$ "". In general, the *checkTuple* method verifies that tuple t satisfies all the constraints of node n. The method keeps track of its nesting through path p. If a value constraint is specified on n, the method evaluates the condition on the value that tuple n exhibits at path p (line 3). Satisfying the value constraint vc_n of node n is a prerequisite to match the remaining matching subtree rooted at n. The verification of the subtree is done recursively in depth-first order. In iterating over n's children, we distinguish two cases: (i) If a child node c of n refers to an attribute typed as nested collection, the algorithm further checks potential cardinality constraints on c by calling the *checkCol* method (see Algorithm 4). (ii) If the attribute is a tuple, the method calls itself to match the child node c reachable via the path $p.name_c$, where $name_c$ represents the attribute name. (iii) If the attribute is of primitive type, the recursion terminates.

To verify cardinality constraints, the *checkCol* function in Algorithm 4 first retrieves the collection COL by evaluation path p on t. Then, it iterates over the *elements* in COL, counting the nested tuples that match the sub-tree of M rooted in n. Since n is, in general, the root of a sub-tree, the algorithm has to validate all constraints of this whole sub-tree. That is why the algorithm calls *checkTuple* in line 4. Only if all constraints on the nested tuple hold, it increments the counter *cnt*. Then, it checks if a cardinality constraint cc_n is defined. If so, the algorithm returns true when cnt is within the range required

Algorithm 3: *checkTuple(t, n, p)*	**Algorithm 4:** *checkCol(t, n, p)*
Input: tuple t, node $n \in N_M$, path p	**Input:** tuple t, node $n \in N_M$, path p
Output: boolean value indicating if t matches constraints of subtree of M rooted at n (true) or not (false)	**Output:** boolean value indicating if t matches constraints of subtree of M rooted at n (true) or not (false)

```
1  isValid ← true
2  if vc_n ≠ ⊥ then
3  |   isValid ← eval(p^t, vc_n)

4  if isValid then
5  |   for c ∈ childrenOf(n) do
6  |   |   if c matches a collection type
   |   |   then
7  |   |   |   isValid ← isValid ∧
   |   |   |   checkCol(t, c, p.name_c)
8  |   |   else
9  |   |   |   isValid ← isValid ∧
   |   |   |   checkTuple(t, c, p.name_c)

10 return isValid;
```

```
1  COL ← p^t
2  cnt ← 0
3  for el ∈ COL do
4  |   if checkTuple(t, n, p[pos(el)]) then
5  |   |   cnt ← cnt + 1

6  isValid ← true
7  if cc_n ≠ ⊥ then
8  |   isValid ← false
9  |   if min_{cc} ≤ cnt ≤ max_{cc} then
10 |   |   isValid ← true

11 return isValid
```

by the cardinality constraint and false otherwise. Due to space constraints, we omit the details on collecting the values of output nodes. Basically, we maintain maps, which allow us to generate the output tuples based on the output nodes.

5   Implementation and Evaluation

In this section, we discuss the implementation of our distributed tree-pattern matching algorithm and our experimental evaluation.

5.1   Implementation

We implement our distributed tree-pattern matching algorithm in Apache Spark [22]. We choose Spark because this work is part of a larger extension of Spark for provenance management [6,7]. However, note that our algorithm definition is independent of the underlying big data analytics system and can be implemented in other systems in the same way.

Apache Spark's Dataframe API [3] provides well-known operators (e.g., selection, projection, join, flatten, or nesting). Pipelines that consist of these operators undergo a query planning and a query execution phase in Spark (like in relational database management systems). We extend the API with a novel tree-pattern matching operator that developers can use and arbitrarily combine with the other Spark operators when defining data processing pipelines.

The operator separates the implementation of the schema-matching phase from Sect. 4.1 and the data-matching phase from Sect. 4.2. The schema-matching phase integrates into Spark's query planning phase since it only depends on the schema of the data. Like query planning, the schema matching is not distributed across the cluster. It is no bottleneck because the schema typically is orders of magnitude smaller than the data. The data-matching phase is part of the query execution phase and implemented as a user-defined function. Spark calls this function on each non-nested tuple in the input data individually. Thus, Spark can distribute the computation of this phase across the available computing resources in the same way it distributes the computation for a map operator.

When the tree-pattern defines no output nodes, the operator behaves as a filter and returns all matching tuples, structured as they were in the input. Otherwise, the operator yields tuples that are restructured following the specified output nodes. The operator potentially yields multiple output tuples per input tuple, because a tree-pattern may match multiple times on a single input tuple.

5.2 Evaluation

We evaluate our algorithm on a Spark 2.4.0 cluster that has 50 executors with 16 GB main memory each. We average five test runs. We use two nested datasets. (i) Twitter: The dataset has up to 130 million tweets. Each tweet has about 1000 attributes and eight layers of nesting [20]. We define five test scenarios T1–T5 (Table 3). (ii) DBLP: The dataset contains up to 1.5 billion records. Records have one of ten types, such as article or proceeding [13]. They are split by type and upscaled, such that essential characteristics, such as the average number of inproceedings per proceeding are preserved. We define two scenarios D1 and D2 (Table 3). Each dataset has a size of 100 GB (default) to 500 GB.

Table 3. Summary of test scenarios

S	$|\mathcal{M}|$	TPM Ops	Spark Ops	Description (detailed descriptions available in [5])
T1	14	1	33	Returns all *names* occurring in the input
T2	10	2	29	Running example
T3	1	1	6	Computes the *user* and *retweet_count* of tweets with at least three *hashtags* longer than five characters
T4	1	1	6	Computes a nested list of *hashtags* for each *user_mentions*
T5	1	1	12	Selects tweets with at least two *user_mentions* that have *name* longer than 5 characters and at least two *hashtags* containing "BTS"
D1	4	2	8	Selects all inproceedings with their proceedings from the last century that have more than 10 citations
D2	1	1	5	Selects all authors that have at least 2 aliases containing "Mill"

Qualitative Evaluation. Table 3 shows the number of operators in the pipeline with and without tree-pattern matching in columns *TPM Ops* and *Spark Ops*, respectively. The numbers do not include read and write operations at the beginning and end of each pipeline. With tree-pattern matching, the pipelines have at most two operators. Without the matching, they have up to 33 operators (T1). For T1 and T2, the number of operators is particularly high because the pipelines consist of one projection for each occurrence of the attribute *name* in the input data. Further, *name* attributes in nested collections need to be flattened out. In D1, the number is high since the *year* and the *citation* attribute occur multiple times and each occurrence needs a separate operator. In scenarios T3–T5 and D2, the high number of *Spark Ops* arises because the pipelines need to express cardinality constraints over nested collections on which further value constraints apply. To this end, the pipelines require a flatten operator on the nested collection, a filter on the value constraints, and an aggregation to ensure the cardinality constraints. In all the above scenarios, tree-matching significantly reduces the complexity of pipelines, allowing for a faster pipeline development process, lower pipeline maintenance effort, and higher overall productivity.

Scalability. To study scalability, we conduct two experiments. In the first experiment, we gradually increase the input data from 100 GB to 500 GB. In the second experiment, we increase the number of executors to study horizontal scaling on the computing resources. For the Twitter scenarios, we report the runtime results in Fig. 5 and the speedup results in Fig. 6. Due to space constraints, we omit detailed results for the DBLP scenarios, which are in accord with the observations we make on the Twitter scenarios.

Focusing on runtime (Fig. 5), we observe that our tree-pattern matching implementation scales linearly with the input data size across all five scenarios. Scenario T2 has the highest runtime because it validates 10 schema matches $M \in \mathcal{M}$ on the input data. Each match requires multiple values to match the constraints. That is more computationally intensive than validating 14 matches on a single attribute (T1) and than validating only one schema match (T3–T5). Thus, both the complexity of the tree-pattern and the number of schema matches influence the runtime. D1 and D2 also scale linearly with the input size.

Figure 6 reports the speedup factor with an increasing number of executors. Executors represent the computing containers in the Spark cluster. Given the runtime of a scenario with one executor r_1 and with n executors r_n, we report speedup $s = \frac{r_1}{r_n}$. The ideal speedup for n executors is n itself (grey line). In our results, all Twitter scenarios have an almost ideal speedup up to $n \approx 15$. Then, the speedup degrades, mainly because the executors share only 12 dedicated SSD disks, which become the bottleneck. D1 and D2 show similar behavior.

We have also studied the individual runtime of the schema-matching and data-matching phases. Detailed results are omitted due to space constraints. However, we generally observe that schema-matching (i) consistently takes less than 50 ms in all experiments, (ii) is constant over the different dataset sizes, since it is computed independently from the data and (iii) is dependent on the input schema size and the nodes in the tree-pattern. For instance, the schema matching in D1 and D2 is five times faster than the matching in T2 because the tree-patterns are smaller and the input schema has significantly fewer attributes.

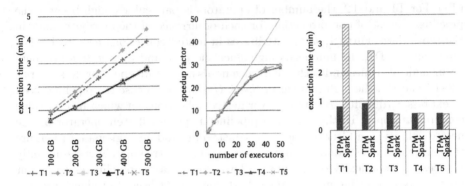

Fig. 5. Runtime for increasing input data

Fig. 6. Speedup for increasing computing resources

Fig. 7. Runtime with tree-pattern matching (TPM) and without (Spark)

Comparative Evaluation. Now, we compare the runtime of the pipelines with tree-pattern matching (TPM) and with standard Spark operators (Spark). Figure 7 shows our results. In T1 and T2, using tree-pattern matching is significantly faster than the "regular" Spark pipelines. The Spark pipelines unify intermediate results in a final step, causing shuffling of data across the computing nodes on the cluster, which imposes unnecessary overhead. Our tree-pattern matching operator does not require any shuffling. In T3 to T5, no shuffling is necessary. Thus, the pipelines using tree-pattern matching are slightly slower. Upon further inspection, we observe that the Spark pipelines are highly optimized, benefitting from, e.g., filter push-downs and custom code-generation for each pipeline. Nevertheless, even our baseline implementation of the tree-pattern matching operator, which has quite some room for improvements, does not significantly affect the runtime. In D1 and D2, the "regular" Spark pipelines are 30% faster than the tree-pattern matching pipelines. They benefit from filter push-downs, e.g., in D1, the filters on year are applied before joining the proceedings and inproceedings.

6   Conclusion and Outlook

We presented a novel operator for big data analytics systems that integrates tree-pattern matching into processing pipelines for nested data. The underlying tree-pattern matching algorithm exploits two properties of these systems: (i) they separate schema from data and (ii) require all tuples of a collection to have the same schema. Thus, the tree-pattern matching can be split into a schema-matching and a data-matching phase. Our experiments on real-world data show that our Spark implementation scales well, reduces the number of operators needed in pipelines, and reduces runtime when avoiding shuffling data. To further improve runtime, we plan to study optimizations of the data-matching phase and to integrate the matching algorithm into Spark's code-generation engine.

Acknowledgements. Partially funded by Deutsche Forschungsgemeinschaft (DFG) under Germany's Excellence Strategy - EXC 2075 - 390740016.

References

1. Afrati, F., Delorey, D., Pasumansky, M., Ullman, J.D.: Storing and querying tree-structured records in Dremel. PVLDB **7**(12), 1131–1142 (2014)
2. Al-Khalifa, S., Jagadish, H.V., Koudas, N., Patel, J., Srivastava, D., Wu, Y.: Structural joins: a primitive for efficient XML query pattern matching. In: ICDE (2002)
3. Armbrust, M., et al.: Spark SQL: relational data processing in spark. In: SIGMOD (2015)
4. Bruno, N., Koudas, N., Srivastava, D.: Holistic twig joins: optimal XML pattern matching. In: SIGMOD (2002)
5. Diestelkämper, R.: Evaluation workload (2020). https://www.ipvs.uni-stuttgart.de/departments/de/resources/pebble/pebble_tpm_workload.pdf
6. Diestelkämper, R., Herschel, M.: Capturing and querying structural provenance in spark with pebble. In: SIGMOD (2019)
7. Diestelkämper, R., Herschel, M.: Tracing nested data with structural provenance for big data analytics. In: EDBT (2020)
8. Grimsmo, N., Bjørklund, T., Hetland, M.: Fast optimal twig joins. PVLDB **3**, 894–905 (2010)
9. Grumbach, S., Milo, T.: Towards tractable algebras for bags. J. Comput. Syst. Sci. **52**(3), 570–588 (1996)
10. Hachicha, M., Darmont, J.: A survey of XML tree patterns. TKDE **25**(1), 29–46 (2013)
11. Izadi, S.K., Härder, T., Haghjoo, M.: S3: evaluation of tree-pattern XML queries supported by structural summaries. Data Knowl. Eng. **68**(1), 126–145 (2009)
12. Kumar, S.: Twitter Data Analytics. SpringerBriefs in Computer Science, 1st edn., p. 77. Springer, New York (2014). https://doi.org/10.1007/978-1-4614-9372-3
13. Ley, M.: DBLP: some lessons learned. PVLDB **2**(2), 1493–1500 (2009)
14. Lu, J., Ling, T., Chan, C.Y., Chen, T.: From region encoding to extended Dewey: on efficient processing of XML twig pattern matching. In: VLDB (2005)
15. Lu, J., Chen, T., Ling, T.W.: Efficient processing of XML twig patterns with parent child edges: A look-ahead approach. In: CIKM (2004)
16. Lu, J., Ling, T.W., Bao, Z., Wang, C.: Extended XML tree pattern matching: theories and algorithms. TKDE **23**(3), 402–416 (2011)
17. Lu, J., Meng, X., Ling, T.W.: Indexing and querying XML using extended Dewey labeling scheme. Data Knowl. Eng. **70**(1), 35–59 (2011)
18. Tahraoui, M., Pinel-Sauvagnat, K., Laitang, C., Boughanem, M., Kheddouci, H., Ning, L.: A survey on tree matching and XML retrieval. Comp. Sci. Rev. **8**, 1–23 (2013)
19. Tchendji, M.T., Tadonfouet, L., Tchendji, T.T.: A tree pattern matching algorithm for XML queries with structural preferences. J. Comput. Commun. **7**, 61–83 (2019)

20. Wang, Z., Chen, S.: Exploiting common patterns for tree-structured data. In: SIG-MOD (2017)
21. Wu, X., Liu, G.: XML twig pattern matching using version tree. Data Knowl. Eng. **64**(3), 580–599 (2008)
22. Zaharia, M., et al.: Apache spark: a unified engine for big data processing. CACM **59**(11), 56–65 (2016)
23. Zhang, C., Naughton, J., DeWitt, D., Luo, Q., Lohman, G.: On supporting containment queries in relational database management systems. In: SIGMOD (2001)

Data Analytics

Iterations for Propensity Score Matching in MonetDB

Michael H. Böhlen, Oksana Dolmatova$^{(\boxtimes)}$, Michael Krauthammer,
Alphonse Mariyagnanaseelan, Jonathan Stahl, and Timo Surbeck

University of Zurich, Zurich, Switzerland
{boehlen,dolmatova}@ifi.uzh.ch, michael.krauthammer@yale.edu,
{alphonse.mariyagnanaseelan,jonathan.stahl,timo.surbeck}@uzh.ch

Abstract. The amount of data that is stored in databases and must be analyzed is growing fast. Many analytical tasks are based on *iterative methods* that approximate optimal solutions. *Propensity score matching* is a technique that is used to reduce bias during cohort building. The main step is the propensity score computation, which is usually implemented via iterative methods such as gradient descent. Our goal is to support efficient and scalable propensity score computation over relations in a column-oriented database. To achieve this goal, we introduce *shape-preserving iterations* that update values in existing tuples until a fix point is reached. Shape-preserving iterations enable gradient descent over relations and, thus, propensity score matching. We also show how to create appropriate input relations for shape-preserving iterations with *randomly initialized relations*. The empirical evaluation compares in-database iterations with the native implementation in MonetDB where iterations are flattened.

Keywords: Gradient descent · Propensity score matching · Column stores · Iterative methods · Data science · MonetDB

1 Introduction

In the era of big data analytics many researchers have to deal with constantly growing data sets that must be analyzed with state-of-the-art data science methods based on iterative methods. *Propensity score matching* is a statistical technique that estimates the effect of medical interventions, e.g., medical treatments. It reduces the bias that exists if we simply compare outcomes among patients that received the treatment versus those that did not. A propensity score is associated with each tuple and can be used to build patient cohorts with comparable patients, i.e., patients with a similar propensity score. The approximation of the propensity score is calculated with a gradient descent method that uses fix point computations and iteratively refines the initial values. Since neither gradient descent nor fix point iterations are available in SQL, applications must export, transform, and import data into statistical analysis environments [1,3] to compute propensity scores.

© Springer Nature Switzerland AG 2020
J. Darmont et al. (Eds.): ADBIS 2020, LNCS 12245, pp. 189–203, 2020.
https://doi.org/10.1007/978-3-030-54832-2_15

The goal of this paper is to enable propensity score matching computation over data that is stored in relations. Towards this goal, we extend SQL with *shape-preserving iterations* that iterate over a relation of constant size (i.e., the number of tuples and attributes does not change). Shape-preserving iterations support methods that repeatedly refine a set of values until a fixed point is reached and, thus, permit in-database propensity score calculation. Shape-preserving iterations start with a *randomly initialized relation*. We show how to randomly initialize a relation that has the required schema and tuples. One important property of shape-preserving iterations is that they iterate over and return relations with *contextual information* [6,7]. Contextual information guarantees that each relation has a proper schema and includes at least one attribute whose values describe and identify tuples in this relation. We discuss the adjustments that are required to support propensity score computation with shape-preserving iterations in a column-oriented database. We show the feasibility of our solution by conducting an experimental evaluation.

Our technical contributions are the following:

- We identify *shape-preserving iterations* as a new type of iterations required for fix point computations over relations. We offer an SQL extension to do in-database propensity score matching.
- We show how to create a starting relation with contextual information for the gradient descent computation using *randomly initialized relations*.
- We describe how to extend the statement tree of MonetDB with a *control loop node* to support in-database query plans with shape-preserving iterations.
- We confirm the feasibility of our approach by empirically comparing the runtime of our solution with a native MonetDB implementation that flattens loops.

The paper is organized as follows. Section 2 describes our application scenario. We introduce basic terminology in Sect. 3. Section 4 gives an overview of related work. We introduce our approach and discuss the extensions required for propensity score computation in Sect. 5. Section 6 describes the implementation in MonetDB and Sect. 7 evaluates our solution. We conclude in Sect. 8.

2   Application Scenario

Figure 1 illustrates a sample of a data set with health information of patients. This is an extract from a right heart catheterization test data set [8] with 63 attributes and 5735 patient records. For example, tuple t1 in relation *rhc* refers to the patient whose PatientID is 394, Age is 67.7 years, Weight is 65.9 kg, and BloodPressure is 125.0 mm Hg. The patient has not received right heart catheter treatment (value of attribute Treatment is zero) and the outcome was positive (value of attribute Death is zero).

rhc

	PatientID	Age	Weight	BloodPressure	Treatment	Death
t1	394	67.7	65.9	125.0	0	0
t2	979	69.7	54.0	58.0	0	1
t3	1198	65.6	75.7	45.0	1	1
t4	4314	68.5	94.1	55.0	0	1

Fig. 1. Excerpt of the right heart catheterization (rhc) data set

The task is to group patients into cohorts, such that each cohort consists of comparable patients. Comparable cohorts allow to compute the true effect of a treatment and decide whether a treatment is successful or not. Treatment success analysis is a common approach to predict the recovery outcome of a medication. Data sets processed in treatment success analysis typically include an additional binary feature variable that indicates whether a patient received treatment. For example, tuple t3 in relation *rhc* represents a patient who received treatment (value of attribute Treatment is 1). Intuitively, one is tempted to divide the input data into a set of patients having received treatment and compare their outcome of recovery to the set of untreated patients. However, this strategy ignores any biases in the data [12]. It is likely that among the patients there are some who would have recovered anyway because of their general health condition, but who still received the treatment. Similarly, it is not enough to separate patients by a recorded feature, such as gender, because groups of male and female patients might be incomparable due to other differences.

Treatment success analysis requires unbiased data, i.e., a data set containing treated and untreated patients, which according to their conditions (i.e., feature values) are comparable. Since most of the data is historical, there is no possibility to randomly assign treatment to patients. Instead, comparable patients must be selected deliberately to form cohorts. The propensity score represents the impact of all characteristic to a treatment and, thus, allows to match patients with similar scores. Thus, the propensity score of a patient is the probability of getting treatment. Typically, the distribution into groups is done via *Propensity Score Matching*. We use shape-preserving iterations to integrate propensity score matching into SQL and MonetDB, and we discuss the details of our solution for the application scenario in Sect. 5.

3   Background

We leverage the extension of SQL with relational matrix operations that supports basic matrix operations, such as multiplication and inversion, over relations [6,7]. A relation is divided into two parts as illustrated in Fig. 2: Contextual information and the application part. The gray cells are the contextual information, and the white cells are the application part. Contextual information identifies and describes each cell in the application part. For example, value 125.0 in relation t1 is the blood pressure of the patient with ID 394. The application part is used

t1			
P	**A**	**B**	**W**
394	67.7	125.0	65.9
979	69.7	58.0	54.0
1198	65.6	45.0	75.7
4314	68.5	55.0	94.1

t2	
P	**T**
394	0
979	0
1198	1
4314	0

$v = \mathtt{cpd}(t1, t2)$

F	**T**
A	65.6
B	45.0
W	75.7

Fig. 2. Input and result relations for cpd

in matrix operations. Each relational matrix operation takes one or two relations with contextual information as input and yields a result relation with contextual information. The contextual information of the result relation is inherited from the contextual information of the input relation and responsible for identifying and describing tuples and attributes. The inheritance is based on the shape of the result relation.

In the SQL extension each input relation r is followed by a list of attributes $\mathbf{U}$ that is the *order schema*. The order schema is a part of the contextual information and determines the order of tuples for the purpose of a matrix operation. The rest of the attributes in r, $\mathcal{R} \setminus \mathbf{U}$, is the *application schema*. For example, the binary relational matrix multiplication is expressed as follows:

```
1  SELECT * FROM MMU(r BY U, s BY V);
```

Here, r and s are input relations, and $\mathbf{U}$ and $\mathbf{V}$ are order schemas that determine the order of tuples for the multiplication. The relational matrix multiplication corresponds to matrix multiplication $a * b$, where a and b are matrices composed of attributes $\mathcal{R} \setminus \mathbf{U}$ of relation r ordered by $\mathbf{U}$ and attributes $\mathcal{S} \setminus \mathbf{V}$ from relation s ordered by $\mathbf{V}$, respectively.

Example 1. Consider relational matrix crossproduct (cpd) between attributes A[1], B, W and attribute T from relation rhc sorted by the values in attribute P:

```
1         SELECT *
2         FROM CPD[F]( ( SELECT P, A, B, W FROM rhc ) AS t1 BY P,
3                      ( SELECT P, T FROM rhc ) AS t2 BY P ) AS v;
```

Figure 2 illustrates the input and result relations of the crossproduct computation. Both subselects include attribute P to sort the tuples in $t1$ and $t2$ for the purpose of cpd operation.

This relational matrix crossproduct corresponds to matrix crossproduct $a^t * b$, where a is the matrix composed of attributes A, B, W of relation rhc ordered by P and b is the matrix composed of attribute T from relation rhc ordered by P. Note that result relation v includes contextual information. It inherits attribute names A, B, and W from $t1$ and attribute name T from $t2$ [7]. The inheritance of these values is based on the cardinalities of the result matrix of the crossproduct.

---

[1] We use the first character of the attribute name to refer to the attributes.

4   Related Work

Currently, there exist two possibilities to perform iterations inside a DBMS: To write an UDF or to use a recursive query. UDFs are expressive and can be used for computing iterative methods inside a database. However, they are not part of the optimization process. In this paper iterations, where both parts, i.e., the iteration body and the exit condition, are SQL expressions. Unlike UDFs, we offer a solution that is deeply integrated into the system and enables optimization for both the iteration body and the exit condition. Recursive queries are based on iterations. After each iteration step, resulting tuples are *added* to an iterated relation until the iteration step returns an empty set of tuples. In our approach we interested in exit conditions that are based on the values of tuples. Since recursive queries do not preserve the shape of the iterated relation, they are not suitable for shape-preserving iterations. Recursive SQL solutions store all (intermediate) result tuples in the iterated relation, which is neither time nor space efficient.

Passing et al. [11] offer iterations over relations in HyPer. The approach introduces iterations on two levels: At the level of SQL iterations are available for a user to program. Iterations are also present as part of operations, such as k-means or PageRank. Although SQL level iterations are similar to our idea, extensions required to implement and integrate them into an optimizer are not discussed. In addition, in [11] iterations do not take the size of the result relation and the contextual information into consideration, while we focus on iterations that preserve the shape and contextual information.

Jankov et al. [9] extend SimSQL with arrays whose elements are relations to integrate neural networks into the relational model. Tables in an array are defined recursively, i.e., each table is defined as the result of a query over previously defined tables. Unlike our approach, each iteration step creates a new table. Unless materialization is stated explicitly, intermediate result tables are not materialized. The optimizer must still handle enormously large query plans. The approach focuses on how to cut plans into pieces, which are optimized and executed independently. This is an NP-hard task, which is approached with greedy heuristics.

Binnig et al. [5] extend SQL with functions that support recursive iterations and multiple-tables assignment operations to add interactivity and procedural behaviour into SQL. New features are implemented with the help of graphs with cycles. Since iterations are available only in functions, this approach is not fully integrated into the optimization process. Binnig offers push-downs of selections and projections in query graphs. More complicated optimization techniques, e.g., join order, are not available.

5   Propensity Score

Propensity score matching builds cohorts based on the estimation of the propensity score. Propensity score matching requires to perform the following steps:

(1) computation of gradient descent between features and a target, e.g., between attributes A, B, W as features and attribute T as target from relation rhc; (2) estimation of the propensity score by multiplying features and the coefficients from the gradient descent; and (3) grouping of estimated propensity scores according to their similarity. We consider these steps in the following subsections.

5.1   Gradient Descent and Shape-Preserving Iterations

Gradient descent [13] is an algorithm that is often used for classification tasks, such as logistic regression. Gradient descent is an approximation method, where a cost function is iteratively minimized, while letting the coefficients converge to the optimum for the given data set [10].

In the context of relations, gradient descent takes three argument relations: The first relation includes the feature attributes, the second relation includes an attribute that represents the target, the third relation includes an attribute with the initially guessed coefficients. Last input relation is also the output relation and its values (i.e., coefficients) are iteratively refined until the coefficients have converged to the real (not guessed) impact of the features to the target. The iteration used in gradient descent has two key properties: (1) it is a fix point iteration with a cost function that must be minimized; (2) the shape of the iterated result relation remains the same (i.e., the iteration refines values, but does not change the number of attributes or tuples). We term such iterations *shape-preserving iterations*.

Shape-preserving iterations are used in iterative methods [16] from numerical analysis that refine matrices with randomly initialized values. Iterative methods are used to solve problems, for which direct methods are very expensive or do not exist, such as logistic regression.

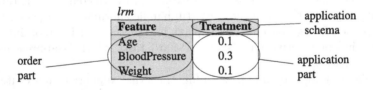

Fig. 3. Structure of an iterated result relation

The division of a relation into contextual information and an application part [6] is satisfied for shape-preserving iterations. Consider relation lrm in Fig. 3. The relation quantifies for each feature its impact on the treatment. The gray cells are the contextual information and remain unchanged during the iteration. The contextual information determines the shape of a relation. The white cells are the application part with the values that are refined during an iteration.

5.2   Randomly Initialized Relations

Gradient descent takes a relation with guessed coefficients as input. The start point is *randomly initialized relation*, i.e., a relation with contextual information and application part over which the iteration is performed to approximate the solution. The values in the application part of a randomly initialized relation are generated randomly. The contextual information is inherited from existing relations.

Relation lrm in Fig. 3 is the start point for the gradient descent. Relation lrm is created as follows (see also Fig. 2):

```
1   CREATE TABLE lrm(F, T) AS (
2       SELECT F, uniform [0, 1] AS T
3       FROM CPD[F]( ( SELECT P, A, B, W FROM rhc ) AS t1 BY P,
4                    ( SELECT P, T FROM rhc ) AS t2 BY P );
```

Relation lrm inherits its contextual information from relations $t1$ and $t2$. The shape and contextual information of lrm are determined by operation cpd. The contextual information of lrm includes the values of attribute F. By definition of cpd, they are the names of attributes A, B, and W, and they describe feature coefficients. The application schema of lrm is attribute T. It is inherited from the application schema of $t2$. The application part of lrm (i.e., values of attribute T) includes random values uniformly distributed between 0 and 1. In order to randomly initialize a relation, the appropriate relational matrix operation is applied to existing relations. The operation provides contextual information, i.e., a skeleton for the application part. The values in the application part are independent of the operation result.

The relational matrix algebra [7] includes an extensive set of operations and provides all possible shapes for randomly initialized relations. For example, if the randomly initialized relation v inherits the attribute values from the application schema of r and the attributes from the application schema of s, operation $cpd(r, s)$ yields the contextual information for v.

5.3   Gradient Descent with Iterations in SQL

We use the WITH clause to perform gradient descent with shape-preserving iterations. Figure 4 illustrates the syntax.

```
1   WITH
2       ITERATED r AS (Q) UNTIL P
3   SELECT * FROM r;
```

Fig. 4. Iterations in SQL

Relation r is a randomly initialized relation. The values in relation r are updated after each iteration step. Query Q computes the new values in r. Predicate P specifies the exit condition. Thus, Q is repeated and relation r is updated until P evaluates to true.

Figure 5 illustrates the SQL statement for gradient descent computation of our application scenario. The gradient descent is computed over attributes A, B, and W as features, and attribute T as a target from relation rhc. Since attribute T includes binary values, the gradient descent is based on standard logistic regression. The SQL statement corresponds to a standard gradient descent algorithm [13], where α is the stepsize, and t is the threshold. The iterative part of the query is framed and consists of Q and P.

```
1  WITH
2      prhc(A, B, W, P) AS (
3          SELECT A, B, W, P
4          FROM rhc ),
5      e(P, T) AS (
6          SELECT P, 1/(1+1/EXP(T)) AS T
7          FROM MMU ( prhc BY P,
8                     lrm BY F )
9      ),
10     ITERATED lrm(F, T) AS (
11         SELECT lrm.F, lrm.T - α*g.T
12         FROM lrm
13         JOIN
14         CPD[F]( prhc BY P,
15                 ( SELECT t1.P, t1.T/t2.N AS T
16                   FROM ( SELECT rhc.P, rhc.T - e.T AS T
17                          FROM rhc JOIN e
18                          ON rhc.P = e.P ) AS t1,
19                        ( SELECT COUNT(*) AS N
20                          FROM rhc ) AS t2
21                 ) AS d BY P
22             ) AS g ON lrm.F = g.F                          Q
23     )
24     UNTIL
25         ( SELECT SUM(-rhc.T*log(e.T)-(1-rhc.T)*log(1-e.T))
26         FROM rhc JOIN e ON rhc.P = e.P )                   P1
27         <
28         ( SELECT t * COUNT(*)
29         FROM rhc )                    P2                   P
30 SELECT * FROM lrm;
```

Fig. 5. Gradient descent over relation rhc (Color figure online)

The gradient descent is performed over randomly initialized relation lrm. The values in attribute F remain unchanged, and the values in attribute T are refined during the computation. Expression $1/(1+1/\text{EXP}(T))$ corresponds to the sigmoid function $\frac{1}{1+e^{-T}}$. Since the sigmoid function takes real values and maps them into a range from zero to one, it is used in gradient descents for logistic regressions.

Subquery Q corresponds to the iteration body of the gradient descent. cpd is performed on lines 14–21 between features from relation rhc and the normalized error from relation d. It yields relation $g(F, T)$. Attribute T is the gradient calculated for the current coefficients. Line 11 states how relation lrm is updated after each iteration: The values in attribute F are preserved, and the gradient is multiplied by the stepsize α and subtracted from the current coefficients. Subquery P corresponds to the exit condition. It determines whether the cost function calculated between the real target values $rhc.T$ and the estimated target values $e.T$ is below the given threshold t. The relational matrix operations are highlighted with red color, and the new constructs for the iteration are highlighted with green color.

Figure 6 illustrates relation lrm during the computation of the gradient descent for our application scenario: Input (lrm_0), intermediate $(lrm_{50}, lrm_{100}, lrm_{200})$, and output (lrm_{266}) relations. The subscript denotes the iteration step, in which the relation is computed. The intermediate relations show how the coefficients converge during the gradient descent. For example, the coefficient for W converges in the beginning while the coefficient for A converges towards the end of the computation.

lrm_0		lrm_{50}		lrm_{100}		lrm_{200}		lrm_{266}	
F	T	F	T	F	T	F	T	F	T
A	0.1	A	0.00	A	0.03	A	0.08	A	0.11
B	0.3	B	-0.06	B	-0.10	B	-0.16	B	-0.20
W	0.1	W	0.03	W	0.03	W	0.03	W	0.03

Fig. 6. Gradient descent: Input, intermediate, and output relations

5.4 Estimation and Matching

The propensity score is estimated by multiplying the features and the result of the gradient descent. After the estimation, groups of propensity scores are formed. Grouping data into percentiles according to propensity scores reduces bias and allows for a proper treatment success analysis [12]. Forming groups of patients with similar propensity scores is accomplished by matching tuples. There exist several approaches to perform the matching, such as stratification matching and caliper matching [4,14]. For stratification matching, the range of propensity scores is split into equally sized buckets, and each tuple is assigned to a bucket. Each bucket holds comparable tuples with treated and untreated patients.

We estimate the propensity score for patients with relational matrix multiplication between features in rhc and coefficients in result relation lrm as follows:

```
1    SELECT P, 1/(1+1/EXP(T)) AS S
2    FROM MMU ( ( SELECT A, B, W, P
3               FROM rhc ) AS t BY P,
4               lrm BY F )
```

Figure 7 shows the result of the multiplication: Relation *propensity_score* has attribute S with an estimate of the probability for a treatment, i.e., the propensity score.

propensity _score			stratification _matching			
P	S		P	I	S	T
394	0.000		394	0	0.000	0
979	0.091		979	0	0.091	0
1198	0.617		1198	3	0.617	1
4314	0.345		4314	1	0.345	0

Fig. 7. Propensity score: estimation and matching

After the propensity score is calculated, the final step is a stratified matching applied to the estimated scores. The propensity scores are distributed into equally sized buckets with size 0.2:

```
1    SELECT P, CAST(S * 10/2 AS INT) AS I, S, T
2    FROM propensity_score NATURAL JOIN rhc;
```

Figure 7 illustrates the final result of propensity score matching with the stratification approach: Attribute I from relation *stratification_matching* states the bucket id for each patient.

6   System Implementation in MonetDB

In this section we discuss the integration of gradient descent and shape-preserving iterations into MonetDB. MonetDB is a column-store DBMS, which offers several routines optimized for column-oriented operations. It stores attributes of relations in *binary association tables* (BAT). A BAT consists of two arrays: One stores the attribute values and the other the object identifier (OID) for each tuple. Each relational operation is represented and executed as a sequence of BAT operations. MonetDB builds the *statement tree* where each node refers to one or more attributes, or the result of the operation on attributes.

6.1   New Types of Nodes and Edges

In order to fully integrate the gradient descent in MonetDB all queries that perform a gradient descent computation go through all stages of query processing. The existing structure of a statement tree is a DAG and does not offer functionality to express iterations. An extension is required to support cycles with an exit condition.

We introduce a new node type and a relationship. A *cloop* node is a *control loop* node that controls the flows in the statement tree. A cloop node contains the predicate and models a loop with an exit condition. The *update* relationship is controlled by a cloop node and substitutes the input BATs of the iteration body with its result BATs.

Consider the statement tree with the cloop node in Fig. 8a, where input and output BATs are shown as gray rectangles. It illustrates the shape-preserving iteration from Fig. 4. The cloop node (denoted by a diamond) is a repeat-until structure expressed as a statement tree that includes predicate P. As input it takes a subtree that represents query Q and additional BATs used for the computation of the predicate P. The output BATs of query Q are connected with the input BATs of this query by an update relationship (denoted with a dashed arrow). After the Q subtree has been traversed and evaluated, the cloop node performs predicate P and decides how to proceed based on its result: Either (1) the output of Q is passed further in the tree if P evaluates to true, or (2) *update* relationship is activated (i.e., the input BATs of Q are updated) and query Q is repeated if P evaluates to false.

Example 2. Consider the SQL query in Fig. 5 and the corresponding statement tree in Fig. 8b. This query has a subquery Q: The part between the AS and UNTIL keywords. Predicate P is based on the cost function of the gradient descent, i.e., the part after the UNTIL keyword. It is included in the cloop node.

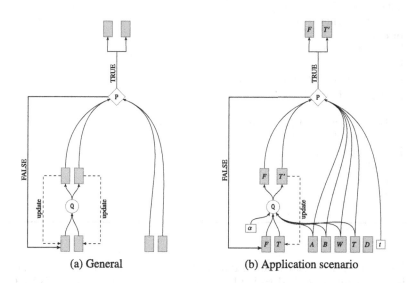

(a) General   (b) Application scenario

Fig. 8. Statement trees with cloop node

The left subtree of the cloop node represents the iteration body, i.e., query Q. One of the output BATs of Q, $T' = \pi_{lrm.T - \alpha * g.T}$, is connected by the update relationship with the leaf node, attribute T from relation lrm. The other children (constant threshold t and selected attributes of relation rhc) of the cloop node are the BATs required to compute predicate P. After the execution of Q, the cloop node evaluates the predicate. If the predicate returns false, T is updated with T' and query Q is repeated, otherwise the result BATs of Q, F and T', are passed further to the next node.

6.2   Implementation

We implement the gradient descent as a new node in the statement tree and a new BAT operation in MonetDB. We compare our implementation with the native MonetDB implementation where the number of iterations is predefined and iterations are flattened in the statement tree.

Node Implementation. In the node implementation we add a gradient descent node to a statement tree and a BAT operation with the gradient descent algorithm.

Algorithm 1: Gradient Descent

Input: BAT C (coefficients, initial guess), list of BATs $\mathbf{A} = (A_1, A_2, ...)$
       (feature vectors), BAT T (target vector), double α (stepsize), double t
       (error threshold)
Output: BAT C (optimized coefficients)

1 $n \leftarrow$ T.length()
2 **repeat**
3   E $\leftarrow$ fill$(0, n)$
4   G $\leftarrow$ []
5   **foreach** $A_i \in \mathbf{A}$, $val \in C$ **do**
6 | E $\leftarrow$ E + $val \cdot A_i$
7   **end**
8   D $\leftarrow$ (sigmoid(E) $-$ T)$/n$
9   **foreach** $A_i \in \mathbf{A}$ **do**
10 | append(G, $A_i \cdot$ D)
11   **end**
12   C $\leftarrow$ C - $\alpha \cdot$ G
13 **until** *cost(C, $\mathbf{A}$, T)* $< t$;
14 **return** C

Algorithm 1 illustrates our implementation of a new BAT operation. The gradient descent is applied to BATs. The algorithm takes as input BAT C with the initial coefficients, list of feature BATs $\mathbf{A}$, target BAT T, gradient descent stepsize α, and error threshold t. The cost function in Eq. 1 is the function we minimize with the gradient descent algorithm.

$$\mathrm{cost}(C, \mathbf{A}, T) = (-\mathrm{T} \cdot \log(\mathrm{sigmoid}(\mathbf{A} \cdot C)) - (1 - \mathrm{T}) \cdot \log(1 - \mathrm{sigmoid}(\mathbf{A} \cdot C)))/n \quad (1)$$

The algorithm returns the updated BAT C with the final coefficients as soon as the exit condition is reached, i.e., the error is smaller than thethreshold.

First, BAT E, which is the non-normalized estimation of target T, is filled with zeros. Then the estimations based on current coefficients C are calculated in lines 5–7. Second, BAT D with the difference of the normalized estimation and the actual target is computed on line 8. BAT G with the current gradient is calculated on lines 9–11. BAT C with the coefficients is updated on line 12.

Example 3. Consider Fig. 9. It illustrates the first iteration step of Algorithm 1 performed over randomly initialized relation *lrm* shown in Fig. 3 and relation *rhc*.

C	A_1	A_2	A_3	T	E	*sigmoid*(E)	D	G	C
0.1	67.7	125.0	65.9	0	50.86	1	0.25	51.45	0.05
0.3	69.7	58.0	54.0	0	29.77	1	0.25	59.50	0.24
0.1	65.6	45.0	75.7	1	27.63	1	0	53.50	0.05
	68.5	55.0	94.1	0	32.76	1	0.25		

Fig. 9. The first step of iteration

BAT C corresponds to attribute T from relation *lrm*, BAT list $\mathbf{A} = (A_1, A_2, A_3)$ corresponds to attributes A, B, W from relation *rhc*, BAT T corresponds to attribute T from relation *rhc*, stepsize α is 0.001, and threshold t is 0.25. BAT E (i.e., the current estimation of the target) is calculated by multiplying $\mathbf{A}$ with C, and the sigmoid function is applied to E. Then BAT D is calculated between the real target T and its estimation *sigmoid*(E). Next, each feature is multiplied with the normalized difference delivering gradient BAT G. Finally, BAT C is updated based on the values in G and the stepsize. After that, the cost function is applied to the refined coefficients C and the predicate is evaluated.

Native MonetDB Implementation. Algorithm 1 is translated to a flattened statement tree where the number of iterations is predefined and the cost function is omitted. Thus, iteration subtree Q is repeated multiple times. The native approach has two major drawbacks. The approach does not scale, since the statement tree grows very fast. The native approach is also not robust in terms of accuracy of the result because of the inability to access and evaluate the intermediate results during the tree creation.

7   Evaluation

We extended MonetDB v11.23.13 with the node implementation and the native implementation. Both server and client are running on the same machine. We use synthetic data for the evaluation. We ran the evaluation on a virtual machine in ScienceCloud [15] with Ubuntu 18.04.3 LTS, 2.593 GHz Intel Haswell 4 CPU, and 16 GB of RAM.

Synthetic data is generated with function make_classification [2], which is a part of the Python library scikit [1]. All features in the generated data sets are informative, i.e., all features affect the target. All preconditions that are used for the generation of regression problems with different numbers of features and tuples are the same.

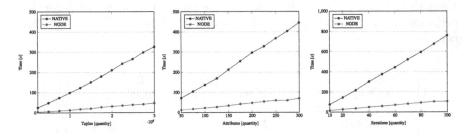

Fig. 10. Runtime of gradient descent for varying number of tuples, attributes and iterations

We perform gradient descent with the node and native implementations over relations of different sizes. We ensure that the node implementation performs as many iterations as the native implementation. For the native implementation we fixed the number of iterations by passing this number within a query. For the node implementation we set the tolerance to zero and additionally pass the maximal number of iterations. This guarantees that both approaches perform the same number of iterations.

Figure 10 illustrates the runtimes of both implementations. The left plot shows the runtimes for gradient descent applied to relations with 150 attributes (i.e., features) and a varying number of tuples. The plot in the middle shows runtimes for relations with 2,000,000 tuples and a varying number of attributes. Both evaluation runs were carried out with 30 iterations. The right plot illustrates the runtimes for relations with 150 attributes and 2,000,000 tuples, but with a varying number of iterations.

The node implementation shows better performance in all cases. Note that the node implementation computes the cost function after each iteration, while the native implementation performs only the iteration body. Since the native implementation flattens the statement tree, it creates huge trees with thousands of nodes, and thus, does not scale.

8   Summary

We introduced shape-preserving iterations and proposed a technique to create randomly initialized relations in order to perform propensity score matching over relations. We integrated shape-preserving iterations into SQL and the MonetDB query tree to support the in-database execution of gradient descent. We illustrated the feasibility of our approach by comparing our implementation of gradient descent with the native MonetDB implementation.

References

1. Scikit-learn: Machine Learning in Python. https://scikit-learn.org/. Accessed 11 Dec 2019
2. sklearn.datasets: Function make_classification. https://scikit-learn.org/stable/modules/generated/sklearn.datasets.make_classification.html. Accessed 05 Mar 2020
3. The R Stats Package: R statistical functions. https://www.rdocumentation.org/packages/stats. Accessed 11 Dec 2019
4. Austin, P.: Optimal caliper widths for propensity-score matching when estimating differences in means and differences in proportions in observational studies. Pharm. Stat. **10**, 150–161 (2011). https://doi.org/10.1002/pst.433
5. Binnig, C., Rehrmann, R., Faerber, F., Riewe, R.: FunSQL: it is time to make SQL functional. In: Proceedings of the 2012 Joint EDBT/ICDT Workshops, pp. 41–46. EDBT-ICDT 2012. ACM, New York (2012). http://doi.acm.org/10.1145/2320765.2320786
6. Dolmatova, O., Augsten, N., Böhlen, M.H.: Preserving contextual information in relational matrix operations. In: Proceedings of the 36th International Conference on Data Engineering. ICDE 2020, p. 4 (2020)
7. Dolmatova, O., Augsten, N., Böhlen, M.H.: A relational matrix algebra and its implementation in a column store. In: International Conference on Management of Data, SIGMOD 2020, Portland, OR, USA, 14–19 June 2020. ACM (2020)
8. Harrell Jr, F.E.: Right Heart Catheterization Dataset. http://biostat.mc.vanderbilt.edu/wiki/pub/Main/DataSets/rhc.csv. Accessed 02 Dec 2019
9. Jankov, D., et al.: Declarative recursive computation on an RDBMS: or, why you should use a database for distributed machine learning. Proc. VLDB Endow. **12**(7), 822–835 (2019). https://doi.org/10.14778/3317315.3317323
10. Martin, J.H., Jurafsky, D.: Speech and Language Processing: An Introduction to Natural Language Processing, Computational Linguistics, and Speech Recognition. Pearson/Prentice Hall, Upper Saddle River (2009)
11. Passing, L., et al.: SQL- and operator-centric data analytics in relational main-memory databases. In: Proceedings of the 20th International Conference on Extending Database Technology, EDBT 2017, Venice, Italy, 21–24 March 2017, pp. 84–95 (2017). https://doi.org/10.5441/002/edbt.2017.09
12. Rosenbaum, P.R., Rubin, D.B.: The central role of the propensity score in observational studies for causal effects. Biometrika **70**(1), 41–55 (1983). http://www.jstor.org/stable/2335942
13. Ruder, S.: An overview of gradient descent optimization algorithms. arXiv preprint arXiv:1609.04747 (2016)
14. Senn, S., Graf, E., Caputo, A.: Stratification for the propensity score compared with linear regression techniques to assess the effect of treatment or exposure. Statistics in Medicine **26**(30), 5529–5544 (2007). https://doi.org/10.1002/sim.3133, https://onlinelibrary.wiley.com/doi/abs/10.1002/sim.3133
15. University of Zurich: ScienceCloud. https://www.zi.uzh.ch/en/teaching-and-research/science-it/infrastructure/. Accessed 18 Mar 2020
16. Varga, R.S.: Matrix Iterative Analysis. Prentice-Hall Series in Automatic Computation. Prentice-Hall, Englewood Cliffs (1962)

The Tell-Tale Cube

Antoine Chédin[1], Matteo Francia[2], Patrick Marcel[1], Verónika Peralta[1], and Stefano Rizzi[2(✉)]

[1] LIFAT, University of Tours, Tours, France
[2] DISI, University of Bologna, Bologna, Italy
stefano.rizzi@unibo.it

Abstract. The Intentional Analytics Model (IAM) has been recently envisioned as a new paradigm to couple OLAP and analytics. It relies on two basic ideas: (i) letting the user explore data by expressing her analysis intentions rather than the data she needs, and (ii) returning enhanced cubes, i.e., multidimensional data annotated with knowledge insights in the form of model components (e.g., clusters). In this paper we provide a proof-of-concept for the IAM vision by delivering an end-to-end implementation of describe, one of the five intention operators introduced by IAM. Among the research challenges left open in IAM, those we address are (i) automatically tuning the size of models (e.g., the number of clusters), (ii) selecting the most effective chart or graph for visualizing each cube depending on its features, and (iii) devising a visual metaphor to display enhanced cubes and interact with them.

1 Introduction

Data warehousing and OLAP (On-Line Analytical Processing) have been progressively gaining a leading role in enabling business analyses over enterprise data since the early 90's. During these thirty years, the underlying technologies have evolved from the early relational implementations (still widely adopted in corporate environments), to the new architectures solicited by Business Intelligence 2.0 scenarios, and up to the challenges posed by the integration with big data settings. However, recently, it has become more and more evident that the OLAP paradigm, alone, is no more sufficient to keep the pace with the increasing needs of new-generation decision makers. Indeed, the enormous success of machine learning techniques has consistently shifted the interest of corporate users towards sophisticated analytical applications.

In this direction, the *Intentional Analytics Model* (IAM) has been envisioned as a way to tightly couple OLAP and analytics [20]. The IAM approach relies on two major cornerstones: (i) the user explores the data space by expressing her analysis *intentions* rather than by explicitly stating what data she needs, and (ii) in return she receives both multidimensional data and knowledge insights in the form of annotations of interesting subsets of data. As to (i), five intention operators are proposed, namely, describe (describes one or more cube measures, possibly focused on one or more level members), assess (judges one or more

© Springer Nature Switzerland AG 2020
J. Darmont et al. (Eds.): ADBIS 2020, LNCS 12245, pp. 204–218, 2020.
https://doi.org/10.1007/978-3-030-54832-2_16

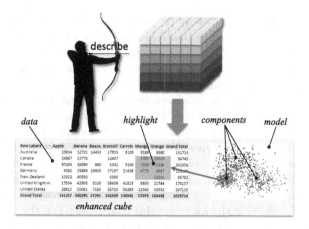

Fig. 1. The IAM approach

cube measures with reference to some baseline), explain (reveals some hidden information in the data the user is observing, for instance in the form of a correlation between two measures), predict (shows data not in the original cubes, derived for instance with regression), and suggest (shows data similar to those the current user, or similar users, have been interested in). As to (ii), first-class citizens of the IAM are *enhanced cubes*, defined as multidimensional cubes coupled with *highlights*, i.e., sets of cube cells associated with interesting components of *models* automatically extracted from cubes [20]. Each operator is applied to an enhanced cube and returns a new enhanced cube. To assess interestingness of model components, a measure based on their (objective) significance and (subjective) surprise is proposed.

An overview of the approach is given in Fig. 1. Noticeably, having different models automatically computed and evaluated in terms of their interestingness relieves the user from the time-wasting effort of trying different possibilities.

Example 1. Let a SALES cube be given, and let the user's intention be

with SALES describe quantity for month ='1997-04' by type using clustering size 3

First, the subset of cells for April 1997 are selected from the SALES cube, aggregated by product type, and projected on measure quantity (in OLAP terms, a slice-and-dice and a roll-up operator are applied). Then, these cells are clustered into 3 clusters based on the values of quantity. Finally, a measure of interestingness is computed for each cluster, and the cells belonging to the cluster with maximum interestingness are highlighted in the results shown to the user.   □

Clearly, the IAM vision raises a number of research challenges, e.g., (i) investigate if there are any other intention operators that should be considered besides the basic ones proposed, and how different operators can be combined; (ii) find techniques for automatically tuning the algorithms that create enhanced cubes by computing models; (iii) enrich the IAM framework with an approach to select the most effective chart or graph for visualizing each cube depending on its features such as number of dimensions, size, etc.; (iv) devise a visual metaphor for displaying enhanced cubes and interacting with them.

The goal of this paper is to provide a proof-of-concept for the IAM vision by delivering an end-to-end implementation of the describe operator. Specifically, we address challenges (ii) by experimenting two techniques to automatically set the number of model components. We also address challenges (iii) and (iv) by proposing a visualization that couples text-based representations and selected graphical representations with a component-driven interaction paradigm. This will save the time it would take to the user to try different visualizations; besides, by automatically selecting the most suitable charts based on the features of each cube, we discourage the user from adopting inappropriate visualizations which might lead her to wrong interpretations of data.

The paper outline is as follows. After introducing a formalism to manipulate cubes and queries in Sect. 2, in Sect. 3 we introduce models, components, and enhanced cubes, and define an interestingness measure. Then, in Sect. 4 we show how an intention is transformed into an execution plan, in Sect. 5 we discuss how to automatically set the model size, i.e., its number of components, and in Sect. 6 we explain how enhanced cubes are visualized. Finally, in Sect. 7 we discuss the related literature, while in Sect. 8 we draw the conclusion.

2   Formalities

To simplify the formalization, we will restrict to consider linear hierarchies (the presence of branches in hierarchies makes Definition 6 overly complex).

Definition 1 (Hierarchy and Cube Schema). *A hierarchy is a triple $h = (L_h, \succeq_h, \geq_h)$ where:*

(i) L_h is a set of categorical levels, each coupled with a domain $Dom(l)$ including a set of members;
(ii) $\succeq_h$ is a roll-up total order of L_h; and
(iii) $\geq_h$ is a part-of partial order of $\bigcup_{l \in L_h} Dom(l)$.

The top level of $\succeq_h$ is called dimension. The part-of partial order is such that, for each couple of levels l and l' such that $l \succeq_h l'$, for each member $u \in Dom(l)$ there is exactly one member $u' \in Dom(l')$ such that $u \geq_h u'$. A cube schema is a couple $\mathcal{C} = (H, M)$ where:

(i) H is a set of hierarchies;
(ii) M is a set of numerical measures, with each measure $m \in M$ coupled with one aggregation operator $op(m) \in \{\mathsf{sum}, \mathsf{avg}, \dots\}$.

Example 2. For our working example it is $\mathsf{SALES} = (H, M)$ where

$H = \{h_{\mathsf{Date}}, h_{\mathsf{Customer}}, h_{\mathsf{Product}}, h_{\mathsf{Store}}\}$, $M = \{\mathsf{quantity}, \mathsf{storeSales}, \mathsf{storeCost}\}$,

$\mathsf{date} \succeq \mathsf{month} \succeq \mathsf{year}$, $\mathsf{customer} \succeq \mathsf{gender}$

$\mathsf{product} \succeq \mathsf{type} \succeq \mathsf{category}$, $\mathsf{store} \succeq \mathsf{city} \succeq \mathsf{country}$

and $op(\mathsf{quantity}) = op(\mathsf{storeSales}) = op(\mathsf{storeCost}) = \mathsf{sum}$. □

Aggregation is the basic mechanism to query cubes, and it is captured by the following definition of group-by set. As normally done when working with the multidimensional model, if a hierarchy h does not appear in a group-by set it is implicitly assumed that a complete aggregation is done along h.

Definition 2 (Group-by Set and Coordinate). *Given cube schema $\mathcal{C} = (H, M)$, a group-by set of $\mathcal{C}$ is a set of levels, at most one from each hierarchy of H. The partial order induced on the set of all group-by sets of $\mathcal{C}$ by the roll-up orders of the hierarchies in H, is denoted with $\succeq_H$. A coordinate of group-by set G is a tuple of members, one for each level of G. Given coordinate γ of group-by set G and another group-by set G' such that $G \succeq_H G'$, we will denote with $rup_{G'}(\gamma)$ the coordinate of G' whose members are related to the corresponding members of γ in the part-of orders, and we will say that γ roll-ups to $rup_{G'}(\gamma)$. By definition, $rup_G(\gamma) = \gamma$.*

Example 3. Two group-by sets of SALES are $G_1 = \{\mathsf{date}, \mathsf{type}, \mathsf{country}\}$ and $G_2 = \{\mathsf{month}, \mathsf{category}\}$, where $G_1 \succeq_H G_2$. G_1 aggregates sales by date, product type, and store country (for all customers), G_2 by month and category. Example of coordinates of the two group-by sets are, respectively, $\gamma_1 = \langle 1997\text{-}04\text{-}15, \mathsf{Fresh\ Fruit}, \mathsf{Italy} \rangle$ and $\gamma_2 = \langle 1997\text{-}04, \mathsf{Fruit} \rangle$, where $rup_{G_2}(\gamma_1) = \gamma_2$. □

Definition 3 (Cube). *A cube over $\mathcal{C}$ is a tuple $C = (G_C, M_C, \omega_C)$ where:*

(i) G_C is a group-by set of $\mathcal{C}$;
(ii) $M_C \subseteq M$;
(iii) ω_C is a partial function that maps the coordinates of G_C to a numerical value for each measure $m \in M_C$.

Each coordinate that participates in ω_C, with its associated measure values, is called a *cell* of C. With a slight abuse of notation, we will write $\gamma \in C$ to state that γ is a cell of C. A cube whose group-by set G_C includes all and only the dimensions of the hierarchies in H and such that $M_C = M$, is called a *base cube*, the others are called *derived cubes*. In OLAP terms, a derived cube is the result of either a roll-up, a slice-and-dice, or a projection made over a base cube; this is formalized as follows.

Definition 4 (Cube Query). *A query over cube schema $\mathcal{C}$ is a triple $q = (G_q, P_q, M_q)$ where:*

(i) G_q is a group-by set of H;

(ii) P_q is a (possibly empty) set of selection predicates each expressed over one
level of H;

(iii) $M_q \subseteq M$.

Let C_0 be a base cube over C. The result of applying q to C_0 is a derived cube C
such that (i) $G_C = G_q$, (ii) $M_C = M_q$, and (iii) ω_C assigns to each coordinate
$\gamma \in C$ satisfying the conjunction of the predicates in P_q and to each measure
$m \in M_C$ the value computed by applying $op(m)$ to the values of m for all the
coordinates of C_0 that roll-up to γ.

Example 4. The cube query over SALES used in Example 1 is $q = (G_q, P_q, M_q)$
where $G_q = \{type\}$, $P_q = \{month = \text{'1997-04'}\}$, and $M_q = \{quantity\}$. A cell of
the resulting cube is $\langle$Canned Fruit$\rangle$ with associated value 138 for quantity. □

3   Enhancing Cubes with Models

Models are concise, information-rich knowledge artifacts [19] that represent relationships hiding in the cube cells. The possible models range from simple functions and measure correlations to more elaborate techniques such as decision
trees, clusterings, etc. A model is bound to (i.e., is computed over the lev-
els/measures of) one cube, and is made of a set of components (e.g., a clustering
model is made of a set of clusters). In the IAM, a relevant role is taken by data-
to-model mappings. Indeed, a model partitions the cube on which it is computed
into two or more subsets of cells, one for each component (e.g., the subsets of
cells belonging to each cluster).

Definition 5 (Model and Component). *A model is a tuple* $\mathcal{M} =$
$(t, alg, C, In, Out, \mu)$ *where:*

(i) t is the model type;

(ii) alg is the algorithm used to compute $\mathcal{M}$

(iii) C is the cube to which $\mathcal{M}$ is bound;

(iv) In is the tuple of levels/measures of C and parameter values supplied to alg
to compute $\mathcal{M}$;

(v) Out is the set of components that make up $\mathcal{M}$;

(vi) μ is a function mapping each cell of C to one component of Out.

*Each model component is a tuple of a component identifier plus a variable num-
ber of properties that describe that component.*

In the scope of this work, it is $t \in \{\text{top-k, bottom-k, skyline, outliers,}$
$\text{clustering}\}$. The components for these model types are as follows:

1. For $t = $ top-k, there are two components: one for top-k cells, one for the
   others (similarly for bottom-k). Each component is described by the average
   z-score of its cells.

2. For $t =$ skyline, there are two components: one for the cells in the skyline, one for the others.
3. For $t =$ outliers, there are two components: one for outlier cells, one for the others. Each component is described by its outlierness.
4. For $t =$ clustering, there is one component for each cluster. Each component is described by the centroid of the corresponding cluster.

Example 5. A possible model over the SALES cube is characterized by

$$t = \text{clustering, } alg = \text{K-Means, } C = \text{SALES,}$$
$$In = \langle \text{quantity}, n = 5, rndSeed = 0 \rangle, \; Out = \{c1, \dots, c5\},$$
$$\mu(\langle \text{Bagels} \rangle) = \mu(\langle \text{Batteries} \rangle) = \mu(\langle \text{Wine} \rangle) = \mu(\langle \text{Beer} \rangle) = c1;$$
$$\mu(\langle \text{Canned Fruit} \rangle) = \mu(\langle \text{Muffins} \rangle) = \mu(\langle \text{Fresh Fruit} \rangle) = c2; \; \dots$$

where n is the desired number of clusters and $rndSeed$ is the seed to be used by the k-means algorithm to randomly generate the 5 seed clusters. Component $c1$ is characterized by property *centroid* with value 151.3.   □

As the last step in the IAM approach, the cube is enhanced by associating it with a highlight, i.e., with the subset of cells corresponding to the most interesting component of the model; these cells are determined via function μ. The measure proposed in [20] to asses the interestingness of each component is based on the idea of *prior belief* [3]: specifically, it defines the *surprise* of a component as the difference of belief for corresponding cells in the cube before (C) and after (C') the application of the intention. This requires first of all to define the concept of "corresponding cell(s)" in C of each cell γ' of C', which is done through a *proxy* function. To simplify this function, we will assume that the intention does not change both the cube group-by set and its selection predicate. Intuitively, if the intention changes the group-by set, the corresponding cell(s) of γ' are determined via the part-of order; if the intention changes the selection predicate, the corresponding cell of γ' is γ' itself if it is part of C, the whole cube C otherwise.

Definition 6 (Proxy Cells). *Let C and C' be two cubes over cube schema $\mathcal{C}$, and let q and q' the queries producing C and C', respectively. Let γ' be a coordinate of C'. The proxy cells of γ' over C are defined as*

$$proxy(\gamma') = \begin{cases} \{\gamma : rup_{G_{q'}}(\gamma) = \gamma'\}, \text{ if } G_q \succ_H G_{q'} \\ \{rup_{G_q}(\gamma')\}, \text{ if } G_{q'} \succ_H G_q \end{cases} \text{, if } G_{q'} \neq G_q \; (P_{q'} = P_q);$$

$$proxy(\gamma') = \begin{cases} \{\gamma'\}, \text{ if } \gamma' \in C \\ \{\gamma : \gamma \in C\}, \text{ if } \gamma' \notin C \end{cases} \text{, if } P_{q'} \neq P_q \; (G_{q'} = G_q);$$

$$proxy(\gamma') = \{\gamma'\}, \text{ otherwise.}$$

For the first intention, the starting cube C is the base cube; since in this case the user has no prior belief, we put $proxy(\gamma') = \varnothing$ for all $\gamma' \in C'$.

Definition 7 (Interestingness). *Let* $\mathcal{M} = (t, alg, C', In, Out, \mu)$ *be a model and* $c \in Out$ *be one of its components. The* interestingness *of* c *is defined as*

$$int(c) = avg_{\gamma' \in \mu^{-1}(c)}\{surprise(\gamma')\}, \text{ where}$$
$$surprise(\gamma') = max_{m \in C'}\{z_m(\gamma') - avg_{\gamma \in proxy(\gamma')}\{z_m(\gamma)\}\}$$

and function $z_m()$ *returns the z-score of a cell for measure* m *over the whole cube that cell belongs to.*

Definition 8. *An* enhanced cube E *is a triple of a cube* C, *a set of models* $\{\mathcal{M}_1, \ldots, \mathcal{M}_r\}$ *bound to* C, *and a* highlight $c_{high} = argmax_{\{c \in \bigcup_{i=1}^{r} Out_i\}}(int(c))$.

Example 6. Let

> with SALES describe quantity for month = '1997-04' by type
>
> with SALES describe quantity for month = '1997-04' by category

be a sequence of two intentions formulated by the user. While the plan generated for the first intention relies on query q defined in Example 4, the one for the second intention relies on $q' = (G_{q'}, P_{q'}, M_{q'})$ where $G_{q'} = \{category\}$, $P_{q'} = \{month = \text{'1997-04'}\}$, and $M_{q'} = \{quantity\}$. Let C and C' be the cubes resulting from q and q', respectively. In practice, q' corresponds to a roll-up of q, so the proxy cells of each cell in C' are determined using the *rup* operator as shown in Fig. 2 (red lines). The figure also shows the z-score for each cell of C and C', and the surprise of each cell of C'. Then, let $\mathcal{M}$ be the model of type top-k, with $k = 1$, computed on C'; this model has two components: c_1, including only the top-1 cell, and c_2, including all the others (shown in green and yellow in the figure). The interestingness values for these two components are $int(c_1) = 1.5$ and $int(c_2) = 0.8$, respectively. So, the enhanced cube resulting from the second intention includes C', $\mathcal{M}$, and the highlight c_1. $\qquad\square$

type	quantity	z-score		category	quantity	z-score	surprise
Bagels	48	-1,0		Beer and Wine	564	-0,9	-1,1
Beer	116	-0,6		Bread	519	-1,1	-0,8
Bologna	192	-0,2		Fruit	936	0,8	-0,4
Canned Fruit	138	-0,5		Meat	999	1,1	1,5
Deli Meats	211	-0,1					
Fresh Chicken	64	-0,9					
Fresh Fruit	798	3,0					
Frozen Chicken	237	0,0					
Hamburger	141	-0,5					
Hot Dogs	154	-0,4					
Muffins	205	-0,1					
Sliced Bread	266	0,2					
Wine	448	1,1					

Fig. 2. Cubes C (left) and C' (right) in Example 6; in green and yellow two components for the top-k model, in red the proxy relationship for two cells in C' (Color figure online)

4   Execution Plans for Describe intentions

The describe operator provides an answer to the user asking "show me my business" by describing one or more cube measures, possibly focused on one or more level members, at some given granularity [20]. The cube is enhanced by showing either the top/bottom-k cells, the skyline, the outliers, or clusters of cells.

The basic idea we followed to define the syntax for describe is that the user will work in sessions, similarly to the OLAP paradigm. As a consequence, the group-by set (by clause) and the selection predicate (for clause) of each intention are formulated as increments over those of the previous intention.

Let C be a cube returned by executing query $q = (G_q, P_q, M_q)$ over base cube C_0 having cube schema $\mathcal{C} = (H, M)$. The general syntax for describe is

with C describe $m_1, \ldots, m_z$ [for P'] [by l'] [using $t_1, \ldots, t_r$] [size k]

where $m_1, \ldots, m_z \in M$ are measures of $\mathcal{C}$, P' is a set of selection predicates each over one level of H, l' is a level of H, $t_1, \ldots, t_r$ are model types, and k is the desired size to be applied to all the models returned as explained in point 2 below (optional parts of the syntax are in brackets).

Now let l be the level in G_q belonging to the same hierarchy of l', and let $P \subseteq P_q$ be the set of predicates in P_q expressed over levels belonging to the same hierarchies than those over which the predicate in P' are expressed. The plan corresponding to a fully-specified intention with C, i.e., one where all optional clauses have been specified, is:

1. Execute query $q' = (G_{q'}, P_{q'}, \{m_1, \ldots, m_z\})$, where $G_{q'} = G_q \setminus \{l\} \cup \{l'\}$ and $P_{q'} = P_q \setminus P \cup P'$. Let C' be the cube resulting from the execution of q' over C_0.
2. For $1 \leq i \leq r$, compute model $\mathcal{M}_i = (t_i, alg_i, C', In_i, Out_i, \mu_i)$ and for each $c \in Out_i$, compute $int(c)$. Size k is used for clustering to determine the number of clusters to be computed, for top-k and bottom-k to determine the number of cells to be returned, for outliers to determine the number of outliers; it is neglected for the skyline.
3. Find the highlight $c_{high} = argmax_{\{c \in \bigcup_i Out_i\}}(int(c))$.
4. Return the enhanced cube consisting of C', $\{\mathcal{M}_1, \ldots \mathcal{M}_r\}$, and highlight c_{high}.

Partially-specified intentions are interpreted as follows:

- If the for P' clause has not been specified, we consider $P_{q'} = P_q$.
- If the by l' clause has not been specified, we consider $G_{q'} = G_q$.
- If the using $t_1, \ldots, t_r$ clause has not been specified, all model types listed in Sect. 3 are computed over C' (the skyline is computed only if $z > 1$, i.e., at least two measures have been specified).
- If the size k clause has not been specified, the value of k is determined automatically as discussed in Sect. 5.

When the first intention is issued on a cube, to constrain the size of the data to be returned it is required that either the by or the for clauses are specified at least.

Example 7. Consider the following session on the SALES cube:

> with SALES describe quantity for month = '1997-04' by type
> with SALES describe quantity by category using clustering size 3
> with SALES describe quantity, storeSales for country = 'Italy' using skyline

The queries corresponding to the first two intentions are q in Example 6 and q' in Example 6, respectively. The query corresponding to the third intention is q'' characterized by $G_{q''} = \{\text{category}\}$, $P_{q''} = \{\text{month} = \text{'1997-04'}, \text{country} = \text{'Italy'}\}$, and $M_{q''} = \{\text{quantity}, \text{storeSales}\}$. The models computed for the first intention are top-k, bottom-k, clustering, and outliers (computing the skyline for a single measure makes no sense). For the second and the third intentions, a clustering producing 3 clusters and the skyline are computed, respectively. □

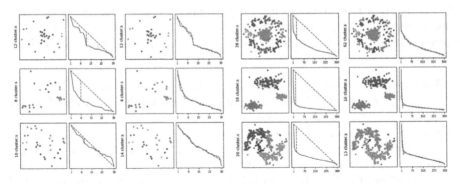

Fig. 3. Results on the 30 (left) and 300 (right) samples data for Kneedle (columns 1 and 3) and L-method (columns 2 and 4)

5   Setting the Model Size

Our approach to find the best value for the size parameter k when it is not specified in the intention is based on good practices in hierarchical clustering, especially when single-linkage is used, meaning that inter-cluster distance is measured by the closest two points of the clusters. The best separation of clusters can then be found by finding the knee of the evaluation graph of the clustering algorithm, which is a two dimensional plot where the x-axis is the number of clusters produced and the y-axis is one classical clustering evaluation metric (error, silhouette, etc.) considering x clusters. In hierarchical clustering, since the cost for merging clusters constantly increases, the evaluation graph often looks like an L-shaped curve with a more or less defined knee. The assumption usually made is that the best merging cost threshold is at the curve knee, where the curve switches from a sharp slope to a low decreasing line.

We tested two solutions from the literature, namely L-method [15] and Kneedle [18], which have been proposed to find the knee in a curve of discrete data. These methods were compared using 3-dimensional non-random toy datasets specifically created for the experiment with the *Scikit-Learn* Python package, varying the size (6, 30, and 300 samples) and the shape of clusters, defining a ground truth. Due to lack of space, we only report the main findings. The code for generating the datasets and the tests is available at https://github.com/antoinechedin/descriptive-clustering.

While both methods achieve similar good results for knee detection, the L-method takes longer to execute and tends to shift the knee on large data sets. This can be seen, for instance, in Fig. 3 on the top right graph. The right knee seems to be located at $x = 25$ but the method returned a knee at $x = 62$. Since Kneedle is quicker and provides more consistent results, we have adopted it to determine k, both for clustering (k being the number of clusters), top/bottom-k (where k is the number of points in the first cluster, i.e., the one with higher values) and outliers (where k is the number of points in the first and last cluster).

6   Visualizing Enhanced Cubes

In this section we discuss how to provide an effective description of an enhanced cube by coupling text-based representations (a pivot table and a ranked component list) and graphical representations (one or more charts) with an ad-hoc interaction paradigm. The guidelines we adopt to this end are explained below:

(i) For visualization purposes, we assume that an intention can select at most three measures ($1 \leq z \leq 3$) and three group-by levels ($1 \leq n \leq 3$). This is actually not a strong limitation, considering that a visualization of four or more dimensions and/or measures using a single table or chart is hardly feasible and definitely not intuitive.

(ii) Since we are focusing on intentions aimed at *describing* data, we believe that providing multiple visualizations from different points of view should be preferred to just picking the "most effective one". Indeed, the effectiveness of a visualization type largely depends on the skills and personal tastes of each user.

(iii) We restrict to considering visualization types that can be easily understood both by lay users and skilled users, and are suitable for multidimensional data.

(iv) Clearly, the effectiveness of a visualization type also depends on the features of the specific dataset. Using an unsuitable visualization can generate confusion and misunderstandings in users, and can lead them to wrong conclusions. Thus, for each intention we visualize only the charts that are recognized to be suitable given the characteristics of the data to be shown.

(v) Models and components play a key role in the IAM approach. Thus, the visualizations we provide aims at showing not only dimension and measure values, but also the different components of a model using a color code. For the same reason, the interaction paradigm should be component-driven.

The visualization we provide for enhanced cube E based on guidelines (ii) and (v) includes three distinct but inter-related areas: a *table* area that shows the cube cells using a pivot table; a *chart* area that complements the table area by representing the cube cells through one or more charts; a *component* area that shows a list of model components sorted by their interestingness. The chart types we consider following guidelines (i) and (iii) are multiple line graphs, grouped column charts, heat maps, bubble graphs, and scatter plots. The heuristics we adopt to decide whether using or not each chart type for a given enhanced cube E (guideline (iv)) was inspired by [10]. The features of E we take into account to this end are the number n of dimensions, the number z of measures, and the domain cardinality and type of the dimensions. The pseudocode is shown in Algorithm 1; an example of heuristics we use is: if $n = 2$ and $z = 1$, draw a bubble graph using the X and Y axes for the two dimensions, the bubble size for the measure, and the bubble color for the model components.

The interaction paradigm we adopt is component-driven (guideline (v)). Specifically, clicking on one component c in the component area leads to emphasizing the corresponding cube cells (i.e., those that map to c via function μ) both in the table area and in the chart area. The highlight is the top component in the list and is selected by default.

Algorithm 1. Chart area creation

Require: $D = \{d_1, \ldots, d_n\}$: sets of dimensions, $M = \{m_1, \ldots, m_z\}$: set of measures, $T = \langle t_1, \ldots, t_r \rangle$: list of models sorted by interestingness
1: **if** $n = 1$ and $isDate(d_1)$ **then**   ▷ Visualize multiple line graph
2:     $MultipleLineGraph(X : d_1, Y_1 : m_1, \ldots, Y_z : m_z)$
3: **if** $z = 1$ and $card(d_1) \leq 50$ **then**   ▷ Visualize grouped column chart
4:     **if** $n = 1$ **then**
5:         $GroupedColumnChart(X : d_1, height : m_1, color : t_1)$
6:     **else**
7:         **if** $n = 2$ and $card(d_2) \leq 8$ **then**
8:             $GroupedColumnChart(X : d_1, height : m_1, color : d_2)$
9: **if** $n = 2$ and $z = 1$ **then**   ▷ Visualize heat map
10:     $HeatMap(X : d_1, Y : d_2, color : m_1)$
11: **else**
12:     **if** $n = 1$ **then**
13:         $HeatMap(X : d_1, Y_1 : m_1, \ldots, Y_z : m_z)$
14: **if** $z = 1$ **then**   ▷ Visualize bubble chart
15:     **switch** n **do**
16:         **case** 2
17:             $BubbleChart(X : d_1, Y : d_2, size : m_1, color : t_1)$
18:         **case** 3
19:             $BubbleChart(X : d_1, Y : d_2, Z : d_3, size : m_1, color : t_1)$
20: **switch** z **do**   ▷ Visualize scatter plot
21:     **case** 2
22:         $ScatterPlot(X : m_1, Y : m_2, color : t_1)$
23:     **case** 3
24:         $ScatterPlot(X : m_1, Y : m_2, Z : m_3, color : t_1)$

Example 8. Figure 4 shows the visualization obtained when a session of the two following intentions is formulated:

> with SALES describe storeCost by month
> with SALES describe storeCost by category

On the top left, the table area; on the right, the chart area; on the bottom left, the component area (the three areas have been repositioned in the figure to save space). Here it is $n = 2$ and $z = 1$, so a heat map and a bubble chart have been selected. The top-interestingness component is a cluster, so a color has been assigned to each component of clustering (i.e., to each cluster) and is uniformly used in all three areas. The highlight (in green) is currently selected and is emphasized using a thicker border in all areas. Note that a tooltip with all the details about a single cell is also shown (in yellow).

7   Related Work

The idea of coupling data and analytical models was born in the 90's with inductive databases, where data were coupled with patterns meant as generalizations of the data [14]. Later on, data-to-model unification was addressed in MauveDB

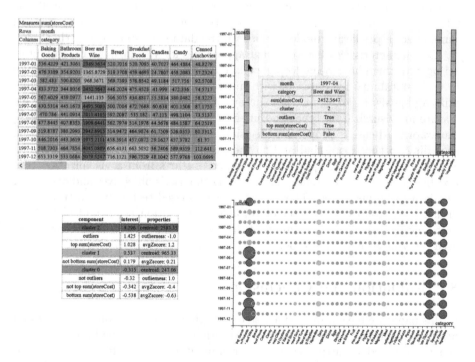

Fig. 4. The visualization obtained for the session in Example 8 (Color figure online)

[7], which provides a language for specifying model-based views of data using common statistical models. However, achieving a unified view of data and models was still seen as a research challenge in business intelligence a few years later [13]. More recently, Northstar [12] has been proposed as a system to support interactive data science by enabling users to switch between data exploration and model building, adopting a real-time strategy for hyper-parameter tuning. Finally, the coupling of data and models is at the core of the IAM vision [20], on which this paper relies. The three basic pillars of IAM are (i) the redefinition of query as expressing the user's intention rather than explicitly declaring what data are to be retrieved, (ii) the extension of query results from plain data cubes to cubes enhanced with models and highlights, and (iii) the characterization of model components in terms of their interestingness to users.

The coupling of the OLAP paradigm and data mining to create an approach where concise patterns are extracted from multidimensional data for user's evaluation, was the goal of some approaches commonly labeled as OLAM [11]. In this context, k-means clustering is used in [2] to dynamically create semantically-rich aggregates of facts other than those statically provided by dimension hierarchies. Similarly, the shrink operator is proposed in [9] to compute small-size approximations of a cube via agglomerative clustering. Other operators that enrich data with knowledge extraction results are DIFF [16], which returns a set of tuples that most successfully describe the difference of values between two cells of a cube, and RELAX [17], which verifies whether a pattern observed at a certain level of detail is also present at a coarser level of detail, too. Finally, in [6] the OLAP paradigm is reused to explore prediction cubes, i.e., cubes where each cell summarizes a predictive model trained on the data corresponding to that cell.

The characteristics of the different approaches for visualizing data and interacting with them have been deeply explored in the literature, also with reference to their suitability for datasets with different features and users with varying skills and goals. In [4], the author surveys the classifications proposed in the literature for visualization types and integrates them into a single comprehensive framework. Abela [1] proposes a decision tree to select the best visualization according to the user's goal and to the main features of data. More recently, SkyViz —to which our approach is inspired— starts from a visualization context based on seven coordinates for assessing the user's objectives and describing the data to be visualized. Then it uses skyline-based techniques to translate a visualization context into a set of suitable visualization types and to find the best bindings between the columns of the dataset and the graphical coordinates used by each visualization type.

8   Evaluation and Conclusion

In this paper we have proposed a visual metaphor to display enhanced cubes for describe intentions according to the IAM vision. The prototype implementation can be accessed at http://semantic.csr.unibo.it/describe/. It uses the simple multidimensional engine described in [8], which in turn relies on the MySQL

DBMS to execute queries on a star schema based on multidimensional metadata (in principle, the prototype could work on top of any other multidimensional engine). The mining models are imported from the Scikit-Learn Python library. Finally, the web-based visualization is implemented in JavaScript and exploits the D3 library for chart visualization.

To evaluate the feasibility of our approach from the computational point of view, we made some preliminary performance tests; to this end we populated the SALES cube using the FoodMart data (https://github.com/julianhyde/foodmart-data-mysql). We considered the worst case, in which all five models are computed on cubes obtained by progressively including in the group-by set the three dimensions with highest cardinality. The tests were run on an Intel(R) Core(TM)i7-6700 CPU@3.40 GHz CPU with 8 GB RAM. Table 1 shows the time necessary to query the base cube, to compute the models, to measure the interestingness, and to generate the pivot table returned to the browser. Remarkably, it turns out that at most 6.38 s are necessary to retrieve and visualize an enhanced cube of 86829 cells.

The main directions for future research we wish to pursue are: (i) evaluate the effectiveness of the approach by experimenting it with real users; (ii) extend the approach to the other intention operators and to operate with *dashboards* of enhanced cubes; and (iii) experiment other interestingness metrics [5].

Table 1. Execution time in seconds for increasing cube cardinalities

Cardinality	Query	Model	Interestingness	Pivot	Total
323	0.88	1.45	0.03	0.03	2.39
77832	0.64	3.61	0.39	0.51	5.14
86829	0.69	3.66	0.48	1.56	6.38

References

1. Abela, A.: Advanced Presentations by Design. Pfeiffer, Hoboken (2008)
2. Bentayeb, F., Favre, C.: RoK: roll-up with the k-means clustering method for recommending OLAP queries. In: Bhowmick, S.S., Küng, J., Wagner, R. (eds.) DEXA 2009. LNCS, vol. 5690, pp. 501–515. Springer, Heidelberg (2009). https://doi.org/10.1007/978-3-642-03573-9_43
3. Bie, T.: Subjective interestingness in exploratory data mining. In: Tucker, A., Höppner, F., Siebes, A., Swift, S. (eds.) IDA 2013. LNCS, vol. 8207, pp. 19–31. Springer, Heidelberg (2013). https://doi.org/10.1007/978-3-642-41398-8_3
4. Börner, K.: Atlas of Knowledge: Anyone Can Map. MIT Press, Cambridge (2015)
5. Chanson, A., Crulis, B., Drushku, K., Labroche, N., Marcel, P.: Profiling user belief in BI exploration for measuring subjective interestingness. In: Proceedings of DOLAP (2019)

6. Chen, B., Chen, L., Lin, Y., Ramakrishnan, R.: Prediction cubes. In: Proceedings of VLDB, pp. 982–993 (2005)
7. Deshpande, A., Madden, S.: MauveDB: supporting model-based user views in database systems. In: Proceedings of SIGMOD, pp. 73–84 (2006)
8. Francia, M., Gallinucci, E., Golfarelli, M.: Towards conversational OLAP. In: Proceedings of DOLAP, pp. 6–15 (2020)
9. Golfarelli, M., Graziani, S., Rizzi, S.: Shrink: an OLAP operation for balancing precision and size of pivot tables. Data Knowl. Eng. **93**, 19–41 (2014)
10. Golfarelli, M., Rizzi, S.: A model-driven approach to automate data visualization in big data analytics. Inf. Vis. **19**(1), 24–47 (2020)
11. Han, J.: OLAP mining: integration of OLAP with data mining. In: Proceedings of Working Conference on Database Semantics, pp. 3–20 (1997)
12. Kraska, T.: Northstar: an interactive data science system. PVLDB **11**(12), 2150–2164 (2018)
13. Pedersen, T.B.: Warehousing the world: a vision for data warehouse research. In: Kozielski, S., Wrembel, R. (eds.) New Trends in Data Warehousing and Data Analysis. Annals of Information Systems, vol. 3, pp. 1–17. Springer, Boston (2009). https://doi.org/10.1007/978-0-387-87431-9_1
14. Raedt, L.D.: A perspective on inductive databases. SIGKDD Explor. **4**(2), 69–77 (2002)
15. Salvador, S., Chan, P.: Determining the number of clusters/segments in hierarchical clustering/segmentation algorithms. In: Proceedings of ICTAI, pp. 576–584 (2004)
16. Sarawagi, S.: Explaining differences in multidimensional aggregates. In: Proceedings of VLDB, pp. 42–53 (1999)
17. Sathe, G., Sarawagi, S.: Intelligent rollups in multidimensional OLAP data. In: Proceedings of VLDB, pp. 531–540 (2001)
18. Satopaa, V., Albrecht, J.R., Irwin, D.E., Raghavan, B.: Finding a "kneedle" in a haystack: Detecting knee points in system behavior. In: Proceedings of ICDCS, pp. 166–171 (2011)
19. Terrovitis, M., et al.: Modeling and language support for the management of pattern-bases. Data Knowl. Eng. **62**(2), 368–397 (2007)
20. Vassiliadis, P., Marcel, P., Rizzi, S.: Beyond roll-up's and drill-down's: an intentional analytics model to reinvent OLAP. Inf. Syst. **85**, 68–91 (2019)

Correction to: An Efficient Index for Reachability Queries in Public Transport Networks

Bezaye Tesfaye, Nikolaus Augsten, Mateusz Pawlik,
Michael H. Böhlen, and Christian S. Jensen

Correction to:
Chapter "An Efficient Index for Reachability Queries in Public Transport Networks" in: J. Darmont et al. (Eds.):
Advances in Databases and Information Systems, **LNCS 12245,**
https://doi.org/10.1007/978-3-030-54832-2_5

The chapter was originally published without open access. With the author(s)' decision to opt for retrospective open access the copyright of the chapter changed to © The Author(s) 2020 and the chapter is now available under a CC BY 4.0 license at link. springer.com.

The updated version of this chapter can be found at
https://doi.org/10.1007/978-3-030-54832-2_5

J. Darmont et al. (Eds.): ADBIS 2020, LNCS 12245, p. C1, 2020.
https://doi.org/10.1007/978-3-030-54832-2_17

Author Index

Printed in the United States
By Bookmasters